Bugger Bugger Shit!

My quest for resilience.

Angharad Candlin

Copyright © 2024 Justine Martin
First Published in Australia in 2024
By Morpheus Publishing
Geelong Victoria 3216
www.morpheuspublishing.com.au

All rights reserved. No part of this publication may be reproduced, stored in a retrieval system, or transmitted in any form or by any means, electronic, mechanical, photocopying, recording or otherwise, without the prior
written permission of the publisher or author.

BUGGER BUGGER SHIT!

ISBN:	978-1-7636985-7-4
Author:	**Angharad Candlin**
Publisher:	**Justine Martin**
Editor:	**Suzie Veitch**
Sub-editor:	**Jackie Garnett**
Cover Graphics:	**Lynny Ingles**

A catalogue record for this book is available
from the **National Library of Australia**.

DISCLAIMER

The information contained in this book is for general informational purposes only. The author and publisher are not offering any medical, legal or professional advice. While every effort has been made to ensure the accuracy and completeness of the information provided, the author and publisher assume no responsibility for errors or omissions or any outcomes or consequences resulting from the use of this book's content.

COPYRIGHT

All original material in this book is the sole property of the author and Morpheus Publishing.

DISTRIBUTION

This book is distributed by Morpheus Publishing and is available through authorised distributors, booksellers, Morpheus Publishing website and Angharad Candlin website www.angharadcandlin.com

COPYRIGHT PERMISSIONS

For copyright permissions or any other inquiries, please contact:

PUBLISHER: Morpheus Publishing
www.morpheuspublishing.com.au
hello@justinemartin.com.au
0403 564 942

AUTHOR: Angharad Candlin
www.angharadcandlin.com
hello@angharadcandlin.com

Dedication

For Bryn and Skye.
The bravest boy and girl I know.

 **Bugger Bugger Shit!**

Acknowledgements

I need to first and foremost express my heartfelt thanks to Jackie; my former English teacher. She was the first person to read each chapter; give me feedback and correct my grammar. Every single semi-colon in the book is due to Jackie, every grammatical error is entirely my own. It was a lovely experience to be back in the 'classroom' under your tutelage. You were the person who lit the fire in me and taught me how to love literature and poetry. You always believed in me. I am so grateful for your continued presence in my life.

To my sister Naomi; Sebastian, Elliott, Lewis, Skye and Bryn - you are the very embodiment of the word resilience. Your bravery and courage in the absolute worst of times are breathtaking. I definitely don't say it enough, so I wanted to write it here for everyone to read. You are all amazing; individually in your unique ways and together, as a group, you are the storm.

To K and M with my love always; no other words are necessary x

Thanks must also go to Jonathan and Sara who, along with Jackie and I, make up our little online, international book group; you fill my cup to overflowing. I love and trust each of you and your feedback is always valued. Thank you for being willing to read the book first and to listen as it came to life. Jonathan, you have always encouraged me to think deeper; even when we were at school. You hold me accountable for the, often unplanned, things that come out of my mouth. I appreciate you so incredibly much.

To my colleagues in the 'Arena' with me; particularly Andree and Anthony who, whilst they aren't mentioned in the book, have been side by side with me for three decades. Our shared sense of the ridiculous and sense of humour have kept us sane in the most trying moments and we have held each other and wept in the darkest moments. You are passionate and dedicated and I could absolutely not have done it without you. I honour you.

Jorgia, you are a gift; this house would not function without you and I don't know what I would do without you. Thank you for looking after us.

Tina (2ni to her friends) - thank you for taking the time to go walking in the forest, camera in hand and late night conversations via messenger. You are incredibly talented and I'm glad to be able to call you my friend.

Nadine - thank you for your friendship and your secret hidden expertise with an iPhone and a camera. Who knew? Well, clearly you did! You make me laugh uproariously with your wicked, wicked questions and look how it paid off!

The Morpheus Inner Circle Writers' Group; my thanks for the enthusiasm and encouragement you have all provided over the last 12 months. Look what we did! Justine, my publisher, you had an idea and ran with it; you knew I had a story to tell and believed in me.

Finally, to the hundreds of clients I worked with over the last 30 plus years; you are the reason I kept showing up and striving to be better. Your combined resilience is the impetus for this book. I carry you in my heart.

Bugger Bugger Shit!

You may write me down in history
With your bitter, twisted lies,
You may trod me in the very dirt
But still, like dust, I'll rise.

Does my sassiness upset you?
Why are you beset with gloom?
'Cause I walk like I've got oil wells
Pumping in my living room.

Just like moons and like suns,
With the certainty of tides,
Just like hopes springing high,
Still I'll rise.

Did you want to see me broken?
Bowed head and lowered eyes?
Shoulders falling down like teardrops,
Weakened by my soulful cries?

Does my haughtiness offend you?
Don't you take it awful hard
'Cause I laugh like I've got gold mines
Diggin' in my own backyard.

You may shoot me with your words,
You may cut me with your eyes,
You may kill me with your hatefulness,
But still, like air, I'll rise.

Bugger Bugger Shit!

Does my sexiness upset you?
Does it come as a surprise
That I dance like I've got diamonds
At the meeting of my thighs?

Out of the huts of history's shame
I rise
Up from a past that's rooted in pain
I rise
I'm a black ocean, leaping and wide,
Welling and swelling I bear in the tide.

Leaving behind nights of terror and fear
I rise
Into a daybreak that's wondrously clear
I rise
Bringing the gifts that my ancestors gave,
I am the dream and the hope of the slave.
I rise
I rise
I rise.

Still I Rise
in And Still I Rise
Maya Angelou
1978 Random House

Table of Contents

Dedication iii

Acknowledgements v

Foreword xi

Introduction 1

Chapter 1: Lessons in Bungee Jumping 11

Chapter 2: Bugger Bugger Shit 27

Chapter 3: Keep Singing 51

Chapter 4: The War Zone 63

Chapter 5: The Front Line 84

Chapter 6: Why Not Me 93

Chapter 7: They've Got Knives! 113

Chapter 8: Bite Me! 135

Chapter 9: The Arena 148

Chapter 10: I Carry Your Heart 158

Bugger Bugger Shit!

Chapter 11: Tears Are The Rivers of Life 167

Chapter 12: Boyfriend Trouble 178

Chapter 13: You Have to Be Kidding Me! 193

Chapter 14: Would You Like Fries With That 203

Chapter 15: WTF!!!! 220

Chapter 16: I'm Not Disabled I'm Just Bloody Stubborn 234

Chapter 17: Entitlement is Not a Disability 243

Chapter 18: Ruby 258

Chapter 19: Anxiety Is Just An Emotion 283

Chapter 20: That Offends Me 292

Chapter 21: The Quest 302

Recommended Reading 308

About the Author 309

Foreword

Aristotle said 'Give me a child at 7 and I'll show you the man'. This assertion was examined in Michael Apted's wonderful docu-series 'Seven up' in which he followed several children over a period of almost 50 years. However, that focus on a socio-economic start seems too simplistic today, in a world in which the need for well being and mindfulness has come to the fore. Where we start, how we learn and who we meet does not necessarily prepare us for what happens next. We will always need to think, to adapt and to prioritise our emotional development.

I have known Angharad for a long time, from when she was a pupil in my English class at a secondary school in the north of England. I remember her as an enthusiastic pupil; very keen to learn and determined to make progress. She loved reading and she loved to ask questions. I remember detailed conversations which sought answers to 'Why?' and 'How?' It was a delight to witness her progress and achievements. I knew her elder sister and family and the context to some early events in her life.

Although teachers inevitably lose touch with pupils as they grow and leave school, Angharad and I were able to re-connect through social media many years later and even to meet up in person in recent years when she has visited the UK. Together with two of her friends who were also in the same class at school, she invited me to join a monthly Book Club, which we could conduct across the world using current media communication. It is a lovely way for us to meet regularly and to chat meaningfully despite coping with different time zones! I was very excited when she told us of her plans to write a book herself and consequently invited me to read it. When I saw the subject matter, I recognised her insight into the need for resilience in our lives and appreciated the ways in which her professional knowledge could help others to identify times and ways in which to maintain the positive approach we need if we are to thrive as humans.

Angharad's life to date has been very interesting and, in many ways, very challenging. There have been times of tragedy and grief, of physical and medical setbacks. She writes about resilience from a personal point of view, which makes the subject matter non-threatening. The book includes scientific information and detail where necessary but it is presented in an accessible manner. Moreover, the character I have always known shines through. She has a wonderful sense of energy and she knows her own opinions. Her strong moral sense is present in so many situations and she is passionate about treating others fairly, kindly and with the correct consideration we all deserve. We are never in any doubt of what she feels are priorities. Her humour is evident, yet used deftly so that it does not detract from the seriousness of her subject matter. She is also self-deprecating; there is no sense that she would act any differently from anyone else or that she deserves any more consideration than anyone else. It is easy to laugh alongside her, knowing that she is not too serious about her own dignity. Just as some of her comments made to me years ago as a pupil would make me stop and think, so do some of the situations raised in the book make me continue to ponder long after the page has been closed.

This is a book with tremendous drive. There are no easy answers but there is the information to help us make sense of why we think and react as we

Foreword

do. Plenty of alternatives are offered for us to contemplate. I smile when she makes her feelings clear because there is no room for misinterpretation. Everyone should have the opportunity to participate in society fully; everyone should be surrounded by a supporting atmosphere to thrive; everyone has a right to be accepted as equals. That will never make us all the same because we may need more time, more skills and a more safe environment to enable resilience. Nevertheless, resilience is shown to be the key to further progress and development.

I feel sure that Angharad, the pupil, would have not seen herself as a writer at all. Yet she is even more than that. Her profile describes her as an author, thought leader, speaker, consultant, trainer and recently retired psychologist. She is an expert in her field of assisting families. I can confirm that she is a tour de force; someone who uses any setback to be even more creative to become enabled. She is not frightened to set off around Australia to deliver talks or to book a journey across the world, which she will manage herself, with her wheelchair, Ruby! I am so incredibly proud to know her and to witness that she is still reading, still writing, still determined and still passionately alive.

When I look back, my memories of Angharad are always centred in the classroom. The classroom is the most special place for any teacher. This is the cauldron of learning; where information is shared alongside enthusiasm and where relationships are nurtured by everyone feeling safe to share any concerns and knowledge. Only last year, Angharad told me that what she loves to do is deliver her talks; where she can share her professional knowledge and skills with others and where her audiences, without a doubt, will leave with more ideas and ways in which to improve their futures. Her friendly, dynamic and caring personality will stay with you in this book, as will her lively interest in her subject matter and the exciting, contemporary manner she has found to deliver her message. Too often, people are described as inspiring - but inspiring is definitely the right word to describe Angharad. She is personable, funny, controlled and confident and it is this final trait which is most pleasing to witness.

Jackie Garnett

May 2024

Introduction

If we do not honour our past
We lose our future
If we destroy our roots
We cannot grow

Hundertwasser
KunstHausWien
(Hundertwasser Museum)
Vienna, Opened April 1991

In the late 1990s, I was in Vienna during a trip to Europe. I saw some of the buildings Friedensreich Hundertwasser had designed. He was an Austrian Architect and Visual Artist; well known for his colourful and bright public works and government housing. In fact he retired to New Zealand and his final gift to the world was to design some public toilets in Kawakawa. There is a museum in his honour in Vienna and so I decided to go and find out some more about the man.

He has a fascinating history. Whilst I was wandering around the museum I came across a torn piece of what looked like butchers' paper stuck randomly to the wall. It had the quote above written on it. I stopped in my tracks. I had been working in the field of adoption for about seven years

Bugger Bugger Shit!

and I realised the quote described adoption perfectly. It wasn't just adoption that it described though; it described a fundamental truth of life.

There are two women in my world that I have been best friends with since early childhood. They know each other but their paths didn't really cross when we were children. For their privacy I am going to use pseudonyms for them. We don't see each other very often but when we do, it is as if time has stood still. I was introduced to Rosie* when we were both four, following our family's move into Lancaster from a nearby village; our parents were part of the same circle of friends. I met my second friend Laura*, when she moved to Lancaster two years later; we were introduced during the summer holidays and we became firm forever friends.

The flicker in my imagination for this book was lit in 2019 after a conversation I had with Laura. I had gone to the UK to attend Rosie's wedding. Unfortunately that trip didn't go quite as planned. Rosie had experienced numerous traumatic events as an adult and whilst I was there, it was apparent that her mental health wasn't good. In the end, instead of attending her wedding, I had to support her partner in organising for her to be involuntarily admitted to a mental health unit.

That day was truly awful. I received a phone call from her partner one evening expressing his concern about her. I promised him I would be there the next morning. When I arrived, Rosie was clearly experiencing psychosis. Her partner had called her GP who had already attended their home. It requires two doctors to agree for a person to be involuntarily admitted so she had organised a second doctor to visit. This doctor arrived shortly after I did. He was satisfied that Rosie needed to have in-patient care and set the wheels in motion.

Introduction

My beautiful, darling friend Rosie was scared and experiencing paranoia but she trusted me. At one point I held her face with my hands, looked into her eyes and said, "I know this is overwhelming and scary for you. You know me don't you?" "Yes," she replied, "Do you trust me?" "Yes," she replied. "Then I am with you and I am going to stay with you and we are going to get through this together" I promised. A wonderful mental health social worker arrived soon after and she waited with us for the ambulance to arrive.

It took almost the whole day; such is the crisis in the UK's health care system at the moment. When Rosie was taken away in the ambulance, the social worker hugged me. She reassured me that her partner and I had done the right thing. I was in no doubt, such was Rosie's distress, that we had, but her compassion in the moment was so kind. Rosie called me a few days later to let me know she was ok and a couple of weeks later, when I was at the airport ready to return to Australia, we had a video call. She was calm, peaceful and cared for beautifully.

A few days later, I visited Laura and also found her with poor mental health. I had known that she had experienced a traumatic medical event a few years previously but I had no idea her mental health had been so impacted. Laura asked me a question that I had no idea how to answer. She said, "You, Rosie and I have had really similar lives so why is it that Rosie and I are a mess but you've got everything together?"

She was right, we did have really similar lives and experiences; including premature loss of a significant family member and trauma. We each have very similar personalities, very similar belief systems and very similar ways of looking at the world. As adults we had all experienced different but very difficult situations. Why was it then that I had come through apparently intact whilst Rosie and Laura both had mental ill health? I'm not sure that we will ever be able to define exactly why the outcomes are different for us but I believe we can find the answers through the pages of this book.

This book is a quest for resilience. I am a psychologist with over 30 years' experience working in the community sector. I have a very difficult family and personal history. Having spent over 30 years maintaining my privacy and focusing on the needs of the clients I have worked with, I decided that if this book was to be at all helpful, I needed it to be very honest.

It is a very vulnerable feeling when one chooses to expose their life to others but I have always strived to be authentic in the work that I do and so I need to be authentic now. Some of the stories in this book have never been shared but the value is in reflecting on how I rose above my various situations so that others may be able to apply the learnings to their own lives in their quest for resilience. I truly hope that it is helpful.

Towards the end of the book I have added a number of chapters with my psychologist hat on for those who wish to explore resilience at a more theoretical level. I think it's important that everyone has the opportunity to think more deeply and to understand ourselves and the people around us in ways we may never have done before. My experience, working in the community as a psychologist, is that people have found it helpful to understand that there are often physical and contextual reasons for how we experience the ups and downs of life; when we realise we're not alone in our experiences it helps our resilience grow and gives us fuel to continue through the hard times.

To give context, I should explain the basics of my life. I am the second of four children to Chris and Sally; Halina-Jane, myself (Angharad), Kit and Naomi. Halina married Eddie but she died in 1987 aged 22, three weeks after their wedding. Eddie continues to be an integral part of our family; he still lives in the UK. Naomi married Tim. Naomi and Tim have four boys; Seb, Elliott, Lewis* and Bryn currently ranging in age from 14

Introduction

to 21. They were all in primary school when their dad died in 2014. Nine months after Tim died, my dad died.

Following Tim and Dad's deaths, Naomi, Mum and I all decided to build a house together; well let's face it, we didn't actually build the house, we paid an architect to design it and we paid a builder to put it together. Whilst the three of us have many talents; designing and building houses are not high on the list but we are all quite expert at spending money. Building a house is not for the faint hearted, especially when one has a neighbour like the one we had at the beginning of the adventure. He was a bully and he obviously rubbed his hands together with glee when he discovered that three women were building the house next door to the one he was building. It was, in hindsight, a recipe for disaster.

My first experience of him was when he called me one day. I was on a boat, sailing in the Whitsundays at the time. Sometimes when I'm distracted, it takes a while for my brain to engage. This was one of them. I really shouldn't have answered the phone. The conversation went something like this: Neighbour, "Hi, I'm Tim" (apologies to all Tim's out there, I just randomly made up a name for him to avoid getting sued). "I'm building my house next door to yours so I just wanted to introduce myself. I'm really looking forward to our house being finished and being able to sit on the patio with a beer and look at the view of those trees". I didn't say anything at the time but I did think to myself, "He's not going to have a view of the trees because our house is going to be built between his patio and the trees". We had the view of the trees, he didn't.

He had bought his side of the subdivision first so he did actually have an opportunity to buy the piece of land with a view of the trees but he didn't; he opted for the smaller and cheaper piece of land. He simply assumed that we would build our house at the bottom of the hill we had

Bugger Bugger Shit!

bought. Seriously? Who's going to do that when they could build a house at the top of the hill with a view of the trees?

He went on to say, "I wanted to talk to you about your front door." "Oh, ok" I replied, somewhat distracted by what the sails were doing. "Your front door is right next to where we're putting our swimming pool." "Ok", I said wondering why on earth he was disturbing a lovely day's sailing with a conversation about our front door and his swimming pool and quite frankly, my care factor was zero. "Well, it's right next to our pool and my children will be swimming in it". "Ok" I said, still not entirely sure where this conversation was going. "Well, when you and your visitors come in and out of your front door, our children will be in the pool right next to it." I was very confused by this, "But there'll be a fence." "Yes," he said "but our pool will still be right next to your front door. You'll need to move your front door."

I wondered whether he was a sandwich short of a picnic to be honest and quite frankly he was interrupting a glorious day of sailing, so wanting to get him off the phone, I said, "There's going to be a fence so no one will be able to see into your pool." "Yes, but they'll still be next to our pool when they're standing at your front door." "There's going to be a fence." I repeated, wondering whether I was in fact not speaking English; "No," he continued, "Can you move your front door?" "Can you move your pool?" I could hear him becoming quite apoplectic, he was breathing hard, clearly no one had ever said no to him before. "I can't move our pool." "No, well we can't move our front door either." He hung up the phone.

This was just the first of a thousand complaints by this man, clearly he had declared war on the brazen women next door who had dared to say no to him. There is a reason this book is called Bugger Bugger Shit and boy was he about to realise that. What he didn't know was that we had been through so much crap in our lives that one irritating man next door was

Introduction

nothing to us; in fact in true Candlin women fashion, we quite enjoyed rising to the occasion.

He became known as "Pool Tool" amongst my colleagues at work as I regaled them with his various episodes of obnoxious behaviour. Each complaint was more ridiculous than the last. The last one however was the icing on the cake and just as ridiculous as his first complaint. After we moved in, we received notice from our local Council that a neighbour had made a complaint. "Here we go again." I thought, as I read the letter. The subject of the complaint was the "unauthorised use of a wardrobe." A wardrobe? Seriously? How can you use a wardrobe in an unauthorised way? And how did he know? Had he secretly had a key cut to come and see what was happening in our wardrobes? Had he installed hidden cameras in our downlights so that he could spy on us? Were there hidden microphones as well? What were we doing in our wardrobes that was so unauthorised? Our minds boggled! I mean, I know there are some people who like to push the boundaries of acceptable behaviour in public but what could we be doing in our own home that was so unacceptable as to cause a complaint to Council? It's not like our wardrobes are particularly big either. And our Council was taking this seriously? Apparently so, because they needed to inspect our 'unauthorised use of a wardrobe'.

He was resentful that we had 'stolen' his view and was going to try and get the top storey of our house removed in whatever way he could. We worked out that the unauthorised use of a wardrobe was in my sister's sewing studio; she is a Milliner and Costume Designer and spends her time creating the most beautiful items, often late into the evening. Apparently the Council had to follow up the complaint so they girded their loins and turned up at our house one day. Three Council Officers arrived to check out this wardrobe and its unauthorised use. I wondered if they were so suspicious of this unauthorised use that they decided there was safety in

Bugger Bugger Shit!

numbers hence why it took three of them to check it out? They were just as bemused as we were.

It turns out that he had studied our plans with a magnifying glass down to the most minute detail; on the plans, the wardrobe label was printed slightly to the left of where it was supposed to be. He alleged that the whole studio was a wardrobe and therefore shouldn't have any lights on, no music playing and certainly no noise of a sewing machine. We realised he had 'busted' us with the Oompa Loompas my sister was clearly using as slaves in her studio, oops, sorry, wardrobe.

No complaint was ever held up, our upper storey remains. Eventually he surrendered and sold his house a couple of years later. We may have taken a little bit of pleasure in knowing it took him months to sell and for a much lower amount that he had initially set. Personally, I hope he's enjoying his pool and his view with no neighbours whatsoever, far far away from any other humans.

Mum now has dementia and lives in a nursing home close by. Naomi, her four sons, our foster daughter, Skye, and I continue to live in Sydney in the house that we built. We also have about 40,000 bees in a hive (which I'm allergic to), five mice, three cats, two dogs, one turtle and a partridge in a pear tree. Yes I know, it's a recipe for disaster; we don't really have a partridge in a pear tree just in case you thought I was serious about that one but we did have two goats, four guinea pigs and six chickens at one point. The number of mice also tends to change, depending on their age, health and whether the cats have managed to complete Houdini-like acts when no one is looking.

In between writing this paragraph and the first edits; the mice have reduced to two but I'm confident in a few weeks they'll be back up to five or perhaps even six if Skye gets her way. More chickens are on the agenda, just as soon as we can secure the pen so that the local fox doesn't get them (again); we're also bracing ourselves for the potential addition of a snake

Introduction

called Zeus and another dog; it's best not to ask. We have also recently been adopted by a duck and a brush turkey occasionally attempts to try his luck.

I'm beginning to understand how Gerald Durrell felt in his book "My Family and Other Animals". And no, we don't live on a property in the bush; just a normal suburban block, entirely surrounded by other houses and fences so I am a little bemused as to how (or indeed why) the duck made its way into our garden and set up house.

Whilst we live in Australia, I was born in New Haven, Connecticut, USA and moved to the UK when I was a few months old. My siblings were all born in the UK. We mostly grew up in the North West of England, just south of the Lake District. A completely beautiful, if usually wet and cold, part of the country; think Beatrix Potter. My family migrated to Australia in 1987 and I followed on Christmas Eve 1990. I was planning on coming to Australia for a year but somehow I didn't get on that plane to go back and I've now lived in Australia longer than I lived in the UK.

Our memories are not like video recordings of our lives; they provide us with snapshots of feelings, experiences, places and people and our brains then stitch them together to form a narrative. This book is composed of my memories and perceptions of events. My siblings and others involved will probably recall things differently because of their ages and levels of involvement in the stories that I have told.

I have tried to be as accurate as possible. Where necessary, I have changed the names of people to maintain their anonymity. I have gained permission to talk about others. Just in case you start wondering as you read through this account, all of the stories I tell, particularly the ones involving various mishaps to myself, are 100% true. They haven't been exaggerated one iota. I may have smooshed some non-essential bits together in places for easier reading but yes, they have all happened.

I have chosen to be vulnerable in this book because research tells us that our western society is getting less and less resilient over time and something has to change. If I am going to be part of the change then I have to lead by example and that means sharing my story; warts and all. There are many difficult stories in this book but there are equally uplifting, poignant and downright hilarious stories.

The stories are hilarious because I don't take myself too seriously and fully embrace the ridiculous things that this thing called life throws at us. I feel confident in saying that I am generally a resilient person. I think people who know me would agree. Does that mean I don't have doubts, areas of vulnerability or times when I get it so completely wrong that it's surprising those involved got out of bed the next day? Of course not, but what I have learned doing this thing called life is that, as Kent Hoffman from the Circle of Security would say, unless we can look at ourselves and deal with the difficult stuff, we're just putting 'icing over shit'.

I hope through my stories and experiences you will discover your own roadmap as to how you can contribute to the solution. We can't all do everything but we can all do something to turn this thing around. Mostly, I hope that my own *quest for resilience* can be one little tiny part of one other person's quest for resilience. If it does that, then it was all worth it.

Bryn and the goats NSW Central Coast 2022

Alfie and Archie the goats just part of the menagerie

Chapter 1

Lessons in Bungee Jumping

Resilience is the happy knack of being able to bungee jump through life. When the inevitable pitfalls and setbacks of life occur, it is as if you have an elasticised rope around your middle that helps you to bounce back from hard times.

Andrew Fuller
Ten Hints for Creating Resilient Families
https://andrewfuller.com.au/resource/ten-hints-for-creating-resilient-families/
Sighted 12th February 2024

"What are the characteristics of a resilient person?" I asked the group of parents sitting in a semi-circle in front of me. There was a pause whilst everyone thought about it and then the first person said, "Strong". With that, there was a wave of responses which I scribed onto the whiteboard.

This is an activity that we facilitate as part of the Keeping Kids in Mind post-separation parenting course. We want parents to start thinking about what their children might need to develop or grow in order to get through the tumult of the family breakdown. It's never a definitive list but it is always an interesting conversation. Many things are repeated from group to group; strong, optimistic, a sense of humour, assertive, vulnerable, an ability to accept influence, previously getting through a difficult experience, supported, thoughtful, determined and optimistic. I would add that in addition to these characteristics, having an 'Internal Locus of Control' is crucial.

Sometimes a group finds it difficult to find the words so I ask them to think of a well known resilient person to prompt their responses. We have had many people listed; Nelson Mandela, Turia Pitt, a group of children stuck in a cave in Indonesia and 33 miners in Chile, are just some of the responses.

Whenever conferences had put out calls for papers, I had always ignored them. I thought they were for 'other' people and that no one would be interested in what I had to say. After I had been in a management position for a couple of years I decided that the work my team and I were doing was important; my passion for the work overcame my discomfort about standing up and speaking in front of a bunch of people. I invited two members of my team to work on the presentation with me and to deliver the paper alongside me. We worked really hard preparing it as we knew we were speaking on a contentious topic.

When we arrived at the conference, I asked which room we would be speaking in. I was horrified to discover the organisers had allocated us to the Ballroom and we were presenting on the first day, just before lunch. Nevertheless, not wanting to freak my team members out, I put on a brave and confident face.

Lessons in Bungee Jumping

We had rehearsed the presentation and fine tuned it down to the second. I explained this to the session Convenor and asked her to let the participants know that we would be happy to answer questions into the lunch break. There were a couple of hundred delegates in the session. My team and I presented really well, our preparation had paid off.

The Convenor, as agreed, got up onto the stage with us and stood behind the lectern to explain the situation regarding the questions. As she took her place, I politely took a step back - completely off the side of the stage! There was a gasp that ran around the room. My two colleagues were sitting on the stage and, hearing the gasp, slowly looked around to discover that I had disappeared.

As I was falling, I had a Roadrunner moment. I felt like time had stood still and I was hanging in mid air. All I remember was my urgent internal prayer, "Please God don't let me land on my bum". I didn't; I landed on my feet, which was a significant accomplishment given I was wearing high heels, thank God I was wearing pants and not a skirt! What to do now? In that split second I decided I could either fold over in humiliation or I could rise. I rose. I put my hands in the air like an Olympian, walked around to the front of the stage, climbed up the steps and carried on, as if nothing had happened.

The questions were coming in thick and fast about our presentation and it took about 30 minutes until the last person left the room. As the room emptied, I walked down off the stage and sat down on the front row. I put my head in my hands and laughed uncontrollably. My colleagues initially thought I was crying so they rushed over to comfort me. I lifted my head; they could see the tears of laughter. My response was to say through my snorting breaths, "Oh my goodness that was hilarious! I wish I could have seen it". My colleague promptly called out to the AV guy and asked

Bugger Bugger Shit!

him if he'd recorded it. He apologetically said no, he had switched off the video camera when the questions began.

About a year later, I was at a professional development session and was talking to one of the participants. Somehow we got onto the subject of the conference. She said to me in a concerned, hushed tone, "I was there, were you ok? I've been worrying about you ever since". I reassured her that I was completely fine and thought the whole episode incredibly funny. She replied, "Thank goodness for that, from where I was sitting, it looked like the Convenor had shoved you off the stage". I laughed at the vision in my mind and confirmed that no, I hadn't been shoved off the stage; I had simply thought I was standing directly behind her when I took a step backwards and didn't realise I was oriented towards the side.

Since then I have presented at numerous conferences and large events. Disappointingly, none of them have been quite as adventurous. To be honest, some of the presentations I've sat through could have done with a little physical comedy to make them a tad more interesting. What it did do however, was give me an opportunity to reassure many subsequent colleagues who expressed their anxiety about public speaking, that the worst thing imaginable had happened to me and I had survived. No matter how badly it might go for them, they were unlikely to fall off a stage. And bounce back up.

That conference was the year I found my voice. The last session was a large plenary session. A conversation was happening amongst the hundreds of participants and the experts on the stage. My team and I felt uncomfortable about the way the conversation was headed. One of them looked at me and whispered, "You have to say something." Following my falling off the stage episode, I decided I was reasonably invincible so I put my hand up and made a comment in opposition to what was being discussed. The sky didn't fall on my head. In fact it was the moment when I actively chose resilience.

According to D.E. Alexander in 2013, the term resilience was first added to a dictionary in 1656 by Thomas Blount. The term has been around for a very long time. The psychological concept of Locus of Control was developed by Julian Rotter in the 1950s and published in the mid 1960s. A Locus of Control could be described at its most basic as a way of experiencing the world; there are two types; Internal and External.

I like to describe it in the following way. If someone generally has an External Locus of Control it's like they are in the passenger seat of their life; they see things as happening by chance, that they have no control of events or things happen to them because of the actions of others.

People who have an Internal Locus of Control, on the other hand, tend to be in the driver's seat of the car of their life. They see their lives as being their own responsibility, irrespective of whether things go well or poorly and they can influence their world and their experiences through their actions and choices.

Infants have an External Locus of Control because they are solely reliant on other people for their very survival. As we mature however and start to have influence in our lives, the hope is that we would move towards an Internal Locus of Control. Nobody has an Internal Locus of Control all of the time. Neither should they; if we're in trouble and we need to get out of it, then it's totally fine to do whatever it takes to keep safe. The problem arises however when someone generally lives within an External Locus of Control frame all the time.

Jean Twenge has completed a vast amount of research in this area and she is clear; there has been a significantly increasing trend towards an External Locus of Control since the 1960s. There has also been a plethora of research that draws the conclusion that people who tend to view the

Bugger Bugger Shit!

world through an External Locus of Control lens have a much poorer outcome in terms of wellbeing, anxiety & depression and levels of psycho social success. These can all be grouped together into one simple concept; the population of the world is becoming less resilient over time.

We know that if you place a baby into a swimming pool they will instinctively start to swim towards the surface. We all have an innate desire to succeed; to survive; so what happens? Why are some people more resilient than others and how can we become more resilient? Yes, there are certainly some people whose personalities and temperaments tend to lean more towards having resilient qualities; like being optimistic; being able to see the funny side of things; being confident. But these are not the only things that support resilience. There are a myriad of things that form resilience and we can support children and adults to become more resilient if we know what to look for, what to focus on, what things that can be changed and what things can't.

There are three key protective factors to consider when exploring resilience; not only in children but also in adults. These are:

- Things that we are good at
- Things that we enjoy doing
- People who support us

When we are good at something, we get great satisfaction from our successes. We are given positive feedback by others which builds our self esteem. The dopamine in our brains increases which gives us a sense of pleasure and satisfaction which, in turn, motivates us to do better.

When we enjoy doing something we get a sense of happiness and joy. The serotonin in our brain increases and that influences our capacity to be optimistic and satisfied.

When we are surrounded by people who support us, we feel connected and less alone. The oxytocin in our brains increases our capacity to attach, to trust and to love.

These three neurochemicals or hormones, along with endorphins are commonly referred to as DOSE (Dopamine, Oxytocin, Serotonin, Endorphins). They influence our wellbeing which in turn, improves resilience. They form the basis for brain growth and healthy development.

On the other hand; adrenaline and cortisol flood our brains when we are in a state of threat. When our brains are flooded, over a period of time, with these neurochemicals, we are solely focussed on survival, which is detrimental to our wellbeing. They prevent us from using the higher order processing part of the brain to analyse, rationalise, problem solve, manage our emotions and ultimately make good decisions. All of these neurochemicals are essential but when our brains are flooded with only one or two of them over a long period of time, rather than a fluid combination of all of them over time, it negatively impacts our health.

The term brain plasticity has been talked about since the 1990s when the development of Functional MRI machines gave us the opportunity to see inside a living brain; rather than post mortem in a clinical setting. Whilst the machines of the 1990s were not as sensitive as the machines we have today, some 30 years later, we could see how the brain functions in certain settings and what influences different parts of the brain.

The 1990s really was the decade of the brain. We can test brain chemicals now with a simple saliva test. Not only can we plot the different regions of the brain, we can plot the ebb and flow of neurochemicals throughout the day and night. We can see how the brain changes over time; plasticity. I prefer the term malleability however; things which are plastic can easily break and snap whereas things that are malleable can shape-shift and remain intact.

Being able to think things through, see other people's perspectives and manage our emotions are all key when it comes to moving from an External to Internal Locus of Control and in turn build resilience.

John Gottman is a well known and respected Psychologist and Researcher who, along with his wife Julie, have been examining couple and family relationships for decades. In the 1990s, Gottman was able to prove that parents can impact children's wellbeing and emotional maturity by Emotion Coaching them.

Infants and young children have no concept of emotions; they just have an experience within themselves in response to certain stimuli. Adults understand these experiences as happy, sad, angry or afraid but they are abstract concepts which children cannot comprehend unless someone first gives them the language to describe their internal experience.

Emotions aren't concrete objects that can be touched or have a label stuck onto them. What children need their carers to do, is label the emotion for them so that they can link their internal state with an external word. It is only when a child can link the label with the feeling that they can understand their experience and therefore manage their emotions.

I often hear parents say to their children, "Use your words" when they are exhibiting a strong emotion. The fundamental point that adults need to understand is that children don't have words until adults give them the words. We can't ask a child, "How are you feeling?" because they genuinely don't know. Adults need to remember that all behaviour is language. Children tell us how they feel through their behaviour; what adults need to do is to label the emotion behind the behaviour so that children can, for now and in the future, understand that this internal state I am experiencing is happy or sad or disappointed or afraid or confused etc.

In his book 'Raising an Emotionally Intelligent Child', Gottman outlines five simple steps for Emotion Coaching. It is essential that they are carried out in the order listed to work effectively. Too often we all like to jump in to solve problems for other people. When we leap to solve problems for someone, we are denying them the opportunity to solve it themselves and more significantly, we are denying them an opportunity to strengthen their resilience.

Before we can problem solve, however, we need to 'feel felt' as Dan Siegel, Clinical Chair of Psychiatry (UCLA) would say. When we 'feel felt', our brains down-regulate the adrenaline and cortisol neurochemicals and up-regulate the DOSE neurochemicals.

I like to use the mnemonic RIVER to help people remember the steps:

1. **Recognise** - that your child is experiencing an emotion and needs you to help them and recognise how you feel about your child's feelings

2. **Intimacy** - see it as an opportunity for intimacy and to truly connect with your child rather than dismissing or disapproving of their emotion or behaviour

3. **Verbalise** - provide your child with the words associated with the emotions they are experiencing, don't ask them, tell them what emotions you can see or hear in their behaviour

4. **Empathise** - with your child, stay with them in the depth of their emotions until they are ready to move

5. **Resolution** - help your child problem solve and understand their emotions and the situation and, if appropriate, how they might handle it differently next time

Having worked as a psychologist for over 30 years I firmly believe that Emotion Coaching is the one fundamental skill that all humans need to learn and to practise. Whilst Gottman talks about children, Emotion Coaching is not age specific. We all need to be supported with our emotions

Bugger Bugger Shit!

in order to be able to regulate them and we need to frequently practise regulating our emotions so that we can lay down strong neural pathways for emotional regulation. Being able to manage our emotions is a fundamental key to wellbeing, resilience and developing an internal locus of control.

Managing our emotions is not about pushing them down or ignoring them, or indeed indulging them; it's about understanding that they are a fundamental part of us. Emotions are often misunderstood and seen as the 'truth' of an experience; they aren't. Emotions simply tell us how we are experiencing something and if we are to build long lasting resilience then we have to fundamentally understand that we can manage our emotions, and if we can manage our emotions, we can change our experience. If we can change our experience we can take control of our lives and we can take responsibility for our lives. We can move from an External to an Internal Locus of Control.

Referring back to the list of characteristics of a resilient person, one of them is having been through a difficult experience and survived; or even thrived. When I think of my life, there is no doubt that it has been impacted by trauma, loss and ill health. It has also been impacted significantly by protective factors.

I was good at English and Ballet, I loved them both and was encouraged and praised for my skills. We travelled a lot with Dad's job so we saw the world; the good and the bad. We changed schools numerous times so we understood at an early age that loss is part of life but it also gave us the experience of making new friends. I have innate characteristics, inherited from both Grampa and my dad, which are; to see the sense of the ridiculous in anything and everything; a healthy sense of humour; a desire to have fun and an optimistic temperament.

There have been many people in my life who have supported me and therefore helped my resilience grow. I have siblings who have been through the same pitfalls that I have; we have a shared history which validates our experiences. It wasn't just me; it was all of us. I have extended family members who cheer me on when I succeed and commiserate with me when I don't. As the Circle of Security parenting program outlines; they have, and still do, provide me with a secure base and a safe haven. I have colleagues who have willingly stepped into the Arena with a shared passion, sense of social justice and commitment to the clients we have worked with. I have a multitude of deep and long lasting relationships with friends from school, university and adulthood; including one teacher who was a shining light for all of us who had the privilege to be taught by her.

Jackie started teaching the same year that my cohort commenced secondary school. She was our English teacher. In the scheme of things she wasn't really that much older than us. She was and still is passionate about education and children. She recognises that every child has potential and she worked hard so that we too could see it in ourselves. Jackie didn't teach me for my first couple of years of high school but once we were streamed into sets for English and Maths I was lucky enough to go into her class. She taught Set 1. This was a class of highly motivated students who loved English; grammar and literature. We were a class who got on well and we encouraged each other to do better.

Jackie was our champion. I still remember one lesson. We all sat down and Jackie told us to pull out some paper and a pen. She put some music on and invited us to write. "Write what?" we asked. "Anything." she replied. She encouraged us to write creatively whatever came into our heads. I mentioned this particular lesson to her last year, she said that she wanted this group of children from the North West of England to have a place where they could just find their creativity.

We read and analysed books and poetry that many of us still love and talk about; 'The Woman in White' by Wilkie Collins; 'Testament of Youth'

Bugger Bugger Shit!

by Vera Britain; '1984" by George Orwell; Shakespeare's 'Taming of the Shrew', the poetry of WH Auden; WB Yeats and many more. She arranged trips to the theatre for us. It wasn't just English though; Jackie was a person to bounce ideas off, go to with concerns, consolidate ideas and helped us think about our futures.

We were in Lancashire and generally speaking, support for our future careers was limited. If you were a girl it was assumed you would work in an office, be a teacher or be a nurse. If you were a boy, it was working on the family farm, learning a trade or joining the Armed Services. There is nothing fundamentally wrong with any of these careers; it was simply the lack of imagination that children from the north could aspire to do anything else.

A friend recently told me of a conversation he had with Jackie when he was ready to leave school. He asked her if she would be a referee on his application for the Armed Services; this was the alternative he had come up with after telling the Career's Advisor he wanted to complete his A Levels and go to University; he was, instead, advised to become a welder.

He didn't particularly want to be in the forces but didn't really see any other career avenues to move forward with, certainly not being a welder. Jackie reluctantly said she would provide a reference if he really wanted to join up but she saw a much bigger future for him and wanted him to go to university. As a result of this conversation and good A Level results, he was the first person in his family to go to university and he has had a very successful career in an area no one from Lancaster would ever have thought possible. Like my friend, Jackie was enthusiastic about me going to university to study Psychology and was highly supportive.

The magic of social media has meant that a few of us have been able to renew our relationship with Jackie years later. She is still our biggest advocate but now as adults. We are in a book group together and my eternal thanks lie with her for agreeing to be the first person to read through my book for feedback. I wish that everyone could have a Jackie; a teacher who sees potential and draws it out. A teacher who unequivocally supports her students. Teachers or coaches like Jackie are a key factor in building resilience. I would encourage everyone to think of a younger person they can be that person for.

Another key protective person for my siblings and me was a long standing friend of my parents; Greta. Greta worked with my dad and was great friends with Mum. She has known me since I was a few months old. She was our unofficial second Mum. When I am talking to parents, I invariably talk to them about the importance of 'the village'. Greta was part of our 'village'. Greta's home was our home. She babysat us when we were little; I stayed with her on many occasions as a teenager and young adult. She has been to Australia to visit us and we always see her when we go to the UK.

I had been steeling myself for the news of her death at some point given she was over 90 years old but still fit as a fiddle and sharp as a tack. Just as this book was getting ready to go to print we got the news that she had died, suddenly at home, after a fall. I had sent her an email 2 weeks prior to let her know I would be seeing her in a couple of months when I visited the UK.

When I saw her in 2023, we talked about Mum and Dad. It was cathartic to be able to speak to someone who was friends with them and had a different perspective than ours. We talked a lot about the impact of Mum's multiple sclerosis (MS) on her and the limitations of her parenting. We also talked about the complexities of being married to my dad; a person who was larger than life and travelled constantly. Greta was one of the keys in my development of resilience and I will be eternally thankful for her.

We also had a 'surrogate grandmother' who lived next door; Joan. When I was four, her husband died. After school, I used to trot off down

Bugger Bugger Shit!

to her house; she would make me a white bread sandwich with Stork margarine and jam - we didn't have white bread or Stork margarine in our house so it was a real treat. We used to sit on her doorstep, with our sandwich, have a chat and then I would trot home again. She only told me years later, when I was a young adult, that the conversations we had all revolved around her husband dying and death in general. I was very apologetic for my four year old lack of tact. She reassured me that actually the conversations were very helpful for her in working through her loss. Sometimes it is the little ones who are our biggest teachers.

Everyone has a choice, irrespective of the circumstances; we can be like Henny Penny who thought the sky was falling in when an acorn hit her on the head. Or we can be like Paddington Bear who was resilient enough to stow away on his own from Darkest Peru on his quest for adventure. We can purposefully practise moving from sitting in the passenger seat with an External Locus of Control to driving with an Internal Locus of Control. Personally I have always preferred Paddington to Henny Penny and I much prefer driving to being a passenger.

Ripley St Thomas Secondary School Lancaster

Lessons in Bungee Jumping

Greta and I, Lancaster 2019

Bugger Bugger Shit!

Jackie Ripley School Lancaster 1986

Jackie Ripley School Lancaster 2019

Chapter 2

Bugger Bugger Shit

> *"You may not control all the events that happen to you but you can decide not to be reduced by them."*
>
> **Maya Angelou**
> Letter to My Daughter
> 2008, Random House

I was about seven when the phone rang one day. My mum was around somewhere, and my dad was away with work, so I answered the phone. It was my dad's secretary, Anne, who asked to speak to Mum. We lived in a big house, so I yelled for Mum to come to the phone. She didn't answer me, so I told Anne I couldn't find her. Anne told me she had an important message for me to give to Mum. She told me that Dad had missed his flight. She asked me to repeat it and to make sure I told Mum as soon as I could. I promised her I would, but I have to admit, I thought she was making a big deal out of Dad missing his flight. I hung up the phone and promptly went off to play and forgot all about it.

A couple of hours later, I wandered back into the kitchen where Mum, my toddler brother and my big sister were. Mum was on the phone, looking

Bugger Bugger Shit!

really worried. She was quiet and listening and then said, "Bugger". She listened some more and said, "Bugger" again. Then she looked even more worried and scared and then said, "Shit". She hung up the phone. My sister and I asked her what the matter was, and she told us that the plane Dad had been on had crashed. It slowly dawned on me that I had completely forgotten to give Mum the message from Anne, so I burst out and said, "Oh no, he wasn't on the plane. Anne rang and told me to tell you that he had missed his flight, but I forgot!"

Silence. Relief. Then my brother broke the stunned silence by loudly proclaiming, "Bugger, bugger, shit!" as clear as a bell and with a big smile on his face. He was immensely pleased with himself that he had managed to put together a three-word sentence for the first time.

That was the day 'bugger bugger shit' came into being. Bugger bugger shit is reserved in my family for the really bad things. It can't be just average bad. It has to be really bad. A few years later, my mum was diagnosed with MS. That was a bugger bugger shit moment. My older sister was diagnosed with malignant melanoma just before she turned 18. That was a bugger bugger shit moment too. Many years later, my younger sister's husband was diagnosed with a terminal brain tumour. Bugger bugger shit. A few years later, my dad was told the prostate cancer he had developed had become terminal. Bugger bugger shit. I was diagnosed with endometriosis, infertility, psoriatic arthritis and multiple sclerosis. Seriously! Bugger Bugger Bugger Shit Shit Shit!

My apologies to those with a sensitive disposition but sometimes, really, the only words you can use to describe the horror of a situation are inappropriate in polite company.

Bugger Bugger Shit!

Bugger Bugger Shit

My dad was 27 when I was born. When I think about that now, he and my mum were almost children themselves but at the time 27 was pretty standard, if not old. He was completing his post-graduate studies in Linguistics at Yale University, having gained his undergraduate degree from Jesus College, Oxford. I was born in New Haven, Connecticut at 3.45pm on the 17th May 1967. Mum and Dad had been living in New Haven since late 1964 but had returned from the US, temporarily, in 1965 for Mum to give birth to my older sister. They returned to the US following the birth of their first child but decided to stay there for my birth. I was born in the same hospital where Mum had been working as a midwife. They returned to the UK 'permanently' a couple of months after I was born.

When I was 10, we were driving across the USA en route to Hawaii where we were going to live for a year whilst Dad was on sabbatical at the University of Hawaii. Mum and Dad made a special stop in New Haven so I could visit my birthplace. Dad took my siblings for the afternoon whilst Mum took me into the maternity unit. Colleagues she had worked with were still working there so it was a lovely reunion for Mum and for them to see the baby they had delivered.

I was shown the room where I was born. Mum and her friends told me the story of my birth which had entailed all of them slipping into the delivery room at various stages of her labour. They were told off at one point by the Sister for making too much noise as she declared, "Women are in labour here." obviously missing the point that Mum too was in labour.

My siblings were all born in the UK where we lived permanently, so it wasn't a big deal for them but Mum and Dad inherently knew that for me, I needed to be able to stand on the spot where I entered the world. Standing and centring myself in place and time has become something that's important for me and I put it down to being separated from where I became

Bugger Bugger Shit!

at a very early age. This day was the day when I could put my being in this world into context.

My dad was a force to be reckoned with. He was big and loud and confident. He had three daughters and a son and was, as far as I can remember, always a feminist. I think that really was the undoing of our relationship. I was being raised to be strong and confident. I had red hair, a fiery temper, called a spade "a bloody shovel" and could not and still can't stand hypocrisy in any shape or form.

My dad had no idea what to do with me. Whilst he wanted independent and strong girls, I think he got more than he bargained for when I came along. My older sister was reasonably compliant but I would, and still do, question everything. That meant questioning him - which he found extremely difficult.

When I was growing up, my dad was shouty. He had a temper and could be violent with me. He had no idea how to parent this strong and intelligent girl he was raising and so used his hands quite regularly to shut me down. There are a number of incidents from my childhood that I will never forget but one in particular is an interesting statement on how domestic violence and child protection was viewed in the 1970s and 80s in the North West of England.

My dad was packing to go on a work trip somewhere and wanted me to clean my bedroom. I, for some reason, decided I wasn't going to. Dad was clearly tired of arguing with me about it. He had his wash bag in his hand so he whacked me round the head with it several times. It really hurt, so I put my hand up to protect my head and he whacked my hand. This resulted in my finger breaking because there was a glass bottle of aftershave in the bag that he had forgotten about. He was mortified when he realised.

Obviously I was in pain, so Mum took me down to Emergency and whilst she was parking the car, I checked myself in. The receptionist asked me what had happened so I told her my dad hit me. She said, "Let's just put it down as a domestic accident." I was annoyed at the time but now as an adult and a Psychologist who has worked alongside family violence and child protection for decades, I am enraged by the attitude of the staff.

Needless to say, my relationship with my dad was pretty fragile and I was always relieved when he was away for work. When he was at home, even into my early adulthood, if we were in a room together, I always made sure I was near the exit. My mum was pretty bad but she certainly wasn't as violent as Dad.

She and Dad argued almost every single day of their married life. As kids we hated it. As an adult I hated it. When Dad was away, at least there was relative peace and quiet. Of course nobody knew this was what it was like at home. To all intents and purposes we were a functioning (whatever that actually means) and reasonably privileged family; professional parents with fairly academic, compliant and well rounded kids.

This of course isn't the whole story. Humans are generally complex beings and Dad was no different. Dad's personality entered a room five feet in front of him. He was very funny, generous to a fault, incredibly kind and well liked by almost everyone. Dad loved the world, he loved to travel, he loved to explore different cultures and was fluent in German and French. He tried his hand at Mandarin which beat him but apart from that he could pick up almost any language and run with it.

Dad travelled constantly. He missed more birthdays than he attended and as my sister and I were sorting through Mum and Dad's accumulated stuff, this summer, I found in the 'precious' folder a telegram to me for my first birthday, which he was in India for. That was just the first of many telegrams sent for a birthday he had missed. We all got used to organising our lives around Dad's but when my younger sister had to rearrange her

Bugger Bugger Shit!

wedding date to accommodate Dad's travel plans, he was on very shaky ground.

One of Dad's favourite times was Christmas. He loved everything about it. He loved the shopping; for gifts and food. He loved writing and sending cards, he loved wrapping presents and cooking the Christmas Day feast. Most of all though, he loved being Father Christmas for his children. In our house we had various working fireplaces. On Christmas Eve though there was never a fire lit in the living room fireplace because of course, Father Christmas was going to descend the chimney. What we did on Christmas Eve every year was kneel in front of the fireplace and call up the chimney to Father Christmas. Imagine our surprise the first time that Father Christmas answered! We had complete conversations with him. We told him what presents we wanted, he reminded us to leave out drinks and snacks for himself and the reindeer.

This ritual went on for years because we had a whole tribe of children of different ages who still believed in Father Christmas even as the older ones realised the truth. One year we were all kneeling around the fireplace; my younger siblings Naomi and Kit still believed in Father Christmas so we were carrying on the tradition. I went out of the living room to get something whilst the Father Christmas conversation was going on and imagine my complete surprise to find Dad hiding behind the living room door talking into a saucepan! I had worked out that Dad was playing the part but I had no idea he did it by talking into a saucepan!

After we moved to Australia, we of course, were all grown up and the tradition had temporarily ended until the next generation came along but one year we had some friends from Iran staying over Christmas. These friends were long standing friends from the UK who were in Australia temporarily. Even though they were Muslim, they had always come to our house on the afternoon of Christmas Day. This particular year, their daughter was old enough to participate in the Father Christmas conversation. The tricky thing was that we didn't have a chimney so we just thought she could call up into the night sky. So, as we had done so often before, we created an opportunity for her to have a chat with Santa and we even managed to trick her into thinking she saw the reindeer and sleigh as he flew past.

The next day was Christmas so we opened presents and had a feast as usual. At the end of the day though, our friend's daughter was a little upset. We initially thought it was because she wanted more or different presents but no, it was because she desperately wanted to say thank you to Santa for such a wonderful day and her beautiful presents. Not to be phased by this, Dad jumped back on Father Christmas duty so she could say thank you.

Dad loved being a grandfather and being able to once again put on his Father Christmas hat for his grandsons. By this time however, technology had taken over so not only could the boys talk to Father Christmas they could sit on Dad's lap and track Father Christmas' journey on the computer. We all struggled with Christmas for a time after my sister Halina died but since my brother-in-law and Dad's deaths less than a year apart from each other, Christmas is simply not the same. Now, we endure Christmas rather than enjoy it.

I travelled around Australia with Mum for my long service leave in 2002 and we met Dad in Adelaide for a few days. Whilst we were there we got the ferry over to Kangaroo Island for two nights. We stayed in a lovely Bed and Breakfast (B&B) place in a paddock seemingly in the middle of nowhere. During the night there was an enormous storm that hit Adelaide and the bottom half of South Australia, including Kangaroo Island. I think it was one of the biggest storms they had ever had. Needless to say the power went out, which was a bit of a problem because the toilets at the B&B were off the mainline sewage and needed electricity to flush. We woke up not

Bugger Bugger Shit!

only to no toilets but to pouring rain and freezing cold weather. What to do? This was one of those occasions that either brought out the worst or best in people. There was no in between. Fortunately for all three of us we decided to make the most of it.

We got into our rental car and set off to see the sights of the island. We saw the seals on the beach in the pouring rain. We looked for koalas in the trees in the pouring rain and then we went to Remarkable Rocks. It had been raining pretty hard before but now it was absolutely torrential. Mum somewhat sensibly decided to stay in the car, but Dad and I decided we were going to venture into the weather. We raced down to the viewing area and saw absolutely nothing. It was a complete white out from the sheer volume of water. We raced back to the car again, leapt in as fast as we could, completely soaked and shivering but laughing hysterically. Mum asked how the rocks were, "Remarkable!" we both bellowed in unison, through tears of laughter, "We couldn't see a thing".

We decided we really needed to dry out after that episode so drove to the National Parks office and cafe. Whilst we were warming up, I started to read the local paper that had been left on our table. I turned to the police section and was delighted to see that the most serious criminal activity of the week had been the theft of someone's garden gnomes. We all thought this was fantastic and such a quintessential small community incident. When my sister and I were going through Mum and Dad's boxes, I found a copy of the newspaper with the report. They had kept it for posterity.

Once we left the cafe we were driving along the road and came to a car in front of us that had stopped. We couldn't see any apparent reason for the car stopping but given we were on Kangaroo Island we decided we needed to be patient. Eventually the car in front moved on and we discovered the problem. A kangaroo was standing in the middle of the road. The poor thing was completely soaked through and looked very forlorn. We attempted to drive around it but it hopped in front of the car, so we pointed the car in the other direction and eased forward, he hopped in front of us again. Then he, well I'm saying he, it could quite easily have been a she, not being an expert on the sexing of kangaroos and really not wanting to get close enough to double check, he/she came to the passenger window and stuck his head in, clearly saying, "Can you just give me a lift? I'm sopping wet and cold and it's a bloody long way to get home."

We were so tempted to just let him in the back of the car with Mum but images of boxing kangaroos, the thought of kangaroo pooh in the rental car, the seats being soaked from this semi-drowned kangaroo, held us back. Funnily enough, not the idea that he might just sit on Mum and squeeze the life out of her. We continued the car v kangaroo dance. It took us ages to finally get past him, I still wonder whether someone took pity on him and gave him a lift home.

Dad had a mop of bright white hair. He was also tall and broad. He was always in an airport and his friends and colleagues were never surprised to see ahead of them, in a crowded random airport, a mop of white hair attached to a body heading for a gate to some far off country. Dad loved flying. He always said it was the one place that no one could track him down. He put his headphones on and caught up with movies and music that he had missed.

He was incredibly excited after one particular trip. Mum had joined him and they were flying with a fairly new airline; Emirates. He had booked Business Class tickets which were being offered at Economy Class prices as a promotional deal for Frequent Flyer members. It involved being able to book a free limousine pick up to drive them to the airport, sheer luxury! Once they were checking in, the airline said that they were going to upgrade Mum and Dad to first class. They couldn't believe their luck.

Bugger Bugger Shit!

Into the plane they went and turned left instead of right and then walked right down to the pointy end. They had two seats together but joy oh joy, it had a screen between the two seats that you could just press and it would automatically raise and lower; Dad jokingly called it the 'anti-wife' device; Mum agreed whole-heartedly that she too could press the button and eliminate Dad's snoring when it was time for a nap. He told me all about the mirror that was surrounded by lights which then folded down into a tv screen and the over 300 options for entertainment; the food; the drinks and the butler-like silver service. When I picked them up from the airport, Dad was like an 8-year old boy with a new train set as he told me all about it.

There was however an earlier, somewhat less marvellous experience. He and Mum had gone for a holiday, I think to Greece, and left the children with our grandparents. Whilst they were in Greece, Dad decided that they really needed to purchase a blow up dinghy. I'm not entirely sure why he decided he had to have one from Greece, rather than get one in the UK, but once he had an idea in his mind there was no stopping him. He put the deflated dinghy in his suitcase and the oars, which came apart, were wrapped in brown paper. Dad of course took the suitcases, with said dinghy inside, and typically, because of the speed and sense of purpose with which Dad walked, Mum followed about 10 paces behind, carrying the oars.

Mum in the 70s had black, cropped hair and she was wearing a Mackintosh when she got her passport photo taken; it really wasn't an attractive photo of her and definitely looked like a mug shot. As we all know, in the 1970s, airline travel was beset with terrorist activities. There were regular stories on the news of planes being held up or blown up. What was Dad thinking? Clearly he wasn't, because he really didn't connect the dots and carried on, regardless, in his mission to get this dinghy and oars back to the UK.

Neither dad or mum contemplated the notion that a woman in her 30s walking through an airport with a long pole-like object wrapped in brown paper under her arm, might look a trifle suspicious. Unbeknownst to Mum and Dad (and the rest of the general public), Interpol had put out a warning for a female terrorist who happened to look exactly like Mum in her exceptionally dodgy passport photo. It really doesn't take a lot of imagination to work out what happened next.

Disbelief at the very idea that this fire-arm shaped brown paper packaged item might be the oars for a dinghy, Mum was stopped by multiple uniformed men with guns and interrogated. She didn't speak Greek, they didn't speak English; it was a recipe for disaster. Dad in the meantime was still 10 paces ahead, completely oblivious as to what was happening with his wife, after all he had the associated dinghy hidden away in his suitcase. We still have the offending passport photo and Mum has been reminded of her passing resemblance to a terrorist on many occasions.

Apart from constant travelling, Dad was infamous for falling asleep - everywhere. I was singing in the choir once at school, and at the end of the performance, I looked out into the audience and there was Dad fast asleep in his chair. As everyone started clapping he jumped and immediately started clapping along with everyone else. He even fell asleep when he was giving me driving lessons. Probably the best one of all though was when he fell asleep in a restaurant in the middle of ordering his meal with the waiter. Unsurprisingly, he was eventually diagnosed with sleep apnoea years later but as far as I know he never used his CPAP machine.

Dad finished studying at Yale when I was an infant and he and Mum came back to the UK with my toddler sister, Halina and me, the babe in arms. There have been many incredibly funny stories told by Mum, my dad's colleagues and friends over the years about Dad's various practical failings in comparison with his professional success. One of the typical Dad

Bugger Bugger Shit!

stories from my infancy was about how we lived in a dodgy flat in Leeds in the late 1960s when Mum and Dad returned from the US.

The floor we lived on was mostly empty except for another flat at the end of the corridor. After we moved in, Dad had put some shelves up on the wall for his growing book collection. One day Mum lay me on the floor on my blanket and the resident of the other flat started hammering nails into their own walls. The hammering of the nails reverberated through all of the empty flats and because Dad was never skilled at any kind of odd jobs, the shelves he put up in our flat collapsed right on top of me. Apparently I was saved by a shelf that landed over me and managed to deflect the incredibly heavy textbooks from squashing me.

After a short time in Leeds, Dad successfully applied for a job with the English Department at Lancaster University in the North West of England, just south of the Lake District. Dad and a couple of young and enthusiastic colleagues set up the Linguistics Department at the new Lancaster University, out of the English Department. It was here that Dad's career really took off. He and a few other pioneers really developed the discipline of linguistics into what it is today. According to the QS World rankings, Lancaster University's Linguistics Course is now ranked 10th in the world of all university courses. He was eventually awarded with the inaugural Chair of Linguistics at Lancaster where he worked for 20 years until he decided to move the family to Australia.

With Dad's new job, we relocated to a little house in a village outside Lancaster called Halton and a few years later, when Mum was pregnant with my brother, we moved into Lancaster. The house we moved into was an old farmhouse that had been extended a number of times. It was in a state of disrepair when Mum and Dad bought it but my two earliest memories are from just before and just after we moved in. The owners of the house invited us over for a picnic in the garden before my parents

Bugger Bugger Shit

bought the house. It was 1970 and they wanted to make sure the house was sold to the 'right' people. Not right in any snobbish way but a family who would love the house, just as much as they had. I fully understand that viewpoint because when we eventually sold the house, I wanted to interview any potential owners to make sure they would love the house as much as we had.

My first memory is of that picnic when I was 3-years old. It's not a clear memory, it's a snapshot impression of sun filtering through the trees on a warm afternoon, snippets of the picnic blanket, the sun on my face, playing on the grass with my sister. My first clear memory was after we moved in; eating fish and chips off the top of the dishwasher. I asked Mum and Dad once if that was accurate and why that was the case. It was accurate because Mum and Dad had organised major renovations and restoration of the house and the dishwasher was the only flat, clean surface we could eat off. There was a cement mixer in the kitchen and the only working toilet was in the cellar.

The house is at the top of a long hill and my friends who still live or visit Lancaster still refer to it as our house. So do I. My younger sister and I have an ambition to buy it back at some point in our lives so that it can be ours again. For a family that was so mired in conflict, it astounds me that we loved the house so much we would do almost anything to live there again. Despite the conflicts, we have many, many happy memories in that house.

My dad was always a great shopper. As they brought the house into a habitable condition, Dad was always off looking for antiques or other items at great bargain prices to furnish the house. One day we drove to Manchester I think, to go to Habitat. They bought four leather chairs that could be pushed together into two sofas and a coffee table, known as the

Bugger Bugger Shit!

Family Tree. They were clearly of incredible quality because my younger sister and I only got rid of the Family Tree last year; some 50 years later.

How we kids hated that coffee table. We had spent our lives wanting to get rid of it but Mum and Dad wouldn't hear of it. Eventually we managed to leave it outside 'by accident' when we knew it was going to rain. Mum was so disappointed when we had to put it out for the council to pick up but oh how my sister and I celebrated! Those leather sofa chairs also only went to the tip after Dad died in 2015. They would probably still be going strong now if we had kept them, but again, we found an opportunity to 'dispose of them' when Mum sold her house after Dad died.

My siblings wouldn't forgive me if I omitted one particular story about the Family Tree coffee table. As well as having a cat, my parents thought it would be a good idea for us to have pet guinea pigs. Their cage was in my bedroom. One day I went to check on them and found two of them dead with blood splattered around the cage - it was like something from The Evil Dead!

The last remaining guinea pig looked decidedly ill; possibly because it had watched its brothers' demise. Mum rang the vet who said it sounded like the poor things had died from pneumonia which apparently can rupture their lungs. I know, stay with me, I promise it gets funnier. The vet advised Mum to lightly blow warm air on the guinea pig with a hairdryer. Given she was preparing dinner, she passed the task on to the children. We were watching 'The Waltons' at the time. My seven year old younger sister, with significant gravitas, took the task upon herself; she placed the surviving guinea pig tenderly on a towel on The Family Tree and then sat next to it, gently blowing it with the hairdryer.

We were all so engrossed in 'The Waltons' on tv, none of us were keeping an eye on our sister in her role as Vet Nurse. She too was glued to the television and was not watching what she was doing or checking on how

Bugger Bugger Shit

the poor guinea pig was faring. All of a sudden her hand slipped; she accidentally knocked the guinea pig. Momentarily distracted from the tv, we watched the event unfold with open mouths. The poor animal flew through the air in a graceful arc and landed, unceremoniously, on the floor in front of the tv. The guinea pig was as dead as a dodo! Clearly it had become severely bored with The Waltons and expired. My sister had been blow drying a dead guinea pig and none of us had noticed! Bugger Bugger Shit.

Our family really doesn't have a good record with guinea pigs. My sister's boys were given some guinea pigs a few years ago; three died in suspicious circumstances. A few months later, I had a scratch which got infected and developed into cellulitis; I ended up in hospital for 10 days as a result. It was during the pandemic so at least I had a room to myself with a lovely view over the bush. I saw it as a much deserved little spa break where I was waited on hand and foot.

I think the young registrar who was looking after me though has been scarred for life after seeing the mess my skin was in. I would have new nurses come in, clearly surprised that my stay in hospital during a pandemic was so long when I just had a bit of a 'rash'. Then I would lift the sheets and they would invariably look at my skin in horror. What had started as a rash had then turned into purple followed by black welts which had spread considerably and, because I'm on immuno-suppressants, just weren't responding to the medication. Well actually that's not true, it did respond to penicillin - by giving me hives! I'd never had an allergic reaction to penicillin before so this was plain rude and added insult to injury. Eventually it cleared up enough for me to be discharged but I had to continue attending the dermatology outpatients department for months.

The first time I was there, the Professor of Dermatology asked if we had any pets. At that time we just had three cats and the guinea pigs. When she

Bugger Bugger Shit!

heard we had guinea pigs, she yelled so loudly the whole department could hear, "It's the guinea pigs, it's always the bloody guinea pigs! Let them be free, let them go!" I, shocked, said, "We're about to get two goats, are they ok?" She reassured me that goats were fine but not guinea pigs. I was confused about how I could have developed an infection from the guinea pigs. They were kept in a completely separate part of our house to me and, after the exploding lung episode of my childhood, I avoided them like the plague.

I came back from that appointment and told the kids that sadly we would need to find a new home for the guinea pigs. The youngest of the children and owner of two of the surviving guinea pigs was suspiciously quiet. I asked him if he'd taken the guinea pigs into my part of the house. He confirmed that indeed he had; he was spoken to sternly. A few hours later he came and sat next to me on the sofa. He's never been able to lie and we always know eventually he will be so overcome with guilt that he will tell us the full story of whatever misdemeanour he has perpetrated.

Sure enough, he sat next to me and said, "I was tired from school one day and I needed cuddles with the guinea pigs so I got into your bed with them." My head exploded, as it so often does with the antics of my family. The two remaining guinea pigs were promptly re-homed to a friend who has a farm. Just last week my foster daughter who is absolutely crazy about animals sent the family a text message with a photo saying she had just bought a guinea pig. Almost immediately, one of the boys replied in a panic, "No you can't! Auntie A nearly died when we had guinea pigs before." I followed up with confirmation of this but she laughed and said she knew and was just pulling our legs!

We had many overseas holidays as children. Dad would be employed to run a summer school and we would all tag along, stay in someone's house and have a holiday whilst he worked. I am grateful for the opportunity to

Bugger Bugger Shit

have seen so much of the world as a child and my goal since retiring is to return to many of these places as an adult. Dad had two sabbaticals whilst we were children; both in Hawaii. The first when I was 10/11 and the second when I was 16/17 years old.

The first time we went, my parents took the opportunity to drive across America both on the way to and the way back from Hawaii. The first time was in a station wagon where my assigned seat was in the boot along with all of the suitcases. The second time was slightly more dignified; we had a camper van.

On our way through the desert, we stopped at a roadside service station and whilst Dad filled up the van we all piled out to go to the loo. In Hawaii, I had attended a group similar to the Brownies but it was called Girls In Action. I had a yellow t-shirt with 'Girls in Action' emblazoned across the front of it and I was wearing it on this particular day. Dad, ever the feminist, had given Mum a t-shirt that had 'Women Hold Up Half the Sky' printed across the front, which she was wearing.

What had happened the day before however was that early in the morning, my younger brother and sister, whose allotted sleeping quarters were above the cabin of the van, were playing with their toys. Mum and Dad were asleep in the bed below them. In their enthusiastic creative play, one of them had kicked the Play Mobile bus which flew through the air and landed, with quite some force, right on Mum's face; a very rude and painful awakening. The force was so great that Mum developed a significant black eye over the course of the day.

So here we were in this service station filling up with petrol and using the amenities. There were about half a dozen ramshackle looking old men sitting on chairs, all in a row, outside the shop. They looked on in stunned silence as this woman with her feminist t-shirt and a very pronounced black eye got out of the van followed by four messy children; one of whom had an equally feminist slogan on her t-shirt, and a rather tired looking man who filled the van up with petrol. I could feel their eyes following us as we walked past them and even as an 11 year old I could sense the irony of the situation.

I don't remember the constant arguments between my parents prior to and during the first Hawaii sojourn. Our second period of time in Hawaii in 1983, was also generally one where a cease fire appeared to have been called and a lot of time was spent laughing. This may well have been because my older sister had been diagnosed with malignant melanoma just before we left the UK and Mum and Dad were acutely aware of the severity of the situation and how tenuous life can be.

The family returned to the UK in 1984. After a year away we returned to face the awful political and social situation in the UK. Mum and Dad decided they didn't want to continue to raise their family in Margaret Thatcher's Britain. Dad had previously visited Australia and he and Mum decided there would be a much brighter future for the whole family in the land down under. They didn't tell anyone, so it was a massive shock when Dad told us he had successfully applied for the role of Professor of Linguistics at Macquarie University and also became the founder of the National Centre for English Language Teaching and Research.

It was 1987 and the start of the next phase in the life of the Candlins; Dad's wanderlust and passion for other languages, cultures and experiences, saw us move between the UK, the USA and Australia. As a result, I have triple citizenship. This constant movement between countries, although I really didn't like it at the time, I have realised during this quest for resilience, forged the foundations of resilience within me.

Much of my dad's professional life is readily accessible and it culminated in 2016 being posthumously awarded an Officer of the Order of Australia for his service to Higher Education. My dad followed in his own father's footsteps: who had been awarded an Order of the British Empire in 1977, almost 40 years earlier, also for services to Higher Education.

Dad and the Kids Lancaster 1975

Grandma and Grandpa Oxford January 1988

Bugger Bugger Shit!

Mum and Dad Oxford circa 1959

Bugger Bugger Shit

Mum and Dad's Wedding March 1964 Jesus College Oxford

Bugger Bugger Shit!

Northfield House 2023

Bugger Bugger Shit

Our beloved Northfield House For Sale Lancaster 1989

Bugger Bugger Shit!

View towards Lancaster from Quernmore

My Baby Weight Card Leeds 1968

Chapter 3

Keep Singing

Amazing Grace
How sweet the sound that saved a wretch like me
I once was lost but now I'm found
Was blind but now I see

John Newton
Olney Hymns
1779

"Are you missing Bumpa?" I asked "Yes", Elliott replied thoughtfully "But he was quite shouty".

Dad was the oldest of three children. My grandmother was the daughter of the Head Gardener at the Bowes Museum at Barnard Castle and my grandfather was originally a teacher but progressed over time and at the end of his career was the Principal of a College of Further Education. My grandfather was extremely myopic. I remember that he had very thick

Bugger Bugger Shit!

glasses and still needed a magnifying glass to read any printed material. This of course meant that unlike my mother's father; Grampa Hector, Grandpa Frank didn't go away to war. My dad didn't experience what my mother experienced in terms of a family separated by war.

My dad was raised to be strong and confident by two equally strong and confident parents. He was very fond of his younger brother Geoff and adored his baby sister Margaret, just as she adored him. My dad's last conversation, prior to his death, was with his sister, Auntie Margaret. When it was clear Dad only had days to live I called her in the UK and they said their goodbyes. It was deeply moving and sorrowful but I am so glad they had the opportunity to say goodbye. My grandmother outlived my father and she died the following year, aged 100. My grandfather had died previously in the mid 2000's from pancreatic cancer. Dad was 75 when he died.

Grandpa Frank wrote a myriad of academic texts and my grandmother was his typist. I have very fond memories of my grandfather. He was acutely aware that my sister was the favoured oldest child/grandchild so he made sure the two of us had a special relationship not least because our birthdays were very close together. Like my Welsh Grampa, Grandpa Frank was a great story teller and he told me stories he made up on the spot, of Jacko the monkey, who wore a red waistcoat and got up to lots of mischief.

Grandpa was also a great supporter of me. When I came bottom of the class at Primary School, as I regularly did, and in maths at Secondary School; he always told me that it took great skill to be bottom of the class and that it was much better to be bottom of the class than mediocre and in the middle. I never recall him making a big fuss when my sister inevitably came top of the class. He was a breath of fresh air in comparison to the pressure my parents' purveyed.

There is a term we use in family psychology; Differentiation. In brief it is when a parent is able to understand that they and their child can have different experiences or viewpoints of the same thing or the same person and each are equally valid. My mother's relationship with her father-in-law was somewhat tenuous at times. She would describe him, amongst other things, as controlling, particularly towards his wife. I would describe him as loving and caring. Both are equally true.

My grandmother was a force to be reckoned with. She could be a bulldozer as well as being kind and generous; was endlessly interested in what various members of the family were doing and liked to gossip about it, often missing out crucial facts or getting things wrong. She and Grandpa struggled enormously when we all moved to Australia.

She would ring around the family like clockwork on a Sunday morning, oblivious to the inconvenience this caused. One Sunday morning she rang as we were all having breakfast. Mum told her that my brother was cooking himself bacon and eggs. Grandma berated Mum for not cooking it for him. Mum replied that he was fully capable of cooking it himself and that he needed to learn to cook if he was going to be independent. Fair point. Grandma didn't think so.

When I was an adult, Grandma would invariably call me if she had tried to get hold of someone in the family and failed. She found it very difficult to understand that we are all independent beings with independent lives and didn't live in each other's pockets. When I told her I had no idea where people were, I think she struggled to believe me and would imagine that I was keeping secrets from her.

I have outlined my older sister's cancer experience in Chapter 7; however it is significant for a number of other reasons; not least because her death was the beginning of the transformation of my relationship with my dad. My sister's death was incredibly difficult for everyone, particularly my

Bugger Bugger Shit!

dad because it was during this period that his own relationship with his parents temporarily broke down.

It was clear in early November 1987 that my sister was not going to survive. My parents and my younger siblings came back to the UK after only a few months in Australia, with the full knowledge that they would be returning without their eldest child. My sister married her longtime love, Eddie, during this time; not in our church but in Christie's Specialist Cancer Hospital in Manchester.

Only the two immediate families, Halina's best friend, our Vicar and his wife and the medical staff attended the wedding. This was disappointing for the rest of the family but when you realise that the wedding occurred only three weeks before Halina died, the context becomes clearer. My sister was incredibly ill and the doctors made the decision that her visitors should be limited to immediate family and one or two very, very close friends who Halina chose to see. Even my brother and sister didn't see her very much and I only saw her to give Mum and Dad a break.

My parents told their respective parents that Halina was too ill for visitors. Mum's surviving parent, Grampa Hector, told her that he was very disappointed but that he knew the decision had been made in Halina's best interests and thoroughly respected it. Dad's parents however were not so supportive. Grandpa wrote Dad a letter which none of us have ever seen. Mum told me that Dad was distraught by it and he threw the letter in the bin without showing it to her.

When Halina died, the church was full to overflowing but from Dad's side of the family only his father, his brother-in-law and his oldest nephew attended. They sat halfway down the church, didn't attend the burial and didn't attend the wake. My father was completely abandoned by his family in his hour of need. Despite this, my parents, myself and my siblings have never held a grudge towards any other members of the family. My parents saw this as entirely the responsibility of Grandpa and Grandma.

My dad didn't have anything to do with his parents for about ten years after this. I was still living in the UK so I continued to see them but the remainder of my immediate family didn't. The family did however eventually reunite and restore the broken relationships at Grandma and Grandpa's Golden Wedding Anniversary celebration which I think everyone was very thankful for after such a period of hurt.

Mum and Dad had been living in Australia for a number of years when Dad relocated to Hong Kong for a period of time, due to his work. Mum was working in Sydney and so didn't join him immediately. Dad commuted for a time and Mum flew up and down. It was really following Halina's death and this time when Dad was alone in Hong Kong that I saw a gradual change in his demeanour towards me. He started to soften and I saw him being vulnerable for the first time in my life. I was working, training to be a Psychologist and studying for my Masters degree and our relationship changed as Dad started to see me as an adult and he would listen to me when we had conflicting views.

I decided that I really needed to face the reality of my relationship with Dad. If I was going to move forward with my life, I needed to let go of the influence he had over me and the fear I could still feel at times. I sought the advice of two church Ministers that I respected and over a number of meetings I talked in detail of Dad's abuse and violence. There were a lot of ugly tears shed as I chose to forgive Dad for each of the times he had assaulted me and sometimes I needed to do it again and again.

The act of forgiveness takes many forms and for me and Dad I needed to name it, give it shape, bring it into the light in order for its power to be dissolved. I did not need to tell Dad that I forgave him. It was, in fact, nothing to do with him. This was about me taking my history with Dad and taking back my power. Since this episode 30 years ago, I have talked about my dad's abuse only a handful of times, this being one of them. It is not my story nor is it my dad's. It is only part of our respective stories and

Bugger Bugger Shit!

one which has been redeemed since. I do not want my dad to be judged on his past behaviour towards me; that is too simplistic and it's unfair. What he did was not ok. I know it and he knew it but we never needed to speak about it.

He was immensely proud when I gained registration as a Psychologist and was awarded my Masters. I started to look for the exit a little less often than I had and was happy to stay longer when I visited my parents. One day in the late 1990s, Dad announced that he wanted to learn to sail. I decided, on a whim, that this might be a safe way to build our relationship. It worked; we had a shared passion for the water and loved learning together. Dad's work invariably got in the way and I spent much more time on a boat than he did but it was our unique thing and I'm so glad we got to do it together. I love being on a boat and I ended up regularly sailing and racing in the summer Twilight series for about 15 years. Dad loved that I loved sailing and being out on a boat in Pittwater always makes me feel close to him.

Dad was diagnosed with prostate cancer on Mum's birthday of all days in November 2007. He was medically well cared for and no one outside the family knew of the diagnosis. As so many doctors said, men die with prostate cancer not from prostate cancer. It really didn't impact his life very much. That was until it did.

In July 2014 it was apparent that Dad was not at all well. My brother-in-law died on the 1st July 2014. Mum and Dad had been in the UK for the inauguration of Mum's younger brother as Mayor of his local area. They cut their trip short and when I went to pick them up from the airport, Dad was in a wheelchair instead of Mum.

Following Tim, my brother-in-law's funeral, Dad went to see his Oncologist who decided it was time to start chemotherapy. Dad did not do well with the chemo. Does anyone? By Christmas he was a shadow of his former self and at his medical appointment on Christmas Eve, the doctors said that the treatment wasn't working and were going to stop the chemo. Bugger bugger shit.

Christmas that year was terrible. Tim had died only a few months previously and Mum and Dad, without telling us, were reeling from the news delivered the day before that Dad's cancer was now terminal. They told us a few days later. Bizarrely, it was by phone when my brother, sister-in-law, sister and her boys and I were all in the Botanical Gardens to see a performance of the Wind in the Willows. We were sitting on rugs having a pre-performance picnic when Dad called us to relay the news. Perhaps he thought it would be better to tell us when we were all together. Unsurprisingly the adults were all a bit dazed during the performance whilst the boys were oblivious.

Dad was born on 31st March 1940 and died on the 10th May 2015. It was Mothers' Day and a week before my birthday. It had been a long hard slog since late January when he was admitted to hospital after a fall. His consultants decided that he really couldn't go home and was nearing the end of his life.

I was in Brisbane working for a few days when Mum called me to say that the doctors didn't think he had much time left. I had planned to go to Noosa after the training for the Australia Day long weekend for some much needed R&R but whilst I was there, all I wanted to do was jump on a plane and get back to Sydney. I had a bit of a cold so I couldn't have visited Dad anyway. I made the best of a lovely location and a few days' peace and quiet knowing I would probably need some reserves in my emotional tank in the weeks to come.

When I landed in Sydney, I switched on my phone as we were taxiing across the tarmac. It immediately rang and it was Mum. She told me that she and Dad, along with my brother and sister-in-law had had a lovely afternoon planning Dad's funeral, including Dad's desire for me to sing at it. I was somewhat distraught at the matter-of-fact way Mum was chatting

Bugger Bugger Shit!

about it, whilst I was on a packed plane and held back the tears at the thought of not having my dad around for very much longer.

Whilst I very much believe allowing the tears to flow is a healthy thing to do, I wasn't entirely sure I would be able to centre myself enough to disembark and pick up my luggage had I allowed myself to cry. Besides, I really didn't want to howl in front of a bunch of strangers on a plane. I did however race to grab my bags and may have broken the speed limit slightly trying to get to the hospital as quickly as I could.

It was past visiting hours when I got there so I slipped into Dad's room as quietly as I could. I gave him a hug and simply said, "Oh Dad". He reassured me that he was ok and that he had come to terms with his mortality and besides he was, "Going to be with Halina", my elder sister who had died in 1987. I wasn't entirely sure it worked quite like that for a man who had never professed any kind of faith in an afterlife.

That evening was the start of what was to become the most intimate and connected time of my entire life with my dad.

I visited Dad every day in hospital following that fateful Australia Day long weekend. The day after I returned from Queensland, my brother and his partner were at the hospital at the same time as I. We chatted for a while and then we all started making moves to leave. Dad delayed me by asking me to move some things for him. Sensing that he wanted to spend some time with me alone, Kit and his partner left and I sat down next to Dad.

Something prompted me to ask Dad if he wanted me to say a prayer with him. Dad was someone who went to church for weddings and funerals, not even Christmas and Easter, but he did appreciate their architecture and would go out of his way to visit any historical churches whenever he was in Europe. This was a strange question for me to ask him but he said yes. I said a little prayer for a good night's sleep and a prayer for the nurses and doctors and gave Dad a kiss good night and went on my way.

The next day I visited him again after work. We chatted about mundane things and then I said that Mum told me he wanted me to sing at his funeral. He said yes but he wasn't sure what he wanted me to sing. I joked that I probably couldn't pull off Eric Clapton, who he'd been listening to on repeat, but I'd have a think. I suggested a few songs and hymns and then with one of them he couldn't remember what it was so I began to sing it. Dad closed his eyes and seemed to be enjoying it so I carried on singing.

That became our ritual for the next three months. I visited Dad after work, sometimes Mum was there, sometimes a sibling. We would chat and then whoever else was there would leave and I would stay behind and sing to Dad and say a little prayer. One evening, amongst a whole host of others, I sang quite a modern church song and he jumped and said, "That's it, that's the one. I want you to sing that at my funeral".

I sang to Dad every evening from the 28th January to the 9th May; sometimes they were old hymns; sometimes quite modern songs; sometimes songs friends of mine had written.

He was moved from Palliative Care to Hospice Care on the 6th May 2015, much to his distress. When I visited him on the 8th May, Mum was there and was now staying 24 hours with Dad. We chatted for a while, I sang to him and he spoke to his sister on the phone. When I hung up the phone he looked me in the eye and said, "Keep singing". He didn't mean for now; he meant forever.

Those were the last words he spoke. He slipped in and out of consciousness and died on Sunday morning the 10th May 2015, holding Mum's hand just as he had wanted to.

At Dad's funeral, the day before my birthday, a friend and I got up to sing:

All these pieces, broken and scattered
In mercy gathered, mended and whole
Empty-handed, but not forsaken

Bugger Bugger Shit!

I've been set free, I've been set free.
Amazing Grace
How sweet the sound that saved a wretch like me
I once was lost but now I'm found
Was blind but now I see
Oh I can see you now
I can see the love in Your eyes
Laying yourself down
Raising up the broken to life
You take our failure
You take our weakness
You set your treasure in jars of clay
So take this heart Lord
I'll be your vessel, the world to see your life in me.
Amazing Grace
How sweet the sound that saved a wretch like me
I once was lost but now I'm found,
Was blind but now I see

> **Broken Vessels**
> **Jonas Myrin and Joel Houston**
> **2014 Hillsong Worship**

Dad and Elliott Mona Vale 2007 My favourite photo of him caught in a natural moment of being Bumpa

Dad and I New Haven May 1967

Bugger Bugger Shit!

Dad on his travels somewhere

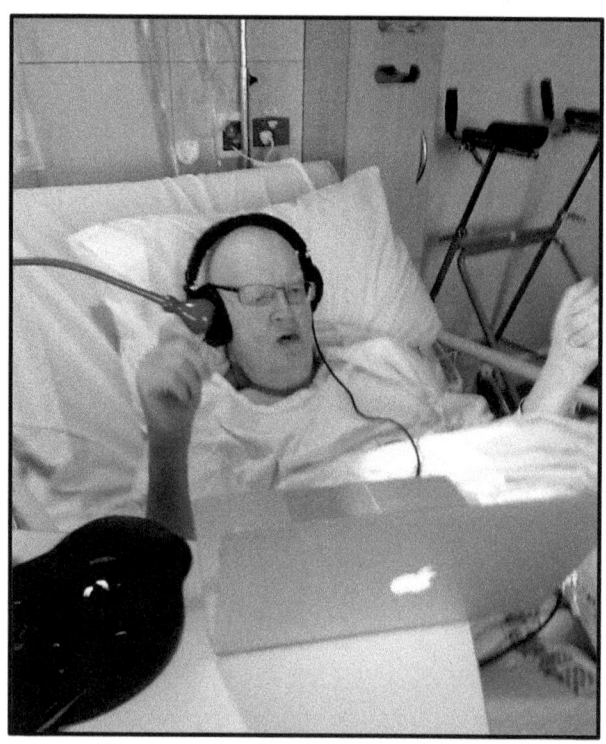

Dad Sydney January 2015 playing air drums to Eric Clapton

Chapter 4

The War Zone

"The past is a foreign country: they do things differently there"

LP Hartley
The Go Between
1953 Hamish Hamilton

In the spring of 2023 our family unexpectedly grew with the addition of the 16 year old friend of Bryn who for various reasons, along with her siblings, wasn't able to live at home with her mum. She came to us in a crisis but stayed to become another member of the family. Skye's arrival meant the family had to make some changes to the bedrooms and so my sister and I were faced with having to finally go through the mountains of boxes that belonged to our parents and had been piled high in what had been Mum's living room.

I naively thought I was almost at the end when I opened a fireproof box that my dad had labelled precious. In it I discovered a treasure trove of letters from Mum to Dad. They were written in 1968, when I was almost a year old. Dad was apparently in India for six weeks of work and Mum had stayed in the UK with their baby and toddler. The letters were affectionate,

Bugger Bugger Shit!

usually starting with, "My Darling Chrissie," and were full of comments about how much she missed Dad, news of us girls, warm comments about family members she had been staying with whilst Dad was away and Mum trying to manage the purchase of our first home.

I read parts of the letters out to my sister, who along with me had trouble managing her facial expressions at this revelation. To say we were shocked would have to be the understatement of the century. Not only had we never heard Mum refer to Dad as Chrissie, we had hardly ever heard her say anything affectionate about Dad or us our entire lives. We wondered whether this really was our mother. We had seen Dad being affectionate with Mum but rarely Mum towards Dad. A few days later we found Dad's letters to Mum. Equally affectionate and adoring. Clearly this was a couple very much in love.

My sister and I have, on and off for years, tried to work out our mother but we have always failed. Her parents were the kindest and most loving grandparents and parents you could wish to ask for. Her brothers could be slightly unusual but always incredibly warm and funny. What had happened to Mum within this family so that she was so harsh and at times cruel? Then I had a profound realisation.

The previous evening, I had been reading a question in one of my MS Facebook Support groups. One of the members had expressed her deep concern that, due to the lesion she had developed in her frontal lobe, found herself being quite mean and wasn't able to control it. As is my habit, I expressed empathy for her and then explained the neuroscience so that she could understand what was happening and then gave her some strategies to manage the situation as well as some books to read.

As I read the letters to my sister, I recalled the online interaction and I also remembered a comment that my sister had made some years before. My sister had attended Mum's Neurology appointment and had seen her

MRI. She commented to me later that Mum's brain looked like Swiss cheese due to the number of lesions she had. I filled my sister in on the Facebook interaction and reminded her of the Swiss cheese comment.

As we often do, we looked at each other knowing exactly what the other was thinking. My sister asked me if I remembered Mum being kind before she was born or had she always been mean. Being nearly eight years older than Naomi, I often have a different understanding of family events, simply because I was older. I thought about it and said it was difficult to remember because there had been so many years of Mum's awful behaviour but I thought that yes, whilst she always had the ability to be a bit mean and strict, I didn't remember her being so consistently abusive.

Naomi and I continued to sort through Mum and Dad's things and we came across a number of boxes that held family photos. Some of these were black and white photos of ancestors long dead, some were of our grandparents and ourselves as younger children. What was of particular interest were the many photos of ourselves as children with Mum and Dad. Of course we had seen the majority of them before and I could remember the events but it was the viewing of them at this particular time and this particular context that was significant.

What we saw with fresh eyes was the warmth and fun displayed in the photos. Pictures of Mum frolicking in the sea with us. Photos of Mum holding her babies with clear love and affection in her eyes. Photos of Mum and Dad looking lovingly at each other. Whilst our most significant memories are of an angry and abusive mother, that is not the whole story.

Our Mum had her first multiple sclerosis attack in 1975, when Naomi was about a year old, although as so many of us with MS know, the symptoms are often around for some time before the first major attack. I remember the incident; she was getting something out of the oven and she

Bugger Bugger Shit!

dropped it because her hand went numb. It took a lot of time for Mum to be diagnosed with MS.

Here was a young mother of four, working full time as a Health Visitor and married to an up and coming academic who often travelled for work. Doctors knew she had MS but were completely unwilling to give her the diagnosis of a progressive neurological disease with no known cure or intervention. Her cousin Jed, who was a doctor, was the one who eventually told her of the diagnosis. Bugger bugger shit.

That afternoon my sister and I were finally able to understand our mum's behaviour. It didn't make anything ok but it did provide an explanation and a reason and we could see, as adults, the complexity of her life.

Mum was born in Cardiff, South Wales in November 1939, just after the Second World War broke out. She was the second of three children. Her oldest brother was 10 years older than her so until Mum's younger brother was born a couple of years later, she was pretty much an only child. Mum told me a story about one of her first memories. It is of her mother, my nanna, standing at the back door of their little house in Bargoed looking over the valleys of South Wales towards Cardiff; watching the bombs raining down and commenting to her young daughter, "Cardiff's really getting it tonight".

My Grampa, Hector, wasn't compelled to join the war due to his age but he did. He went off to France first and then the "Far East" and didn't return for five years. My uncle, Mum's younger brother was a baby when Grampa left and in school by the time he came back. My Nanna, like so many women of her generation, was effectively a single Mum, raising her children in the midst of a war whilst being constantly terrified that her

The War Zone

family would be wiped out or her husband wouldn't return home. It is the story of so many families, over so many years, impacted by whatever international conflict or governmental policies happen to be at the time.

My Grampa returned home physically intact, albeit with a limp due to his 'wooden, left leg, Archie'; however, as an adult and as a psychologist I can reflect on the impact of the war on him through one simple story that he used to tell, to wide eyes and peals of laughter from his respective grandchildren.

When we would ask him to tell us about the war he would settle in for story time. He told us of the day he came across a tiger in the jungle. Faced with certain death from the tiger, Grampa rushed towards it, stuck his hand into the tiger's mouth, all the way through the stomach to its tail which he grabbed hold of, pulled and whipped the tiger inside out. As a child this was wondrous, as an adult I can see the impact of trauma on the man. He never told any stories of what happened to him and his friends during the war. I have no idea specifically of where he served or what he did, other than him being a storeman. He wasn't on the front line fighting, he was back at the camp ensuring supplies were in order but still the horror of war impacted him deeply.

There was another story that he told. He told us about handing out sweets to the local children when he was in India. This was important to us because Grampa was the purveyor of sweets to his grandchildren. After his wife, my Nanna, died on New Year's Eve 1980; he would live with us for several months of the year and every Saturday he would go down to the shops to buy his 'fags', a paper and a chocolate for each of us. He carefully researched which were our individual favourites and without fail he would buy them for us. Grampa died from respiratory failure, aged 84, in 1988; the day before my 21st birthday. His age is a feat given he was considerably

Bugger Bugger Shit!

overweight, did virtually no exercise and smoked a pack of unfiltered cigarettes every day.

Before he died though, he had a home visit from a new doctor; an Indian man, who was a child during the war. Grampa reminisced with him one day about his time in India during the war. The doctor told him his own story about the war; a story about his interactions with the Allied troops, particularly one very kind Welsh soldier who used to give sweets to the local children. Unbelievable!

Growing up in our family was, at times, like being raised in a war zone. We had two parents who bickered constantly. That is not an exaggeration; none of us can remember a single day when Mum and Dad weren't having some argument or passing snarky remarks at each other. I remember one day when I was in the kitchen making a cup of tea or something equally banal. Mum and Dad got into an argument about something meaningless and Mum ended up hurling cans from the grocery shopping she had just bought at Dad. My Mum even managed to pick a fight with my dad when he was in palliative care.

Mum's way of managing their arguments was to go off for a long drive in the car to cool off. My dad's response over the years to his deteriorating relationship with Mum was to simply travel more for work. With Dad being away, there were at least some times where they got on well. Dad often displayed an affectionate side with Mum but it seemed to us that it was rarely reciprocated or initiated by Mum to him. When Dad died we realised just how much he had been a buffer between us and Mum, even though we couldn't see it at the time.

Mum's constant refrain to her daughters was, "You'll be as fat as butter" if anything vaguely unhealthy went into our mouths (despite the fact that we were all stick thin and I was a very fit ballet dancer). She also liked to call us sluts quite regularly. It took me until I was about 16 to realise "slut" in Welsh referred to someone who would probably be described as slovenly rather than slang for a prostitute. She would generally use it if our bedrooms were untidy or we'd left a mess. Nevertheless, the context didn't matter when you are a child and your mother is calling you a slut. Birthday parties were always a drama because Mum would ensure the birthday girl/boy never won any of the games and even if we did she would always give the prize to whoever came second. Her reasoning was that we were getting presents and shouldn't be greedy.

One of the hardest things for me as the second child was always being compared with our older sister, Halina, particularly when it came to academic success. Parent teacher evenings were hell on earth. It didn't matter how many good reports I got from teachers, there were always some where they were pretty average or, when it came to maths, the reports were always terrible. I would get my ear chewed off in the car on the way home. There was never any praise for the things that I did well but there was always intensely personal criticism of my apparent failures.

Our sister Halina could do no wrong. It is often said that parents don't have favourites; well, in our family, there wasn't any point in denying it. Of course what happened was inevitable; Mum and Dad's approval of Halina meant that my relationship with my sister was always compromised.

I remember one day when Mum had, as usual, taken my sister's side in some disagreement we had had. My red hair was often my downfall when it came to managing my temper and this particular day I lost it. I yelled at Mum and she slapped me so I grabbed Mum's hair and refused to let go, so she grabbed my hair and also refused to let go. To be honest, she had an unfair advantage because my hair was long so she had way more to grab hold of! Dad had to literally break up the fight because neither of us would back down.

Bugger Bugger Shit!

I decided very early on that my exit strategy from this home mired in conflict would be to apply to be a boarder at the Northern Ballet School. Ballet was my refuge. I was good at it and I loved it. My focus was on my future as a professional dancer. Unfortunately it wasn't to be because one of my High School classmates, during a particularly rambunctious lunch time, ran at me whilst we were mucking around on the school oval and tackled me to the ground. I irreparably damaged my knee. Ballet was off the cards forever. I was devastated and I was angry, particularly because my parents seemed to have no concept of what this meant for me and were entirely unsympathetic and unsupportive. Bugger bugger shit.

Whilst my younger sister, Naomi, and I were going through our parents' documents we made yet another discovery that left us considerably surprised. Mum hadn't been able to throw away any of our older sister's school work. We had found her uni notes which was bad enough but then we came across her sixth form notes, and later all of her school exercise books. I think there are going to be thousands of rolls of toilet paper created out of the paperwork we have added to the recycling depot during this endeavour. Along with her school notes we found some of her school reports and then as we delved deeper into the boxes we found school reports for all of us. Having spent my childhood and adolescence being compared to Halina academically, I discovered that in fact my grades were often better than hers!

It was even more significant for Naomi. We discovered a very thorough developmental assessment of Naomi when she was in Year Five at Primary School. The assessment utilised a number of well respected and commonly used scales and the report was very well written. Naomi always struggled at school and in a house full of academically inclined people this was a big deal. Naomi always felt 'less than', she would say that she was never expected to even finish school and certainly not go on to University. It is to

The War Zone

her absolute credit that she not only got to University, she completed a double degree and went on to gain her Masters in Education. It wasn't so surprising however once we read this report.

At age ten, her IQ score fell into the above average range and was well on the way to being gifted. A comment on the first page added to the interest. It said that of the three younger children, Naomi was the brightest and that my brother and I were both well below average and in fact, as a younger child, I had been assessed as having special needs and was placed in the special education unit at school.

What is absolutely clear to me now, as a Psychologist reading that report, is that Naomi had Dyslexia and it wasn't picked up. She does in fact have Irlen Syndrome (a visual processing disorder) and despite the fact that her school reports all clearly stated how well she was doing; because she wasn't able to read and spell, she was dismissed. How the education system in the UK, the US and Australia failed my sister; and my parents, despite their academic and medical training, fell into the same category of not understanding that Naomi clearly had a disability.

Had this been picked up and early intervention support been put in place, she would have a very different story to tell. Now, living in the same house with my sister as adults, it is abundantly clear how intelligent she is. She knows and understands far more about the world than I ever will. I may know psychology and neuroscience intimately but I wouldn't have a clue how to work out the problems and concepts that Naomi does in a flash.

I had always known that I had an issue with reading when I was very young but I didn't know I had been placed in the Special Ed unit. It does however explain why I was always confused about why I had two Infants teachers. Mum and Dad had told me that I was desperate to do ballet as a young child so they had enrolled me in classes. An unexpected bonus was

Bugger Bugger Shit!

that within a few weeks of starting ballet classes, my reading age had shot up and I was reading books several years ahead of my classmates.

I spent most of the 'reading time' in primary school sitting in the library corner reading whatever I liked, whilst my peers had to endure Peter and Jane. I think it's fascinating that our bodies and brains are so clearly linked. That moving our bodies in a coordinated way, coordinates our brains. If ever there was a story to support Forest Schools and flexible learning policies this is it. Children are not made to sit behind desks; when children are allowed to move and play and problem solve, as well as hang upside down in trees, or pirouette, their whole system benefits.

It would be remiss of me to not talk about the good times we had growing up. Families are rarely just one thing or another. They are a mix of good and bad, sad and happy. A few years ago I was at a professional development session. As part of the training, a large circle with labelled quadrants was mapped out on the floor. We were asked to consider our Family of Origin and stand in the most appropriate associated section. Despite being engaged in the training, I found this particular exercise completely impossible to do. The trainer suggested I choose the quadrant most similar to my family of origin experience. I explained that the problem lay not in my family being more one thing than the other but that they were ALL of the quadrants equally, just at different periods of time. I couldn't choose one over the other, they were all equally significant and equally valid.

We were always aware of the story of how Mum and Dad met - on a blind date at a bus stop. Mum was in her first year of nursing and Dad was in his last year of school. One of Mum's friends dropped out of a group date because she had a boyfriend and felt guilty about going. Mum also had a boyfriend but apparently that didn't phase her, so off she went.

She and Dad clearly hit it off because their relationship was immediately more than just being friends. They really liked each other. The slight

The War Zone

spanner in the works was that Mum had this boyfriend. Mum's younger brother Dave, decided to sort this situation out. He invited Mum's boyfriend round for afternoon tea. He also invited Dad round for afternoon tea at the same time. There was Mum's deception caught in action. All three of them have enjoyed regaling us on numerous occasions with this story of the slightly awkward afternoon tea. Dad evidently won the 1958 season of Love Island.

Dad loved to tell us about Mum's early years as a student and then qualified midwife. She would cycle through Cardiff and then Oxford when they moved there, to deliver babies at home. We couldn't believe our luck when Call the Midwife was broadcast. This was exactly what Mum had done. It was hard to imagine Mum as a Trixie, Barbara or Jenny but Dad assured us that whenever Mum was on her bicycle, everyone in a car got out of her way. Dad was working to support himself as a bus conductor at the time so he would definitely have known. Mum tells stories of sneaking out late from the Nurses quarters to go off on adventures with her friends or on dates with Dad and then, slightly more problematically, sneaking back in without being discovered by Matron.

Just as much as we argued, we laughed as a family. I was the comedian of the bunch but we all had a healthy sense of the ridiculous. My particular talents lie in unplanned physical comedy and saying exactly the wrong thing at exactly the wrong time. My mouth frequently got me into trouble, ok let's be honest, it still does. On one particular evening, both of my talents occurred simultaneously.

We were having dinner and for some unknown reason we had dessert. We never had dessert. Dad asked me to go downstairs to the cellar to get the ice cream out of the chest freezer. In our house there was a door between the kitchen and the hallway and a second door between the hallway and the

Bugger Bugger Shit!

stairs down to the cellar. This was a very old Victorian House with very thick stone walls. I duly went down to the cellar.

I am not much over five feet now as an adult. As a child, I was tiny. I opened the freezer to discover the ice cream right at the bottom. There was no way I could reach it. Not to be deterred however I used my ballet training. I hitched myself up on the side of the freezer and perfected the art of balancing on the side using my body as a fulcrum so whilst I held the chest freezer open with one hand, I could swing down and grab the ice cream with the other.

It took a couple of goes to calculate the velocity of swinging hard enough and fast enough to reach the bottom of the freezer without losing my grip on the lid of the freezer that I was holding above my head and without actually falling in. I was quite impressed with my genius problem solving to be honest. What I had completely forgotten about was that when I was concentrating hard, I tended to stick my tongue out. As I finally swung down to get the ice cream, my tongue grazed the side of the freezer and got firmly stuck. Bugger!

I had a problem. I couldn't pull my tongue off the freezer without using my right hand, I couldn't let go of the lid of the freezer because it would have crashed down on me and squashed me. What to do? Call for help of course. Have you ever tried to call out when your tongue is firmly stuck to the side of a freezer? No? Well I hadn't either but I thought it can't be that hard. So I gave it a go. "Hellllll" I called. No p because I couldn't close my lips to get the p sound. I also discovered that when one is balancing on the side of a freezer one doesn't have any capacity to use one's diaphragm to amplify the sound and my head was in the freezer so my voice was never going to go anywhere other than down. "Hellllll" I quietly called again. Nothing. Hardly surprising with my whisper of a yell, two doors and some very thick stone walls. "Helllllll". I called with increasing panic rising.

The War Zone

Would anyone realise I hadn't exited the cellar? Would my family be so busy talking they would forget about me? Would they clear up the dinner dishes, sit down and watch a bit of tv and then lock the cellar door on their way to bed, leaving me hanging with my tongue stuck to the freezer for the rest of my life? Can you actually die from a frozen tongue?

Eventually after what I swear was two hours, Dad sent my sister Halina down to find out what the problem was. I'm sure it wasn't because he imagined his second daughter's mouth was stuck to the actual freezer. It was probably just because he wanted his ice cream faster than I was bringing it up. Halina came down, slightly irritated, saw me hanging in the freezer and doubled up in laughter. Not helpful. When she had recovered, she assessed the situation and decided that the easiest thing would be for her to lean in and peel my tongue off the wall of the freezer. I mean it was effective, it worked. Whether my tongue was ever the same again is a question for debate.

Then there was the time that my dad decided to make pea and ham soup. My dad was a fabulous cook and he loved cooking. He didn't like cleaning up so much but he liked to express his creativity in the kitchen. In fact a frequent refrain from us children was, "Please don't fangle the food". We just wanted fish fingers or egg and chips but no, nothing was ever simple when Dad was home. Secretly we really liked it when he was away for work because Mum would give us fish fingers, egg and chips and our absolute favourite; thinly sliced cheese laid on a baking tray and shoved under the grill. No bread, just burnt cheese that we liked to peel off and eat. Heston Blumenthal would have a heart attack if he knew what was going on in our kitchen in the 70s.

Anyway, back to the pea and ham soup. Dad had cooked up the soup and in his infinite wisdom decided that he would pour the hot soup into his latest kitchen "toy"; a blender, to save him having to squash all of the

Bugger Bugger Shit!

peas and get rid of the lumps of ham. No, in case you are wondering, I have no idea what on earth he thought he was doing. Pea and ham soup is best when it's lumpy with ham for goodness sake. Anyway, hot soup, blender, lid on, basic physics. Dad pressed go just as I walked into the kitchen and yes, the lid shot off and I was sprayed with piping hot soup. It tasted nice but it wasn't really how I wanted it to be served and I certainly didn't appreciate the almost third degree burns I ended up with!

I will never forget the time our entire family went to the movies together. It only happened once but it was memorable. Mum and Dad had just moved to Australia, my sister and I were visiting from the UK, and A Fish Called Wanda was released. Perfect. Mum and Dad loved John Cleese, Michael Palin and the like so we all decided to go. I was sitting next to Mum. She laughed so hard I thought she was going to expire, or at the very least pee her pants. She was completely incapable of moving once the film finished. I had never seen her doubled up with mirth before. I think the cinema attendants were ready to switch the lights off and lock up by the time we actually left.

Despite our fractured relationship, Mum and I could still get on. In Australia there is a wonderful concept of Long Service Leave. It was originally developed so that the ten pound poms and other European migrants could get back "home" to see their families. This was before we all took aeroplanes at the drop of a hat. People had to get there and back on a ship which of course took weeks.

After 10 years with an organisation you can apply for about 12 weeks leave. In 2002 it had been over 10 years for me with the same organisation so I took my Long Service leave to travel around Australia. Mum came with me for part of the trip and we genuinely had a lovely time together. If we were sitting down anywhere for a while, Mum would look around and she would spy a person or a couple and she would start to make up a story about them. I would join in and we created the most ridiculous lives for so many people.

We also developed a rating system for public toilets and when one of us had taken advantage of the amenities we would come back and just say a number as we sat down again. If anyone else was with us they would have no clue what we were talking about. One of the most wonderful things we did together was to take the Indian Pacific train from Perth to Adelaide. Mum and I loved it. We sat reading or just looking out of the window. Not really talking. We would look at the desert and outback for hours on end. There was essentially nothing there so whenever we saw a sheep or a dog, we'd just call out, "Sheep". "Dog". Every so often there was a truck. In the middle of nowhere. Neither of us could work out how a truck got to be there when we never saw any dwellings, or people for that matter.

Mum's MS diagnosis and her training as a nurse meant there was no room for anyone in our family to be ill. If we complained of a headache or nausea we were always reminded that we were so much better off than Mum and we had nothing to complain about. As we endured the war zone, people from outside our family who were none the wiser, constantly asked me how Mum was. Mum was fine. She was always fine because in fact her MS was in remission whilst we were growing up.

They were always well meaning and had that look of concern on their face but it made us feel invisible. There was no room to be anything other than fine ourselves. In fact when I was diagnosed with MS on top of my Psoriatic Arthritis, Mum's response was to minimise my MS because hers was so much worse than mine - it wasn't, it was just different - and I had to also manage an equally horrible, aggressive and degenerative form of inflammatory arthritis.

As I grew older and Mum's MS deteriorated, her behaviour became more and more odd, abusive and erratic. Following Dad's death my sister,

Bugger Bugger Shit!

Mum and I pooled our finances and built a house for us all to live in together. This would mean that my sister's sons would have a second adult in a parental role, following the death of my sister's husband; Mum would be cared for as she aged and I would very quickly be mortgage free.

Whilst our house was being built, I lived with Mum in a little villa we had rented. One day she went out to do the grocery shopping in the middle of the afternoon. She drove to the shopping centre she had been going to for over 30 years. When she hadn't come back by about 6pm I started to get a little worried and called my sister, no she hadn't heard from Mum. By 7pm, I was ready to call the police but Mum arrived at that moment.

What had happened was very strange. Mum had done the shopping and then came into the car park and 'lost' her car. This in itself wasn't so odd, who hasn't lost a car in a multi-storey car park? Mum however was completely incapable of finding it. In the end the security officers helped her locate it because they observed an apparently confused little old lady on the CCTV. She explained it away by saying her blood sugar was low so she'd got confused.

Once she had put the shopping in her car, she decided she really needed to get a cup of coffee. Instead of going back into the shopping centre where there were a myriad of cafes, she drove several suburbs away to a centre she knew had a cafe. I assume the cafe closed at about 5 so it took her 2 hours to drive the 20 minutes home.

This wasn't in fact the first episode where she got lost driving on very familiar streets, it had been happening for years. Eventually the Neurologist, who Mum and I share, diagnosed her with MS related Dementia. If we felt like we were in a war zone previously we were now on the front line. Bugger bugger shit!

The War Zone

Dad Halina and I Hawaii 1983

Mum and Dad Church Point circa 2012

Bugger Bugger Shit!

Halina and I Portugal circa 1969

The War Zone

Mum and the kids Hawaii 1984 the year my MS started to grumble

Naomi Kit Me Halina Lancaster circa 1977

Bugger Bugger Shit!

Nanna and Grampa's Wedding December 1929. Nanna and Grampa are seated in the centre

The War Zone

The Family including Grandparents Lancaster 1976 Halina's Confirmation

Chapter 5

The Front Line

There is a crack in everything - that's how the light gets in

Leonard Cohen,
Anthem
1992 Columbia Records

On one particular day Lewis, who was about 10 at the time, came across Mum with her coat on about to go outside. "Where are you going Nain?" (pronounced nine; it's Welsh for Nan), he asked, "To the airport of course, I'm going up to Hong Kong to see Bumpa (my Dad), I'm just going outside to wait for the taxi" she replied. "I tell you what, why don't you go and sit down on your sofa and I'll let you know when the taxi arrives," Lewis responded helpfully, knowing full well that she would quickly forget that she had planned to go to the airport.

Mum's driving had become so erratic and she was getting lost so frequently that I spoke to her Neurologist and asked him to tell her that she

The Front Line

couldn't drive anymore, which he duly did. When I would remind Mum that she wasn't supposed to drive she would get very cross and say that it was only temporary and that she was fine.

The boys would often worriedly tell my sister or I that Nain was going out to the car but we reassured them we had hidden her car keys so she couldn't drive anywhere. I spoke to her Neurologist again and explained he needed to be very firm with Mum and very clearly tell her she couldn't drive anymore at all. He did and finally Mum accepted it and we sold her car so she wouldn't be tempted and it would be one less thing to argue about.

Nobody in our extended family had developed dementia so this was a whole new experience for us. Mum was often violent, broke doors and would daily spit venomous comments at all of us. One day Lewis, myself and Mum were in the kitchen and Mum was yelling at me over some imagined fault. She had a glass of water in her hand and with no warning whatsoever she threw it over me. Not one to be outdone in an argument, I instantly grabbed the hose from the sink that I was standing in front of, aimed it at Mum and turned the tap on full blast. I don't think any of us expected it to be quite as effective as it was, somewhere between a rush of water and a fire hydrant. Given its effectiveness, I'm not entirely sure why the boys weren't more efficient at doing the washing up!

It had its desired effect, Mum who now looked like a drowned rat, stopped yelling and walked into her bedroom without saying a word. There was a moment of silence in the kitchen before Lewis exclaimed, "That was epic!" and we both fell about laughing. Now I know why spraying a hose on fighting domestic animals is highly recommended. It wasn't quite as messy as Dad's pea and ham soup episode but it came close.

On numerous occasions my sister physically lifted our mum up and carried her into Mum's self contained part of the house just to stop her interacting and yelling at everyone. Of course she would never remember

Bugger Bugger Shit!

these incidents; but we would, and even though we knew it was because of dementia, it was unbelievably hard and we had virtually no support from any services. In fact, one of the services I approached once Mum's aged care support funding was approved said they couldn't provide a support worker for her because Mum was in a wheelchair and OH&S rules precluded them from manually handling wheelchairs. Mum was little, frail and weighed about as much as a feather and she had an incredibly light-weight wheelchair. I was astounded that an Agency, funded for aged care support, refused to offer practical assistance for the aged who are in wheelchairs.

One of the most validating experiences was with one of the community nurses who came to visit Mum in 2020. I went out to the car with her to get a sharps bin for Mum's insulin needles. As she shuffled around in her boot she said, "I just want you to know that I know, I can see it". I looked at her, somewhat surprised and replied, "This is Mum on a good day". The nurse looked at me kindly and said, "I can hear it in her tone of voice and I can see it in her facial expressions and I want you to know you and your sister are doing a really good thing but you have to look after yourselves".

As she aged, Mum presented to the outside world as a lovely little frail old granny. As was the case when we were growing up, this was a complete fabrication of our lived experience. During this period of time, Naomi and I had various medical and allied health professionals take us aside to check on our wellbeing. These small conversations meant volumes to us. Someone could finally see what we had endured our whole lives.

Whilst I was writing this chapter, I asked a very good friend who I have known since we were 11 what her experience was of my parents. Her considered response was that our mum was welcoming but that she was always a little bit scared of her because she was always worried she was going to say the wrong thing. On the other hand another good friend has always maintained that she felt safe at our house because, whilst Mum was strict, she was also supportive and my friend always knew where she stood with her. Mum, as we all are, is complex.

Despite Mum's failings as a parent, as a grandmother she was wonderful. She adored her grandsons and they loved her. She was kind, patient and generous. The boys loved going for sleepovers at Nain and Bumpa's house; Christmas and Easters were always full of treats for the boys and Mum was never too busy to read or sing to them when they were babies, teach them how to swim and watch Peppa Pig, the Wiggles, Postman Pat and the like.

Watching Mum with the boys as she sank into dementia has been incredibly difficult. The boys have very few good memories of her because her erratic and aggressive behaviour linked to dementia is at the forefront of their memories. We remind them regularly of how lovely she was as a grandmother but they have now almost lived longer with her with dementia than without.

On the weekend before Australia went into lockdown because of the Covid-19 pandemic, Mum had a fall and hit her head. Naomi and I had always talked about Mum inevitably dying following a fall because she stubbornly refused to use her walker. Despite the danger hospitals posed at the beginning of the pandemic, I took Mum up to Emergency. I stayed with her for a while so that I could explain Mum's medical history to them but once it was clear she was going to be admitted I left her in their capable hands.

Despite the significant knock to her head on a tiled floor, Mum didn't suffer any particular damage but the hospital made the decision for her to go into rehab, partly for her but partly to give us a break. We were incredibly grateful for this decision because it meant that Mum wasn't at home for the lockdown which made it so much easier to manage the changes and know that Mum was being cared for.

Bugger Bugger Shit!

I was the only one in the family who could visit Mum and only for 15 minutes a couple of times a week. Mum's confusion increased and we noticed a pattern with the dementia that she would have a drop, plateau for a while and then drop again. Mum insisted that she was at the University in Dad's office and that all of the nursing staff were lecturers. She would call me to pick her up but most distressing was that she forgot that Dad had died five years before. This meant that almost everyday she would ask where Dad was.

The nursing staff experienced her grief when they told her the first time that he had died and so every time she asked where he was, they would make up some excuse because they felt bad and didn't know how to tell her and be the cause of her distress. What of course happened was that Mum became increasingly angry with Dad for not coming to visit her. I finally had to instruct the nurses to tell Mum he had died when she asked. This was a difficult conversation because generally speaking, the western world struggles with how to break bad news and so we avoid it. All this does though is make everything so much worse and we never learn the skills to talk about difficult things.

Whenever Mum asked me where Dad was I took a breath (because of course it was painful for me to have to re-live Dad's death every time I saw Mum) and said something like, "It's now 2020 and Dad died in 2015." Of course Mum was then distressed so I would have to comfort her but also confused because she had no insight into her dementia. After a few years of this, in a moment of lucidity, Mum said she couldn't remember Dad dying but she could remember me telling her that he died. She doesn't ask me anymore and I think it's not so much that she's remembered that he's died but actually that she only lives in the moment of whoever is visiting her and because Dad isn't visiting her there's no context for her to remember him.

The Front Line

Mum came home after the first lockdown and we carried on in the way that had become normal, with two daughters and four grandsons enduring gaslighting and abuse but continuing to care and look after her because 'that's what you do' and besides which, Naomi and I both said that no matter how horrible Mum had been and continued to be, she was still our Mum and we didn't want to put her in a home. We decided together that we would call time when Mum developed double incontinence and couldn't manage it herself.

Our plans were thwarted by the medical profession. Mum had been home for a few months when she had yet another fall. This time both Naomi and I were out. Usually one of us would have been at home but Naomi had to take her car in to be serviced and so decided to do the shopping whilst she was waiting for it and I was unexpectedly called into the office to support a training session. Fortunately, I decided to leave at lunchtime to finish my day working from home.

As I parked the car, I noticed that Mum's bedroom curtains were still closed. I wondered whether I would be finding Mum's body but as I opened the front door I heard her calling out. She was in her living room on the floor and unable to move. I worked out that the community nurses must have been because they would have called us; Mum wasn't dressed so she must have been on the floor from about 10am. It was now close to 2pm. I couldn't get Mum off the floor but just at that moment my sister arrived and we decided Mum was in so much pain we needed to call an ambulance.

This was the end of November 2020, the NSW Ambulance service was still extremely stretched and overwhelmed from the pandemic and it took over an hour for them to arrive. They took Mum to the hospital but due to the restrictions in the Emergency Department, we weren't able to go with her. Mum had broken her hip. We had multiple phone calls from doctors discussing DNR instructions and the likelihood that Mum wouldn't survive

Bugger Bugger Shit!

the surgery but they had to operate on her because she was in so much pain and because of the type of break.

Mum of course flew through the surgery and was up and mobile with assistance two days later. She had her 83rd birthday in hospital and was then discharged to rehab again. This time her specialist made the call that she couldn't return home because she needed 24 hour care. The social worker was fantastic and even though it was a few days before Christmas, found a respite bed for Mum in a nursing home five minutes drive from us.

The respite bed inevitably became permanent and Mum has been there now for nearly four years as she has gradually declined. I think we are all amazed that Mum has lived this long. She regularly falls because she's stubborn and refuses to use her walker, she refuses to keep the fall alarm mat by her bed and she refuses to wear hip protectors. Staff at the nursing home have called me many times to ask how to manage Mum. In the end I had to say to them that I had no clue what would work and that they are the ones experienced in aged care.

The nursing home involved Dementia NSW in order to better care for Mum. I received a phone call one day from their social worker in order for her to understand Mum a little better. I paused, trying to find an appropriate word to describe Mum but the social worker rescued me by asking me if she'd always been a "mean Mum". "Yes." I said, relieved that someone understood. She confirmed that dementia doesn't really change someone's personality; it just amplifies it. She then read out part of a report she had received which described someone who was manipulative, stubborn, full of her own self importance and abusive. I was lost for words. The social worker said that she assumed that I had provided that information to the nursing home for the report. "No," I said, "I had no idea they were putting a report together for you but that is breathtakingly accurate."

The Front Line

My sister and I have talked about Mum's parenting of us and its impact on many occasions. My sister, as the youngest, had to endure Mum's difficult parenting far longer than I did and she had to do it alone because we had all left home by the time Naomi was a teenager so she had no one to buffer Mum. In one of the conversations, we were trying to work out why I was seemingly less impacted by Mum and was able to visit her in the nursing home relatively unscathed. As I thought about it, I realised that what I had learned to do fairly early on is imagine myself in a castle surrounded by a moat. I choose to lower the drawbridge to engage in a conversation with Mum but then I raise it again. She doesn't have power over me. I put in the boundary, I choose when and how I interact with Mum. I choose the attitude I take into it knowing that I can pull the drawbridge up at any moment.

Whilst the impact of Mum's MS on her behaviour has been a valuable insight and explanation it doesn't make the experiences any easier. What I also understand and talk to many parents about is that the majority of people in the world have been impacted by trauma, either directly or indirectly, through changes to our epigenetics, as a result of generational trauma. Irrespective of how lovely my grandparents were, my mum and uncles were raised by parents who had directly experienced the trauma of war. This has to be taken into account when we take the time to understand the way our parents raised us. Our world needs to be so much more trauma informed but also trauma responsive if we are to make any positive impact on people's mental health and well-being.

I often questioned myself why I could forgive my dad for his physical abuse but why it is so hard to forgive my mum for allowing him to be physically violent. One day she was yelling at one of the boys and said, "He needs a jolly good smack" and I realised that whilst my dad's violence came from a lack of parenting skill and child development knowledge, my mum

Bugger Bugger Shit!

who was a qualified nurse and midwife, had a Bachelor's Degree in Psychology, a Masters in Public Health and a PhD in Nurse Patient Communication, fundamentally believed that assaulting children was a fine way to parent. My Mum should have known better.

Forgiveness is an interesting word. Forgiveness is not about saying something was ok. Forgiveness is about refusing to allow a person or their actions to have power over you anymore. So I suppose without even realising it, I have forgiven my Mum. I raise and lower the drawbridge and I understand that my Mum and my relationship with her is what it is. I cannot change it so I choose to find peace with it.

I have struggled with this chapter because, unlike my dad, there is no redemptive end to the story. It goes on and the impact of my mum on all of her children and grandchildren will continue long after she has died. The lesson I have learned though is to always seek to understand the why.

There is always a reason for someone's behaviour. Behaviour is simply communication. I can understand my mum's behaviour through the lens of psychology and neuroscience. MS lesions in her prefrontal cortex impact her ability to regulate her behaviour. The impact of being raised by parents who were traumatised by war has been passed down to my generation.

My job is to find the crack, understand the light and ensure that it doesn't get passed down any further.

Chapter 6

Why Not Me

As far as my eyes can see
There are shadows approaching me
And to those I left behind
I wanted you to know
You've always shared my deepest thoughts
You follow where I go
And oh when I'm old and wise
Bitter words mean little to me
Autumn Winds will blow right through me
And someday in the mist of time
When they asked me if I knew you
I'd smile and say you were a friend of mine
And the sadness would be lifted from my eyes
Oh when I'm old and wise
As far as my eyes can see
There are shadows surrounding me
And to those I leave behind
I want you all to know
You've always shared my darkest hours

Bugger Bugger Shit!

I'll miss you when I go
And oh, when I'm old and wise
Heavy words that tossed and blew me
Like Autumn winds will blow right through me
And someday in the mist of time
When they ask you if you knew me
Remember that you were a friend of mine
As the final curtain falls before my eyes
Oh when I'm Old and wise
As far as my eyes can see

Old and Wise
Alan Parsons & Eric Woolfson
Arista, 1982

"Why not me is the question, not why me?" my older sister Halina said to me from her hospital bed in Preston Infirmary. She was lying face down with her head in a hole in the bed. She had just had a considerable amount of her back removed due to a malignant melanoma. She had just turned 18, I was 16. She had completed her A levels and I was just finishing my O Levels.

She told me about a woman who was in the plastic surgery unit alongside her who had been burnt in a horrendous fire at her home. Halina went on to say, "I'd much rather it was me than her. I have friends and a family who love me, everything that I need and faith in God, so really, why not me?" The wisdom of those words from such a young woman have stayed with me and have lit my path throughout my adult life.

Why Not Me

Halina was born on the 5th July 1965 at Banbury Hospital. I followed 22 months later. My brother Kit is four years younger than me and my sister Naomi is three years younger than him. In our family we were split up for ease, into 'the girls' and 'the kids'. Halina and I got on and then we hated each other and then we loved each other and then we hated each other again and then we got on; for pretty much our whole lives together. Our relationship was somewhat marred by our parents' constant comparison of the two of us and I was never as good as Halina.

This comparison carried on into school where I was also consistently measured against the successes of my sister and I was told regularly by every teacher that we shared, that I wasn't as bright or well behaved as her. Halina took all the sensible, intelligent, diligent space. I forged my own path and was funny, disorganised and irresponsible. I'm still funny, disorganised and irresponsible. We both had red hair but Halina's was a dark auburn whereas mine was strawberry blond which deepened to a fiery red when I was older.

When the movie 'Brave' was released I went to see it along with a few friends and when Merida came on the screen my friends and I all stared in amazement because Merida seemed to be the epitome of me in looks and character. Halina was the complete opposite of Merida.

When Mum was pregnant with Halina, she and Dad went to see the film 'How Green Was My Valley'. They loved the character and name Angharad, and Mum suggested that they call the baby she was pregnant with Angharad. Dad said no, we've decided to call this baby Halina-Jane, we can call the next one Angharad. Halina-Jane was named in honour of some Polish friends of Mum and Dad; Halina and Jan. I was named after the character in 'How Green Was My Valley' which is a good thing because I am also far more like that character than Halina was. My secret weapon growing up, to be used sparingly for best effect, was that the name Angharad means best loved.

Bugger Bugger Shit!

When I was 16 and Halina 17, Halina had to go into hospital in Preston to have a mole removed from her lower back. It seemed like a fairly straightforward operation to me so I couldn't understand the worried looks and whispered conversations. The afternoon and evening of her operation were a complete nightmare for me. I was impacted by it for years afterwards.

My grandmother took it upon herself to call me constantly to get updates on Halina. I had no idea why she was so worried; it was, after all, just a mole. Grandma rang almost every 20-30 minutes for hours. I couldn't take the phone off the hook in case Mum and Dad were trying to get through. When they finally got home I burst into tears at the stress. I had no idea why Grandma was being so extreme.

Halina had noticed a change in the mole on her back previously but, not knowing how dangerous they can be, had just ignored it until it started to bleed and was making a mess on her school shirts. By then of course it was too late. Halina was diagnosed with a stage 4 malignant melanoma. She went into hospital as soon as she finished her last A level and spent her 18th birthday there.

I was trying to complete my O levels whilst this was all happening. I remember vividly one day we were sitting our English literature exam. I was always in the front row for exams because my last name began with a C. For this exam I was right in front of the teacher's desk. The teacher supervising this exam was Jackie, my all time favourite teacher. Just before the papers were handed out Jackie, knowing what was going on with my sister, asked me how I was doing. I said if X, Y and Z are on the paper I'll be fine, if they're not I'm stuffed.

The exam started and I opened the booklet. Jackie and I looked at each other as we read the questions. Every single area that I needed to be on the exam was there. She smiled at me and we began. I got an A. It's actually the only O level mark that I can remember but it has always been the most significant exam I've ever taken in my life.

My parents had planned to leave the UK for Dad's one year sabbatical in Honolulu very quickly after our exams. Halina was accepted into Homerton College in Cambridge to study Education and Drama but she and my parents decided that it would be better, given the diagnosis, for her to take a year out and come to Hawaii with the family. Halina enrolled at the University of Hawaii to study Drama for the year.

I was put up a grade at high school because it was deemed that the rigour of the UK education system was superior to that of the US so I went into the senior rather than junior class. I was also put into an Advanced English class which is where I made friends. I had found my tribe and thanks to Facebook we continue to be in touch with each other today.

Apart from my friends, I hated school. It was a regimented system, with little room for flexibility and certainly not an environment where adolescents were taught to think. Despite school, my year in Hawaii was filled with great adventures; my warring parents had called a truce and I have very fond memories of the place.

We returned to the UK a year later. I had to go down into the Lower Sixth to complete the two year A level course which was extremely difficult emotionally for me, and Halina went off to Homerton. Halina had worked at a local kebab place, Platos, since she was 14. Everyone who lived in Lancaster in the mid to late 1980s knew Platos. It was nothing like a kebab takeaway place that we know today. The food was fresh and healthy and it eventually expanded, to sell fine wines along with a great deli. It was run by a guy in his 20s called Eddie. Eddie and Halina hit it off immediately and once she returned from Hawaii, aged 19, Eddie thought she was old enough to start a romantic relationship with. Eddie was the great love of Halina's life, as she was for him.

Bugger Bugger Shit!

We all loved Eddie as well; my parents and children alike. He was 10 years older than Halina so he kind of fitted neatly in between our parents and us kids and was easily able to relate to all of us. Eddie had a good friend who was a jeweller and so Halina and I both had some lovely and unique earrings as gifts for both Christmases and Birthdays.

On what was to be Halina's last Christmas; Eddie had given her a pair of gorgeous, dangly, Hematite earrings. They had three balls each increasing in size so they weren't small and they were actually quite heavy. On Boxing Day, Halina had been over at Eddie's house in the evening and was, how do I say this politely? A little worse for wear. I'm not entirely sure what she and Eddie were doing but unexpectedly her earring came off the hook.

The story that she and Eddie told was; not wanting to lose the earring, whilst she was lolling on the sofa, she held the hook and the earring up to the light, eyes squinting with her arms extended, tried desperately and failed repeatedly, to hook it back on. Alas, given the amount of alcohol she had drunk, her coordination and reflexes - as you and I would expect but apparently she didn't - were impaired. Without warning, she dropped the earring - into her mouth and straight down her throat! Apparently her gag reflex was just as impaired as her coordination! Bugger bugger shit!

Halina was devastated, I think they were possibly the nicest earrings Eddie had ever bought for her. The following morning we all heard about the earring disaster; before Eddie and Halina headed up to the Lake District for lunch at the pub at Kirkstone Pass. When they arrived home, Dad, with some level of polite interest, asked them where they went. Quick as a flash, the usually quiet and reserved Eddie jumped in with, "Looking for a jeweller so Halina could have something to eat!" We rolled around laughing.

She spent weeks afterwards checking the toilet bowl just in case the earring 'reappeared' out the other end. It didn't. In fact, if you checked her coffin today, you might just find a rather lovely Hematite earring to match the one that Eddie kept.

Eventually I finished school and headed off to London for University. I was in my first year at Roehampton studying Psychology and Business Studies whilst Halina was in her third year at Cambridge. I would sometimes go up to Cambridge for the weekend to spend time with her. On one notable weekend, the two of us and some friends of Halina's decided to go to the local fondue restaurant; remember this was the 1980s!

None of us drank any alcohol that night, which was a good thing because there was so much alcohol in the cheese followed by chocolate fondues that we rolled home; possibly singing loudly but definitely with a significant amount of falling over, across the common, to Halina's share house. What's that acronym they use in Emergency Departments around the world? PFO - Pissed Fell Over - that was us that night. Our childhood and adolescent relationship was evolving into an adult sibling relationship; not living in the same house or enrolled at the same academic institution was a definite benefit.

Halina had thankfully been cancer free since her initial diagnosis in 1983 but everything changed in 1987. Mum called me at University unexpectedly one day in June 1987. She and Dad were packing up the house and their lives to permanently move to Sydney with my younger brother and sister who were still at High School. Halina and I had decided to stay in the UK for the immediate future despite being granted Permanent Residency along with the rest of the family. They were getting on a plane imminently.

Mum told me that she had had a call from Halina's doctors prior to her routine Oncologist check up, with the results of her latest blood tests. The cancer had returned and they thought someone should come to her appointment with her so she could have support when they told her. Mum

Bugger Bugger Shit!

and Dad of course weren't able to attend, so Mum asked me if I could. I made up some excuse to visit Halina for the weekend. She told me she had a hospital check up on Friday, so I played dumb and said not a problem; I'll just come and hang out at the hospital with you.

I sat in the hospital with Halina whilst she had a series of tests and then we went into the consultant's rooms for the results. He explained to her that the cancer had returned, the prognosis was grim and that there was very little they could do. At that time there was no treatment for malignant melanoma. The worst bugger bugger shit moment ever.

Halina and I walked out of the appointment reeling. For some unknown reason we wandered into the hospital shop. There was a song playing and Halina stopped and listened. It was 'Old and Wise' by the Alan Parsons Project. "This," she said pointing in the air as she listened to the lyrics. "This is what it's all about." From that moment on, Old and Wise has been "our" song. It has no other meaning for me. It is, and can only ever be, about Halina.

Halina and I completed our respective academic years and got on a plane to meet the rest of the family in Sydney. It was our first time in Australia and the middle of winter. We were freezing! We had no understanding of how the weather and seasons worked in the southern hemisphere. Despite that though, the house Mum and Dad had rented had a pool so we made full use of it. We made sure to see the marvellous sights from the Opera House and Harbour Bridge to the Blue Mountains, knowing that this would likely be the only opportunity Halina would ever have of experiencing the rest of the family's new life in Sydney.

We had a running joke that the Three Sisters in the Blue Mountains were a depiction of the Candlin three sisters. We went up Centrepoint Tower and had lunch up there. Dad reasoned if we didn't do it then, we would never do it. He was right, the only time I have ever had a meal up

Centrepoint was in 1987. There was a small fire in the kitchens whilst we were up there so the tower stopped turning and the shutters on the kitchen hatches came down automatically. It was somewhat disconcerting and we wondered whether we were going to have to walk down the endless stairs to get to the bottom. Fortunately they extinguished it and everything resumed as normal.

Over 30 years later, I still have the same favourite views of Sydney that I had then. Driving down the Warringah Freeway towards the city there is a moment where you can see the Harbour Bridge peeking between the buildings of North Sydney. Coming from Macquarie Street onto the Harbour Bridge slipway there is a spot where you can see the sails of the Opera House peeking between the branches of the Palm trees. I still get a thrill driving over the Harbour Bridge. I have done it thousands of times but I still have to pinch myself that I get to call Sydney home. In 1987 I had no idea that three and a half years later, Sydney would become my home town. What an incredible privilege for a girl from the North West of England.

Halina and I did not get on well that holiday. I have no idea why but we both annoyed each other and spent quite a lot of time bickering. I left Sydney before Halina and went home via Hawaii and the US mainland so that I could catch up with my friends from school in Honolulu. Given that Australia is the 'melanoma capital of the world', Halina spent some time getting opinions from Skin Cancer Specialists here. Ultimately though the prognosis was the same as her UK Oncologist.

Halina returned to the UK for the start of the Michaelmas term and was given special approval to complete her teaching practice in Lancaster rather than Cambridge so that she could be with Eddie. Eddie had asked Halina to marry him and they started planning their wedding for the following May.

Bugger Bugger Shit!

When Halina returned to Lancaster, she and Eddie went to see her Oncologist, Dr Neil*, at Christie's Hospital in Manchester, the large cancer hospital for the area. Prior to her appointment she and Eddie went to a nearby pub for some lunch and a drink. Neil told Halina and Eddie about a new drug trial: Interleukin Therapy. He was clear that it wasn't a cure but would hopefully buy her some more time. She asked him how much time. His response was that patients have had anything from an extra 11 weeks to 2 years. He went on to say that given Halina and Eddie had been having a drink in the pub prior to the appointment he doubted that she was in the 11 week category. Halina didn't need to think about it and so she started the Interleukin Therapy.

In early November, Halina had been walking back to our house from the town centre and became so exhausted she had to stop at our surrogate grandmother, Joan's, house which was about half way. She and Mum had become friends not long after we had moved into Lancaster from Halton. Joan was a member of the local Anglican Church, Christ Church, and she was on the home visiting roster. She came to welcome us to the area and despite being many years older than Mum they became firm friends.

Joan lived just down the road from us when we were young but by the time we were at university, had moved down the steep hill to a flat and much more accessible street a few minutes away. Years later when I visited Joan she told me about this incident. A retired nurse, she had been very worried about Halina and could see how seriously ill she was. She called Eddie who came to pick up Halina and the next day they went to Christie's. The news was not good; Halina's cancer had advanced quickly.

Mum and Dad were called and they scrambled to get flights to come back from Australia. I'm not sure who called me but I packed a bag and drove up from London to Manchester. The rest of the family were on a plane and that evening Halina and I had time alone together. Halina apologised to me for being horrible over the break in Australia and I apologised to her. We said what we needed to say to each other, not knowing how long she would have. As it turned out, despite being in the pub before her appointment with Dr Neil, she died 11 weeks after it.

As soon as it was clear that Halina would not live long enough to get married the following May as planned, everyone went into organising mode and arranged for the wedding to be held at Christie's Hospital on the 26th October 1987. Our Vicar conducted the wedding. My brother was the 'best man' because Eddie's best friend, the jeweller of the Hematite Earrings, was pathologically scared of hospitals and couldn't bring himself to be there. Halina's best friend came over from Finland to be the bridesmaid and I did the reading. Mum and the nurses secretly decorated the ward's dayroom the evening prior whilst Halina slept. Halina had started to make her wedding dress and had got as far as the slip. I'm not entirely sure who finished it. I wore a dress that Halina had made for me. The reading Halina and Eddie chose was a passage from 1 Corinthians that is often read at weddings:

Love is patient, love is kind. It does not envy, it does not boast, it is not proud. It does not dishonour others, it is not self-seeking, it is not easily angered, it keeps no record of wrongs. Love does not delight in evil but rejoices with the truth. It always protects, always trusts, always hopes, always perseveres.

That was the hardest piece of public speaking I've ever done in my life. Looking at my sister and her beloved Eddie as I read those words; they meant something they had never meant before, nor since. All of the people in that room knew they were seeing a love story where there was going to be no happy ending. As soon as the wedding ceremony was over, Halina made the nurses take off the wristband that had Halina-Jane Candlin on it and replace it with one that said Halina-Jane Steel. She was so incredibly delighted to be married to Eddie.

Bugger Bugger Shit!

Whilst my sister was at Christie's Hospital, one of the nurses recorded an interview with her for a church group she was involved with. My sister gave me the recording which I've listened to once. I still have it but haven't been able to listen to it again. I think the sound of her voice would undo me.

In the interview, the nurse asked her who had had the most significant influence on her. She replied that I had. She said that she had observed me closely over the years; noted my compassion for others and that, no matter how difficult things were, I had a deep faith and spirituality at my core which meant I was able to stay grounded and connected. I was astounded by these insights and so surprised that she had been so quietly connected to who I was and what I did.

I have been known to have, what I describe, as a wobble when I get bad news but it doesn't last long. I usually take a breath, have a chat with someone about it and then I centre myself and carry on. I thought working in the industry I've worked in for so long was the thing that centres me but it had clearly started long before that.

My sister deteriorated quickly, and in the end was transferred to St John's Hospice in Lancaster. Halina had volunteered at the Hospice and knew Sister Aîné and Sister Callista well. We had previously made the decision that I wouldn't come up to Manchester that weekend so that I could have a weekend of relative normality with my friends in London, but as Halina was moved to the hospice, Mum called me to let me know she had suddenly deteriorated even more quickly than expected and said I should come home.

As I packed my bag I realised I would need to pack something to wear for the funeral. I had nothing suitable in my wardrobe. It took about five agonising hours on public transport, but eventually, I got to Lancaster and immediately went to St John's to see Halina. It was a Thursday evening and as any self-respecting adult would know, it was Top of the Pops. Halina and

I watched it together. Doing something so completely ordinary was just what we both needed.

The following day, Halina and Eddie spent a long time together and everyone was completely shut out of the room as they said what needed to be said. Later, she also had a conversation with Mum and Dad. She told them she was scared of dying. Then she clarified that she wasn't so much scared of death but of the process of dying. Mum reminded her that Halina had previously volunteered at the Hospice so she knew how people died here. She asked her if she'd ever seen anyone have a horrible death there. My sister admitted that she hadn't. Mum reassured her that she wouldn't either. In this conversation, Halina told Mum she wanted to be like Jesus.

Over the next few days, Halina's body started to shut down. I describe it like she died from the bottom up. On the Saturday she was devastated that her hearing went so she couldn't listen to her Taize music and the following day her sight went. Her speech had been gradually declining over days. On the Monday, she drifted in and out of consciousness.

Our Vicar came in the morning to give her communion but she was asleep. He came again in the afternoon and whilst she had been awake she was asleep again when he visited. He came back in the evening. It was completely unplanned but the whole family, including Eddie, were there at the same time. Halina was asleep/unconscious again so our Vicar suggested we stand around the bed and have communion together in Halina's presence.

He handed out the communion and as he put some wine on Halina's lips she opened her eyes and looked directly at Eddie, who was standing next to me at the foot of the bed. Clear as a bell, she said, "I love you" and drifted back into unconsciousness again. She died a few hours later at a little past 1am on the 17th November 1987. Mum and Dad were with her as they were when she came into the world.

Bugger Bugger Shit!

The next day I took my younger brother and sister into the hospice where Mum, Dad and the Sisters let us know that Halina had died overnight. Sister Aîné asked if we would like to see Halina. I said that I would, so she took me into a little room where Halina was dressed in her wedding dress. Halina's was the first dead body I had seen and I knew immediately she wasn't there any more. Halina wasn't her body, my sister was in her 'spirit'.

I stroked Halina's hair and said goodbye to her. Sister Aîné cut that lock of hair off for me to keep. I have no idea of the emotions I experienced in that room. Shock, bewilderment, utter loss. I didn't have a big sister anymore. 'The girls' and 'the kids' ended the moment my sister died. My whole identity changed in an instant. I went from being the second child to being the oldest in everyone else's eyes. Except I wasn't and will never be the eldest. I was, and will always be, a middle child.

I had no way of processing the reality of this loss. I was 20 years old, the only other person of significance to me that had died was my Nanna. I struggled for years when people asked me about my family and siblings. I didn't always want to explain that my sister had died but if I said I only had two siblings I felt like I was betraying my sister.

I struggled when people described me as the eldest. Birth order is a significant thing when it comes to how we function in the world. My younger brother and sister's birth order hadn't changed. They were still middle and youngest children. I was the disorganised, funny and irresponsible middle child and suddenly I was expected to be the responsible, organised and eldest. Over thirty years later I still struggle with being the responsible one and the eldest. I was granted Power of Attorney for my parents, I am the Executor of Mum's Will, I have Mum's Enduring Guardianship. I want none of it. Halina would have been so much better at it than me. It all came naturally to her and she was raised to be that person; I wasn't.

Why Not Me

I continue to struggle explaining my sisters. I was sitting at the lunch table at work aeons ago. One of my colleagues asked me a question about my sister. I didn't know which one she meant so, ever pragmatic, I asked, "Do you mean my dead sister or my alive sister?" Later on I was taken aside and reprimanded for being so blunt and insensitive. Insensitive? Seriously? I was being insensitive? I was the one who's sister had died and somebody felt offended when I needed to clarify a question.

Note to anyone reading this; you don't get to be offended at the language chosen by the bereaved. Everyday they have to get their heads around their loss, their changed world. You don't. Your job is to support them in whatever way they need. By all means feel uncomfortable, feel sad, feel scared but we have to also take the time to look deep within ourselves for the root cause of those emotions. It is the only thing that will halt our feelings of offence because when we understand what it is within ourselves that is often too painful to uncover, we truly understand the human condition.

Mum was initially quite distressed by the way Halina had died. When Sister Callista explored it with her, Mum explained that she had told Halina she wouldn't have an awful death but that the way she died was awful. Callista reminded Mum that Halina had said she wanted to be like Jesus. Mum agreed. Callista responded by asking, "Well how did Jesus die?" Mum replied, "On the cross". Sister Callista pushed her to be more specific and to use her nursing training to think it through from a medical perspective. Mum thought about it and said, "Well I suppose ultimately Jesus choked which caused his death". "Exactly," replied Callista, "and how did Halina die?" Mum thought about it for a minute and realised that medically, Halina had died because she choked. Callista gently said, "She wanted to be like Jesus, and she was".

We drove home from the Hospice with all of Halina's things in the car we had shared. I guess the car that Halina and I had shared was mine now.

Bugger Bugger Shit!

Halina loved the perfume Anais Anais and my car was filled with its scent. It was overwhelming. I haven't been able to bring myself to smell that perfume again. In fact one of the kindest and most sensitive things anyone has ever done for me was by a colleague and friend. Not long after we met, about twenty years ago, I have no recollection of how, but her social work heart was brought to attention by a tiny comment I made, linking Anaïs Anais with my sister. Unbeknownst to me, for years; Anais Anais is her favourite perfume but, at that moment, she made the decision to never wear it around me. She has stuck to that promise. Whilst I would love to free her from that commitment, I just can't.

Halina's funeral was about a week after she died. She had planned it and we carried out her wishes. We all arrived at the church, which was completely packed. Whilst we were waiting for everyone to finish arriving, we were sitting in the front row and our cousin Morag and her young daughter Louise were sitting directly behind us. Halina's coffin was, as expected, at the front of the church. It was the first funeral Louise had ever attended, so her Mum was quietly explaining everything to her. There was a momentary pause in their conversation and Louise suddenly piped up loudly, "I don't want Halina to be in the box. Can she open it and get out?" Morag was mortified, but we cracked up laughing; it was exactly the thing that needed to be asked and her innocent questions were perfect in distracting us from the anguish of the moment.

What it couldn't distract us from was the reality that Eddie wasn't there. I mean Eddie often ran late for everything but we couldn't believe he would actually be late for his own wife's funeral. Everyone was seated (or standing at the back and around the sides of our very large church) when Eddie finally arrived. He walked down the centre aisle of the church to the front bearing a bunch of red roses. Our Vicar came to him and quietly asked him if he wanted to place them on the coffin with our flowers. Eddie declined.

At the end of the funeral we all followed the coffin out with Eddie still holding the bunch of roses. The Funeral Director asked Eddie if he wanted to put his flowers on the coffin. Eddie declined. We followed the hearse to the cemetery; Eddie was still holding the roses. "What's with the roses?" we all wondered.

We arrived at the cemetery and stood around the coffin. Eddie asked the Funeral Director to remove all of the flowers from on top of the coffin and to put his bunch of red roses on top of it. Halina's body was committed to the ground and she was buried with Eddie's red roses.

I asked Eddie later about the story behind the roses. He told me in that long conversation he and Halina had, she had berated him for never buying her red roses. She instructed him that at her funeral, he was to buy a bunch of red roses and walk down the aisle with them so that everyone could see that he had finally bought her red roses. My sister, the eldest child, was still bossing everyone around from her grave!

Thirty six years later it is Australia Day and Professor Georgina Long and Professor Richard Scolyer, Co-Medical Directors of the Melanoma Institute, have been announced as the 2024 Australians of the Year. As I watched the program on the ABC, I cried rivers of tears. This is the meaning-making from my sister's death. This is what that initial trial all those years ago came to. The dream of Georgina and Richard is for a future with zero deaths from melanoma. In 1987 we couldn't possibly imagine it, but in 2024 we might just see it, and much sooner than we thought. It is breathtaking. I am thankful, I am happy, I am sad, but most of all I am hopeful.

Bugger Bugger Shit!

Cutting the Cake

Halina & Eddie Christie's Hospital October 1987

Halina and I Oxford circa 1969

Halina & Eddie utter joy on her face

Bugger Bugger Shit!

Halina's Grave 2023 beautifully cared for by those who loved her

Married! Surrounded by Love

Chapter 7

They've Got Knives!

"The eternal God is my refuge and underneath are His everlasting arms"

> **Deuteronomy 33:27**
> The Bible

My lecturer asked me to stay behind after a Developmental Psychology Seminar in early November 1987. She told me that she had been having a chat with a couple of my other lecturers during the week and they started talking about some of the difficult things students had gone through; all in a two week period. One of them talked about a student whose sister was dying in Christie's Hospital in Manchester; another talked about a student whose car had been broken into and the windows smashed whilst her car was parked in a hospital car park and the third talked about a student who had been assaulted and mugged at knife point in between lectures.

My lecturer went on to say they had put two and two together and realised it wasn't three different students but one student who had experienced all three events. They were horrified that one of their second

Bugger Bugger Shit!

year students was going through so much simultaneously. I wasn't surprised; they had all happened to me the fortnight before. She was kind and checked how I was going. I was surviving and just putting one foot in front of the other. She told me that she had let all of my lecturers know about what was happening and if I needed anything to not hesitate in seeking them out for ongoing support.

About six weeks later, my sister had died and I was sitting in my best friend's room. I was telling him that I was overwhelmed because I was behind on 23 assignments and I wasn't entirely sure what to do. His advice was that I could just put my head down and get on and do the assignments or I could take the rest of my second year off and recommence the following September. I had already delayed starting university because I had to do an extra year of high school due to the year in Hawaii my family had. There was absolutely no way I was going to take a leave of absence in the middle of my degree. He told me years later that he had fully expected and wanted me to opt to take the year off.

What I did instead was go to my Psychology Tutor and tell him I was 23 assignments behind; involving both my Psychology Course and my Business Studies Course. He, then and there, took out a pen and drew a line through the vast majority of assignments that were overdue and told me not to worry about them and to just do the bare minimum that were graded as part of the assessment. He said he would talk to the Business Studies faculty and ensure they were on board. The relief I felt was palpable. That meeting was the only reason I managed to finish my second year and eventually graduate from University in June 1989. Sometimes being, and remaining, resilient means inviting other people in to help us.

They've Got Knives!

When I was looking at options for university I had a non-negotiable. It was going to be in London. I was interested in studying Communication (Marketing), Journalism or Psychology. I was equally interested in all three so was finding it difficult to choose. I decided eventually that Communication Studies and Journalism were going to be very hard to get into because they were so popular and I was not expecting my A Levels to be good enough.

My dad happened to mention Roehampton; a University with four residential colleges. One of his colleagues had been the Principal of one of the colleges and his sister had studied for her teaching qualifications at one of the other colleges. I checked it out. It looked interesting and the bonus was I could kill two birds with one stone and study both Psychology and Business Studies, which included a large component of Marketing. The other interesting thing about Roehampton was that whilst you didn't need particularly high A Level grades to be accepted; you had no option but to complete a double Honours degree. If you failed your first year you were out; there was no option to do a single subject non-Honours course of study.

The University was very forward thinking in understanding that some adolescents gradually mature into academic success rather than exceed at A Level. I had to have an interview though, if I was to be accepted into Psychology. I applied and was invited to interview so I took the train down to London for the day. During the interview, the lecturer commented that I had only managed to get a CSE Grade 3 for Maths in the Fifth form and then a Grade 2 when I re-sat the exam during my Lower Sixth (it was a complicated system no longer in place. Whilst it sounds like a Grade 3 or a 2 was a pass, it wasn't, I had to get a Grade 1 if it was to count). I nonchalantly told him not to worry, I'd get it this time when I sat the exam along with my A Levels. Who was I kidding? At that point, I had absolutely

Bugger Bugger Shit!

no chance of getting a CSE Grade 1. Not getting into your chosen degree course because you couldn't get a high enough maths exam result was stressful.

In the Lower Sixth, there was always a very small smattering of students re-sitting their maths GCE or CSE O Levels. The teacher who took the re-sit group was one with a reputation for being mean and sarcastic. I had managed to avoid him all the way through school so I was pretty worried when I turned up in his class that first day. Everyone was right. He was mean and strict and treated us like we had failed on purpose.

When I turned up again, on the first day of my Upper Sixth, he completely understood that this was an intelligent kid who had a problem with maths. I was, up until that point, the only Upper Sixth student who had to resit maths. I'm probably still the only one, come to think of it because the system changed after we went through. The pressure was on; if I wanted to study a Degree in Psychology I HAD to get a Grade 1. Mr R sat me down at the back of the classroom and I saw a completely different side to him that year. Every lesson, he would set the others some work, make sure they were on task and then come and sit next to me to tell me step-by-step how to do it. He did not give up on me once. He had much more faith in me than I did myself.

I also had a boyfriend at the time who was a bit of a genius. He had fast tracked through school and university and was, despite only being two years older than me, studying for his PhD in Biology at the local university. He was a science nerd and could do maths upside down in a swimming pool whilst twirling a baton if he chose. He took it upon himself to tutor me to try and get me through. I am eternally grateful for the commitment of these two men. I managed to scrape a Grade 1 and was off to London.

I can't remember now why my parents couldn't take me down to college at the beginning of the academic year in 1986 so I needed to find

They've Got Knives!

an alternative. Our Vicar knew of another Vicar in a nearby town whose daughter was at Roehampton starting her second year so he introduced us and they took me down with their daughter Clare*. We were both living in Halls and it turned out we were both in the same House; I was upstairs while she was downstairs. We became firm friends.

My Business Studies subjects were all on site at my college in Wimbledon but my Psychology subjects were about a 10 minute drive away at Roehampton. Wimbledon Common was between the two sites and was a lovely walk if you were so inclined. It also had a number of very nice pubs situated on it, which was a bit of a drawcard for the average university student. I did look to see if I could find any of the Wombles; particularly Great Uncle Bulgaria or Tobermory but failed.

Our college grounds also backed onto The All England Lawn Tennis Club so every summer a huge amount of students applied for jobs there and hopped over the back fence. In my first year of working at Wimbledon in 1988, I surreally ended up having an impromptu picnic lunch at the side of one of the practice courts with Ivan Lendl, Pat Cash and Jimmy Connors.

I ended up with a job as a waitress in the Executive Suites. The bonus working in that section of the Club was that we ate like Royalty for the two weeks of the event. We would arrive early, prepare the room and some of the food, including topping and tailing mountains of strawberries. Then it was on for young and old as the guests of the big Corporate sponsors arrived; we served drinks and beautiful gourmet lunches. Once all the guests had left to go and watch the tennis we would clear away the remainder and then we were allowed to eat the leftovers but out of sight of the patrons.

We would invariably help ourselves to a mountain of food on our plates and then sit under the bar, which was a high trestle table covered in long white table cloths, completely hidden from view. Once we had finished we were allowed to freely access the venue. We could watch as much tennis as

Bugger Bugger Shit!

we liked on the outside courts and if there were spare seats in Centre Court we could slip in and watch any match in play. I enjoyed working at Wimbledon for the camaraderie but I have never really been one for tennis so I certainly didn't appreciate the opportunity. I did however enjoy the financial reward and for most of the students it set us up financially for the rest of the long summer holidays.

My three years at Roehampton remain, despite the deaths of my sister and Grampa whilst I was there, one of the highlights of my life. I lived in Halls throughout my degree and made life-long friends whilst I was there. In fact just last year, five of us met up. We have all seen each other at different times since graduating but we've never actually all been together since we finished. When we met up at London Bridge Station we all cried and then promptly carried on with our friendship as if the intervening 30+ years had never happened.

University was like nothing I had ever experienced before and living in Halls was like a somewhat older version of the Mallory Towers series of books about girls at Boarding School. Everyone got along well and there were constant tricks being played on people. Our room doors were easy to lift off the hinges so doors regularly got swapped around just to confuse everyone (our names and message boards were on the outside of the doors). Toilet seats were cling-wrapped from time to time, short sheeting was a regular occurrence and one exceptionally creative person managed to gain entry to a mate's room and carefully took everything out one day and re-created the entire room on the side of the football pitch. We had end-of-term whole college parties with a plethora of live bands and at the end of each year we had a Summer Ball, complete with ball gowns, tuxedos, fairground rides, live bands and movies being played in the Senior Common Room; the works. I loved it!

They've Got Knives!

It will horrify some readers to know that our Halls of Residence were single sex; until my third year when two of the houses became mixed (but single sex floors); there was one public telephone between the whole building which housed 30-40 students. There was a single bath and two toilets on each floor of up to 16 people and if you were lucky, a couple of showers in each block. We got very creative about the times we bathed.

We weren't supposed to have members of the opposite sex in our rooms, but really this was a home for young adults, who were they kidding? You just had to hope there wasn't a fire drill if you were 'entertaining'. Having sex also needed to be carefully orchestrated because everyone could hear everything.

I remember one night; I was ill, I think, so hadn't gone to some event that was happening. I was woken by the clanging of the radiator and realised one of my co-residents had taken the opportunity of everyone being out to have some intimate time with her boyfriend. Except the bed kept banging against her radiator and the sound ran around the heating pipework in a crescendo of percussive rhythm. I went back to sleep - you do learn to sleep through almost anything when you're living in such close quarters with so many other people. It's amazing actually that there were no meltdowns or arguments or people hating each other.

There were parties galore; especially toga parties! I came back to my room after one in particular and could not for the life of me get my key into the lock of my door and needed to be helped by someone passing by. I fell onto my bed wearing my sheet and promptly fell asleep only to be woken by two of the male students (including one I thought was quite dishy), standing in my room, at the end of my bed, apologising profusely. I had forgotten to lock the door and not getting a response to their knocking (in the middle of the night mind you), tried the door handle and wandered in.

Bugger Bugger Shit!

They continued saying they were sorry repeatedly. "Sorry for what?" I asked somewhat confused and somewhat impacted by alcohol. I was eventually able to ascertain that one of them had been annoyed at his girlfriend and in a show of male bonding, the other had offered to let down the tyres of the girlfriend's car. Instructions were provided as to the colour, make and model of the car and where it was in the (very small) car park. Alas he forgot the colour of the car and seeing a Fiat Uno, despite it not being parked in the allocated spot, he confidently went over to it and let the air out of all of the tyres. Except it was my red Fiat Uno, not the Green Fiat Uno of the girlfriend.

The car park was situated right outside the dining room which had floor to ceiling plate glass windows. My punishment for them was to remove each tyre, take them to the local service station to fill up with air and then replace them - during lunch the following day so they could suffer public humiliation for their stupidity!

It was also at university that I discovered that if you spill red wine on a white carpet and then pour a bottle of white wine over it (because you can't find the cheaper option of a packet of salt) it neutralises the red wine and the carpet stays white. This was in a shared house in South Wimbledon in which, over the years, various combinations of my friends lived.

It was also at this house that I discovered two panadol, half a glass of white wine and an allergy to grapes will not end well. I thought the ground was going to open up and swallow me whole. I spent the evening holding onto my, then boyfriend, trying not to die. That night wasn't a raucous college party, it was just dinner with the few friends that lived in the house, so we were sitting on the floor talking. Well, when I say talking, I was mostly groaning and when my boyfriend turned his head to direct his conversation to someone else, I could feel the world spinning like some sort of psychotic disco ball.

They've Got Knives!

The biggest scandal of my first year though involved the football team. Well, more accurately, the football pitch and goalposts. As far as I know, the truth of this story has never come out; until now. I don't think it would be an exaggeration to say that members of the college football team thought, at various times, that they were 'God's Gift to Womankind'. This may have been because the demographics of college were two thirds women, one third men.

During my first term, a group of female students (the majority of whom were my friends) were out at the pub farewelling one of their friends who had decided to leave college. Reasonably inebriated, the conversation on the way back to college, had got around to the football team and the team's somewhat over inflated egos. The group decided to do something about it. They managed to woman-handle the two sets of goal posts into the middle of the pitch and then ran around all of the residential houses and gathered as many containers of Vim (powdered disinfectant bathroom cleaner) as they could find. They then wrote SOD OFF (name of football team which I will leave nameless to protect the guilty) in gigantic letters of powdered Vim across the entire pitch. It was glorious.

All of them opened their curtains the next day with differing levels of alcohol induced amnesia to behold the site before them, as their memories kicked in. To say this event went down in the annals of history of the college would be an understatement. The Police were called, the entire college population was called to a security meeting; the Student's Union, The Bursar and Principal were all involved. Everyone was asked if they knew anything and of course everyone said no. We lived fairly close to a local council estate and of course the residents were blamed. The assumption was that it must have been a gigantic gang of young men who had breached the security somehow in order for this gross act of war to be instigated.

Bugger Bugger Shit!

As I looked around the room, I saw a number of my friends looking entirely uncomfortable, with a sudden fascination for the floor. Nothing of course ever came of it. There was no evidence to be gathered because no one on the estate was responsible. It was not a gang of burly blokes; it was a group of no more than 5, slight, drunk 18-20 year old young women.

The second major incident whilst I was at college, again involved the football team. My best friend was on the team and in my second and third years my college room overlooked the football pitch. Whilst everyone else was on the sidelines shivering and watching the match, I used to watch it from the comfort of my room, usually with a cup of tea in hand.

In my second year, the team had reached the quarter or semi finals and were playing off against a team they had already played during the season. The game had started and I nipped out to the kitchen to make my cup of tea. As I came back down the corridor, one of my friends ran past and yelled, "They've got knives!" I rushed into my room to see what on earth was going on and sure enough it looked like all hell had broken loose on the pitch. I was extremely worried about my friend and raced down to the mayhem to check he was ok.

The opposing team had arrived with knives and machetes (I kid you not) secreted on their persons and at some, clearly pre-arranged, time all pulled them out at once and laid into this bunch of fairly innocuous university boys. I tried to stay out of trouble as I attempted to find my friend, who fortunately was physically alright, if a little shaken up. Of course the police and ambulances arrived quickly and various players were dispatched to hospital. Fortunately no one was seriously injured but it was a reminder we were in South West London in the 1980s and football had a very bad reputation. So bad in fact that one of the subjects in my social psychology course was the psychology of football hooliganism.

They've Got Knives!

My friend Clare was hilariously accident prone which kept everyone amused for our entire time at college. One day, she was in one of her lectures and was at the front of the room talking to her lecturer; she looked to the ground and somewhat surprisingly, one of the lenses fell out of her glasses; then one of the arms fell off and her glasses quickly disintegrated in front of the entire congregation of students and her lecturer. She came back to Halls and told me about it, in her very comical way.

The following week, she came flying upstairs to my room yelling repeatedly down the corridor, what I thought was, "My glasses have fallen out of the window!" I thought, "That's ridiculous, your glasses just fell off your face in your lecture and you had to get new ones". I thought this was a bit dramatic, even for Clare so helpfully (?) I said, "Well just go downstairs and pick them up." "No," she said, "My glass has fallen out of the window." "Well go and get them then" I said patiently. "NO, YOU DON'T UNDERSTAND!" she said loudly and emphatically, "The pane of glass has fallen out of my window!" Bugger! "How on earth did that happen?" I asked, now fully understanding her panic. "It wouldn't open so I had to really push it and the glass fell out".

We raced downstairs to survey the damage. I was trying to work out how the glass could just fall out of the window even if she had shoved it hard. I gave her a look, and she folded. "I didn't shove it with my hands, I couldn't get it open so I kicked it, my foot slipped and hit the glass instead of the frame." Now it all made sense, but I thought we were going to have to work out a very good story so that the Bursar didn't become suspicious as to how the window ended up on the ground.

This was important because at the beginning of the term, we had all returned from our Christmas Holidays; Clare discovered that her radiator wasn't working, so she decided the air in it needed to be bled. I have no idea how she happened to have one of those little keys that you fit over the nut

Bugger Bugger Shit!

to turn it, but she did. Actually, come to think of it, maybe she didn't, which is why the following disaster unfolded. With some difficulty and possibly a little too much force, she turned the nut and instead of the expected hiss of air, water spurted out like a fire hose; she completely flooded her room, the corridor, down the stairs, under the doors of her neighbours. I mean, it would have been nice to have an indoor, heated swimming pool, but possibly not one created from radiator water and in the middle of a hall of residence.

Every year at many Universities they have what's known as Rag Week. It's a week where all the students basically go slightly mad in an attempt to raise money for charity. My college was no different and every year, the Students' Union thought up wilder and wilder things that could be done. In my third year my friends paid for the guy who I thought was dishy and had let the air out of my tyres to come and read me a bedtime story - the intimate bits out of Lady Chatterley's Lover. Here I was, in bed, in my winter fleecy pyjamas, with the man who I thought was the sexiest guy at college, reading me the steamy bits of a book - with my entire corridor of girls looking on and laughing.

We had various individuals dress up as gnomes and they were paid to follow a particular person around for the entire day. The gnomes did a wonderful job, completely obscuring their identity. One day someone had paid for one of the guys from the Student's Union to be Gnomed. What he didn't know was that his fiancée was one of the gnomes. He couldn't find her during the day, she wasn't in any of their shared lectures. He didn't see her at lunchtime and by dinner time he was getting really worried. All of us who were in the know thought this was very amusing. I'm not sure how long it actually took for him to find out who his Gnome was. Probably not until long after they got married.

They've Got Knives!

Each college had a "Hit Squad". Each year it was done slightly differently depending on who had volunteered to lead it. In my third year, a group from my corridor volunteered. The leader of the gang was a drama student and she encouraged us all to rise to the occasion. We dressed completely in black, with our heads obscured by black stockings and balaclavas. We were given a list of names each day and we chose dinner, when all the students were in the dining room, to strike.

Once everyone was in the dining room, we made our entrance. We all had one person to 'hit' but we would wander slowly and ominously around the room; sitting down next to random people, taking their forks out of their hands and feeding them, toying with their food or just sitting at their table staring at them. If they were still standing with their tray heading towards a seat we might take it off them and carry it to a table. Then we would get up and go to another person and start the whole routine again which really drew out the tension.

We did this for at least half an hour and at a pre-arranged time we would all go and get a paper plate with a custard pie on it, slowly come back into the room, go up to a table and wait. When we were all in place we would smash the custard pie into the relevant target's face and then make our exit. Thinking about it, we had such innocent fun over those three years; I can't imagine those things would be happening now at universities.

Of course however it wasn't all fun. My sister's cancer returned just as I was finishing my first year. I came back to my room one day to discover a card under my door; it was from one of Clare's neighbours on the floor below. The card was very simple and inside, it read, "The eternal God is my refuge and underneath are His everlasting arms" Deuteronomy 33:27. She wrote an incredibly kind message and offered for me to talk to her anytime. Clare had told her about my sister's cancer recurrence and because her Mum had died from cancer only a few years before, she kindly offered me her

Bugger Bugger Shit!

support. We became firm friends after this and she remains one of my closest friends today. I cannot confirm or deny that she might have organised the hit squad in our third year.

That Bible passage has become my life long comfort and I remind myself of it frequently. Faith is often, but not always, a characteristic of resilient people. Whilst at various times my faith has been deeply challenged by the events of my life, I keep my eyes fixed. A friend recently asked me about my faith. I explained that I simply cannot believe the brain in its complexity, symmetry and beauty could develop by accident.

It is my understanding of the brain's precision that holds my faith intact whilst I increasingly find the 'church' a troubling and sometimes destructive institution. I cannot abide what has developed in many church communities, particularly since the pandemic; it is the intricacy of the brain that keeps me grounded.

I developed significant symptoms of multiple sclerosis at the end of my first year of university and I am genuinely grateful that I have been diagnosed with a disease of the nervous system, rather than some other random disease, because I find it fascinating. I also increasingly began to experience symptoms of the psoriatic arthritis I was eventually diagnosed with. They impacted my hands and my lower spine particularly at the time.

The first time I saw my current Neurologist I surprised him by asking him to show me the lesions on my MRI scan and for him to tell me exactly where they are. I explained that I regularly teach about neuroscience so I want to know exactly what's going on. I now receive a link to my MRI images which I check out before my follow up neurology appointments.

I love watching the different aspects of the brain appear within the video images. I know that the issues I have with my balance and my left leg are because I have a lesion in my right parietal lobe. I know that the very first issues I had with my arm are because of where the original lesion was. I fully

They've Got Knives!

understand the symptoms that the lesion at C2/3 causes. When I became aware of the disc rupture and damage at C5/6, I was fully cognisant of the fact that I was potentially looking at para or quadriplegia if the Neurosurgeon didn't repair the damage. I have two very good friends who are both OTs, I knew why they were asking me exactly where the spinal cord damage was - they were assessing quite how bad things could be.

My degree course was very busy. I had chosen two subjects that had very little down time. I basically had Thursday afternoons off and otherwise was shuttling back and forth between the two campuses where my Business Studies and Psychology lectures were held. I loved everything about Psychology but in Business Studies it was really when we got to be able to choose subjects such as Marketing and International Relations that I really enjoyed myself. I struggled with Accounting and Economics; not least because they were boring but also because Economics was gobbledegook and Accountancy seemed to be arbitrarily adding up numbers; which, with my maths incompetence, was nothing short of a trial.

Really though, the thing that kept me going throughout the three years was the community of students. We were all studying and focussed on getting out into the world in our chosen fields. At school, my English teacher Jackie, specifically, and some of my other teachers more generally, had kick started a love of learning within me. University cemented it. I discovered that I love to be challenged, enjoyed complex debates and genuinely wanted to make a difference in my field.

I always struggled with exams but the provisions that were put into place because of my dysfunctional hands; to have a scribe and to complete my exams in the quiet of the health centre were enough for me to scrape through my introductory subject requirement of the first year and move into my second and third years where I could choose the subjects I wanted to immerse myself in. I was definitely a late bloomer when it comes to

Bugger Bugger Shit!

academic success. Throughout my career those critical thinking skills that I developed at university have been essential.

When I had completed my degree, I decided to stay in London, despite my parents moving to Australia, and pursue a career in Marketing. I was successful in my application to become a Marketing Assistant, then Executive with Newsweek International. Whilst I was there I received news of my results for my degree. Despite the devastating family situation and an overwhelming amount of work, I was successful in achieving a 2:2 Honours Degree in Psychology and Business Studies. A few of us on the Marketing Course had been invited to simultaneously study for a postgraduate certificate in Marketing. I passed that as well, so I had a Graduate qualification as well as my degree.

I loved being out in the workforce, although living in London during an IRA bombing campaign was not what I had envisaged. Public transport was regularly disturbed and we got used to finding alternate routes around bomb threats and the like.

A few years after I moved to Australia, I returned to Europe briefly to attend the wedding of my sister's best friend in Finland. I caught up with my uni friends for dinner in London before flying back to Australia. We had decided to go to Covent Garden but at the last minute made a change to Leicester Square. Following our dinner, whilst waiting at Leicester Square tube station, an announcement came over the tannoy, "We apologise for the delay due to a bomb threat at Covent Garden". My friends and I all calmly looked at each other and matter of factly said, "Well thank goodness we chose Leicester Square instead of Covent Garden".

When the 2007 bombs went off in London, one of my team from Australia was on holiday in the UK. We were all very worried about her safety but I reassured my colleagues that if you're going to be anywhere in the world and there's a terrorist threat, the UK is probably the best place you can be because they are so experienced in dealing with them.

They've Got Knives!

One of my jobs when I was first employed at Newsweek was to start quite early once a week; before anyone else was in, and take the headlines that had been telexed into the London office from the News Bureaus around the world and reformat them into a Press Release which was then distributed by courier. Remember, there was no internet or emails in the late 1980s.

In the last quarter of 1989, there had been a lot of rumbling in what was then East Germany, about the movement of people from the Eastern Bloc to the West; and then as we all know, basically by accident, announcements were made about freedom of travel and on the 9th November the Berlin Wall started to come down.

I recall it being quite confusing at the time, with the general public not really immediately understanding the enormity of what was happening. I went into the office, pulled the telexes off and re-typed them into the Press Release which outlined the dismantling of the wall and the end to the Cold War. I had no idea at the time quite how significant that Press Release was in terms of political history.

I worked at Newsweek for 18 months and as I was planning my annual Christmas trip to Sydney I discovered that my passport needed to be renewed. When I renewed it, along with my Permanent Residency Visa, I was told if I didn't establish my permanent residency at that time, by staying in Australia for at least 12 months, then my visa would be revoked.

This news coincided with an experience I had at a tube station on my way home from work one day. I was, as usual, waiting for my tube at Notting Hill station. An announcement came over the tannoy indicating that someone had committed suicide which was delaying the tube service. My immediate thought was, "Why did they have to do it during rush hour?" I was instantly appalled by the thought that came into my head. I couldn't believe I could be so callous at someone's devastation. This was a

Bugger Bugger Shit!

wakeup call for me. I realised that after five years of living in London, I was losing my compassion. Perhaps I had lost it already. Over the next few days I thought about where I would want to live in the UK instead of London; I couldn't think of anywhere I wanted to live, maybe somewhere in Kent, but I wasn't really enthusiastic about it.

Margaret Thatcher was still in power and there was this overwhelming sense of depression that hung over the country. I could see why Dad had wanted to move the entire family to Australia. He could see the writing on the wall and didn't want his family to be part of it - especially when Australia seemed to be so much more hopeful and of course, the weather was so much better.

Graduation Guildford Cathedral 1989

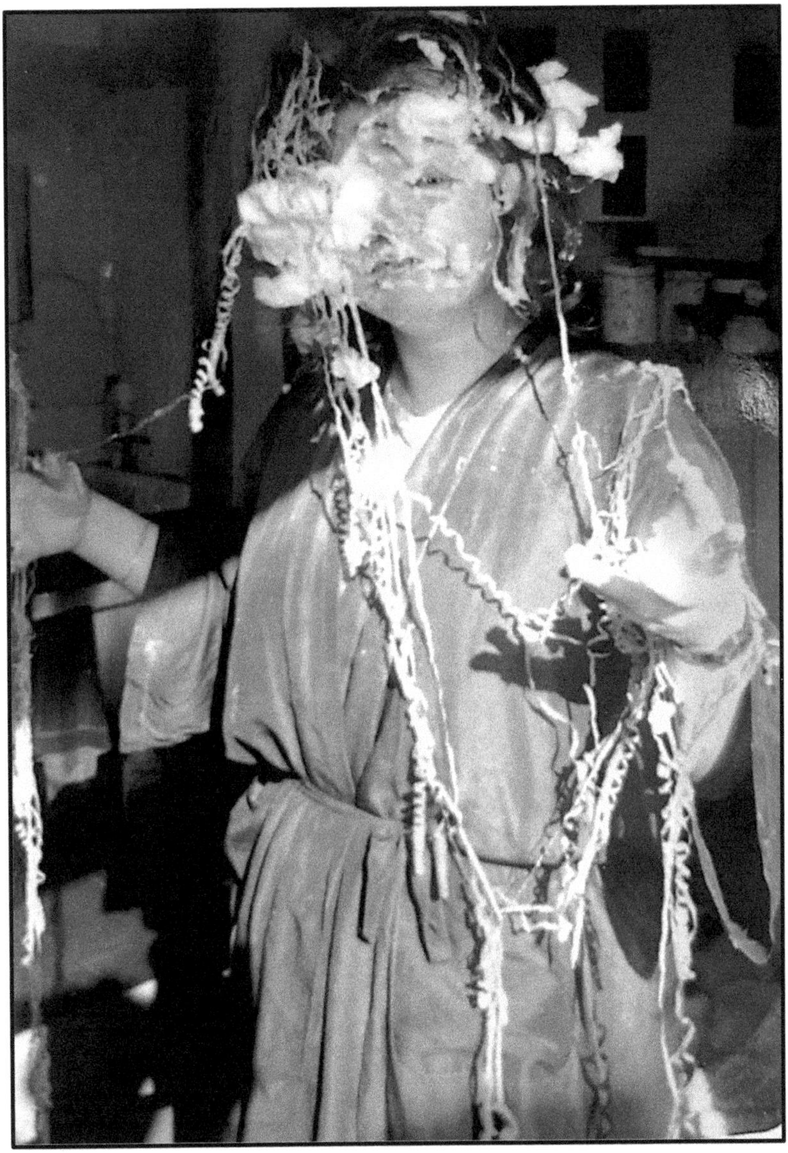

They've Got Knives!

21st Birthday Shenanigans London May 1988

Bugger Bugger Shit!

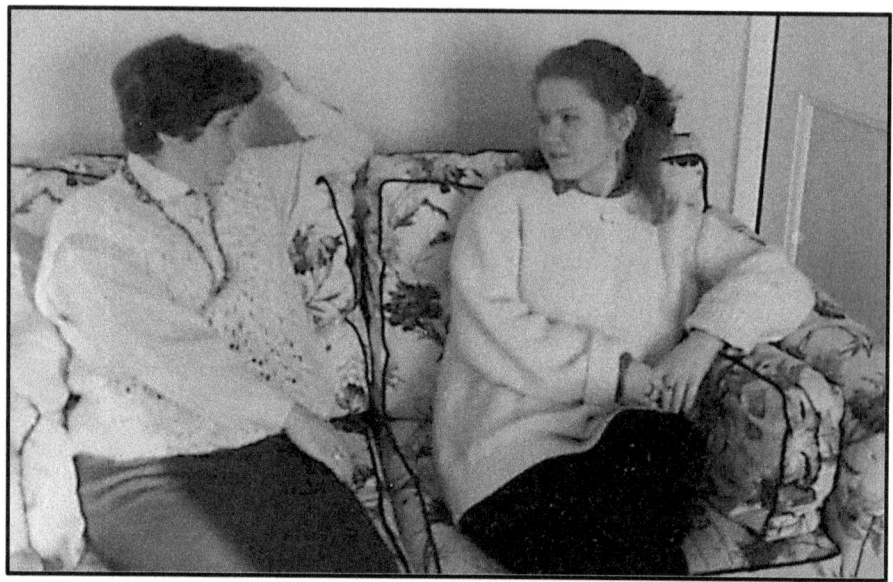

Mum and I Oxford January 1987

My college room London 1989

They've Got Knives!

Perfecting our hit squad disguises

Bugger Bugger Shit!

Post Finals Recreation June 1989

Southlands College Halls of Residence

Chapter 8

Bite Me!

This story's right, this story's true
I would not tell lies to you
Like the promises, they did not keep
And how they fenced us in like sheep
… Said to us, "Come, take our hand"
Set us up on mission land
Taught us to read, to write and pray
Then they took the children away
… Took the children away
The children away
Snatched from their mother's breast
Said, "This is for the best," took them away
… The welfare and the policeman
Said, "You've got to understand
We'll give to them what you can't give
Teach them how to really live"
… "Teach them how to live," they said
Humiliated them instead
Taught them that and taught them this

Bugger Bugger Shit!

And others taught them prejudice
… You took the children away
The children away
Breaking their mother's heart
Tearing us all apart, took them away
… One dark day on Framingham
Came and didn't give a damn
My mother cried, "Go get their Dad"
He came running, fighting mad
… Mother's tears were falling down
And Dad shaped up and stood his ground
He said, "You touch my kids and you fight me"
And they took us from our family
… Took us away
They took us away
Snatched from our mother's breast
Said, "This is for the best," took them away
… Told us what to do and say
Taught us all the white man's ways
Then they split us up again
And gave us gifts to ease the pain
… Sent us off to foster homes
As we grew up, we felt alone
'Cause we were acting white
Yet feeling black
… One sweet day all the children came back
The children came back
The children came back
Back where their hearts grow strong
Back where they all belong

The children came back
Said the children came back
… The children came back
Back where they understand
Back to their mother's land
The children came back
… Back to their mother
Back to their father
Back to their sister
Back to their brother
Back to their people
Back to their land
All the children came back
The children came back
The children came back
Yes I came back

Took The Children Away
Archie Roach
Charcoal Lane
Released September 1990
Mushroom Records

It was the summer of 1976 and my family were on holiday in Greece; I was 9 years old. It was the year everyone around my age and older will remember because it was the summer when the UK was in drought. One day we went to see an ancient monument. I don't recall which one because what happened there took up too much space in my brain for any other memory.

Bugger Bugger Shit!

We were looking at whatever we had gone to see and in front of us was a little family of mum, dad and toddler. I was idly watching the parents take photos of their child. They didn't speak English so I wasn't entirely sure what conversation took place but what it looked like to me was that the photo wasn't as cute as they wanted to be. Without any warning whatsoever, one of the parents slapped the child. The child of course burst into tears. This clearly created the photo that the parents wanted because they expressed their enthusiasm and took lots of photos of their distressed child in front of this monument. I was outraged and as a nine year old, was completely impotent to do anything about it.

I think a lot of people assume I decided to work in the community sector because of my experiences in my family of origin. It wasn't; it was solely attributable to this incident.

Whilst I was working in my marketing position with Newsweek International, one evening a week I volunteered as a counsellor for Childline. Despite the content of the calls, I really loved volunteering at ChildLine, and the opportunity to help children in very difficult situations.

When I moved to Australia, I applied for jobs in the marketing sector and also, because of my experience at ChildLine, in the community sector. It was a 'Sliding Doors' moment when I was unsuccessful with my application to be a Marketing Executive with KLM airlines but successful with my application to become a Direct Care Counsellor in a brand new residential program working therapeutically with adolescent girls unable to live at home because of child protection concerns.

My limited marketing career was over and I began a career that has lasted over 30 years working at the "pointy end" alongside child protection and domestic violence. I love my work. It is hard; it is poorly paid; it is stressful and distressing - but I am incredibly privileged to be able to play a small part in improving the lives of children and families.

Not long after arriving in Australia, I heard a song called 'Took the Children Away' by Archie Roach. It was the first time the plight of Aboriginal people and the associated government practices, over decades, of removing Aboriginal children from their families; as an act of genocide, was brought into the public sphere. I knew nothing of the treatment of First Nations people. I couldn't believe that successive governments could just remove children from their families on a racist whim. How dare they!

I was so incredibly sorry that this had happened that I wrote a letter to Archie Roach via his Management, apologising for what had happened. I have no idea if he got that letter but I do hope so. I was terribly sad when he died recently. He really was a voice for the time. Like so many people, when Prime Minister Rudd stood in Parliament reading the apology to the Stolen Generations, I cried. I have worked with hundreds of people who are part of or impacted by the Stolen Generations. I am grateful for their patient education of a girl from the North West of England who had no idea.

I am privileged to live and work on Darug land. When I sink my feet into the soil, I am reminded of the love and care First Nations people have given; over 60,000 millennia, for the land, sea and sky of this place I get to call home. I am very sorry, I pay my respects to all Aboriginal people and I am reminded to walk gently in this world.

I worked in residential care with young women for two years. There is a reason why caseworkers change so often; the work is profoundly challenging. We had adolescent girls who had all experienced abuse and neglect living together; most of them had no idea how it felt to be cared for, no trust of any adult and no concept of what it felt like to be in a safe environment. They were vulnerable and challenging and all of the staff were

Bugger Bugger Shit!

young. I was one of the very few practitioners in my time who had worked previously and was not straight out of university.

It was during this time that I was introduced to and trained in the work of Milton Erikson; the grandfather of Brief, Solution Focussed Therapy. The innate desire I had to tell stories was developed as I learned the art of therapeutic metaphor. I became a strengths based solution focused practitioner.

We used to take the young women away camping every school holiday. This was always an interesting exercise as this group of young city kids had generally never experienced the great Australian outdoors. Neither had this young practitioner from England. I'd spent years exploring and walking in the Lake District but that was poles apart from the Australian Bush.

The first camping trip was to Kosciuszko National Park in the Snowy Mountains during the long summer holidays. We set up camp; that was an interesting experience in itself. I was slightly nervous, as all non-Australians are, about the risk of snakes and poisonous spiders but it wasn't the snakes or spiders I needed to be worried about, it was something far smaller.

On the evening of the first day, I went back to my tent for something; I shouldn't have. As I stretched up to unzip the tent, something dropped down my top and then I felt the most searing, agonising, burning pain in my breast that I had ever felt in my life. I had been bitten on the boob by a bull ant! What the actual heck!!!! What was this country? I was fully prepared for the snakes and spiders, not the bloody ants!!!! I hadn't even been told to watch out for the ants. I mean what kind of country is this when the ants can kill you?!!

I had visions of my boob getting infected, turning black and having to be chopped off!!! I screamed in agony and tried not to rip off all my clothes and go racing through the camp half naked. One of my colleagues ran towards me as I tried to explain, without using various expletives (after all I

Bite Me!

was at work), that something had bitten me. She grabbed the vinegar. Vinegar? Vinegar? Seriously? This was no time for a culinary exercise. Then she poured it over me. You have to be kidding me! I smelt like a fish and chip shop! She explained vinegar dilutes the sting. Again - YOU HAVE TO BE KIDDING ME!!!! Now, some 30 years later, like all Australians I understand the importance of vinegar - not in the kitchen; in the first aid kit.

That wasn't the last time I got bitten by something very small. A couple of years later I was getting dressed one morning and as I walked past the mirror I saw this huge black welty growth on my side. I did not like the look of it, and being paranoid about malignant melanoma; which also looks black and welty, I was not going to just ignore it.

I duly went to my GP who also did not like the look of it, so she excised it and sent it off to be tested. I went back a few days later for the results. She started reading the report aloud and suddenly her voice elevated as she squeaked, "Oh my God - it was a spider bite!". "What do you mean it was a spider bite???!" I was committed to avoiding the buggers and knew I hadn't had to exterminate any recently. No, it wasn't a Huntsman or a Funnel Web, it was a White Tail spider; a little, tiny, almost invisible, innocuous looking spider with a white tip on its tail which likes to creep around when you're least expecting it, bite you painlessly and cause your skin to develop necrosis! WTAF and bugger bugger shit simultaneously!!!!

After intensively supporting traumatised young women, I needed a change. Fortunately there was a maternity leave locum position with one of the other programs in the division I worked within; an Adoption Specialist role. This random job opportunity was to change the trajectory of my career. I had no idea about adoption when I started, but when I finally moved into a different role, 15 years later, I was an expert.

Bugger Bugger Shit!

Not long after starting in the new role, we had a professional development day. My previous manager was presenting to the rest of the Division the work my colleagues and I had been doing. I was sitting in the back row, near the door, and literally thought to myself, "This will be boring, I'm just going to have a little snooze". What happened next was completely unexpected.

I felt a wave of emotion come over me from my feet up to my head and I bolted out of the room as fast as I possibly could. I ran into the next door building, sat on the stairs and sobbed, great big, body wracking sobs. Another manager who I knew well, came and sat next to me and put her arm around me without saying anything, until the experience passed. I had absolutely no explanation for what had happened. Now I know that I was experiencing Vicarious Trauma.

I commenced my work in adoption during a time of significant change. The NSW Adoption Information Act 1991 had just been proclaimed which meant that Adoptees and their Birth Parents could have information about each other and were able to have contact. It was the very beginning of the open adoption practice we have today. Having worked in the sector for many years, I firmly believe that Australia has the best adoption legislation and practice in the world. We were leagues ahead of the US and the UK at the time. Fortunately, I believe, they are starting to catch up.

To work in adoption means holding grief. There is no one involved in adoption who has not experienced grief. For an adopted person it is the grief of not being raised within their biological family; for parents considering placing a child for adoption it is the grief of not being in a position to parent the child they have created and given birth to; for adoptive parents it is the grief of not being able to parent a biological child. Loss is at the very core of adoption. My sister had died five years previously; if there was something I understood well, it was grief.

There is an ugly past to adoption in Australia; where parents were forced to place their infants for adoption because society would not tolerate 'unwed' mothers. There was no social support; in fact it was the polar opposite. I was profoundly impacted by the individuals I worked with; those whose adoption experience had happened in the past and those adoptions I was supporting in the present.

There is much to be said about adoption. Books have been written on it; television programs have been presented about it, films have been produced. I don't intend to unpack the politics of adoption within the pages of this book. What I will say however, is that every single adoption professional I worked with understood the profundity of the work we did and was deeply impacted by it. I used to say, we can leave the work of adoption but adoption never leaves us.

Early in my adoption career, a film was shown on television called 'The Leaving of Liverpool'. It was about UK Child Migrants who had been shipped to Australia without their parents or families. Many were told that their parents had died; a complete lie. My team was asked to be on hand if there were any telephone calls in the following days from people personally impacted by the film. A colleague and I volunteered to be available. That was the beginning of the work I continued to be involved in; where former child migrants and those who had been committed to the care of an institution, were able to contact us to access their records and to receive counselling if they wished.

It was fascinating and heartbreaking work which still continues today; many former clients subsequently made submissions to the Royal Commission into Institutional Responses to Child Sexual Abuse. I will never forget one particular elderly woman who, with a glint in her eye, told me a story that when any of the children misbehaved they were given bread and dripping to eat. She said that she really liked bread and dripping so she

Bugger Bugger Shit!

proactively broke the rules in order to have some tasty food. That is resilience at its core.

After five years as a practitioner, I was successful in applying for the role of Principal Officer (PO). At 33, I was the youngest ever appointed and the responsibility was enormous. Over the ensuing years, the care and responsibility for thousands of children across NSW sat with me. Most days, as I packed files away and tidied my desk, I would think for a moment; will anybody be in danger or die if I go home now. The answer was usually no, thanks to the skill and dedication of my team, but if the answer was yes, there would be no way I would go home until the issue was resolved. I stayed in that role for eight years and then briefly moved into an Adoption Management position with another Agency.

During my tenure as PO, the NSW Parliamentary Inquiry into Past Adoption Practice was underway. I felt duty bound to 'bear witness' to the horror stories of past adoption practice and attended every hearing. As an Agency we were called to give evidence. In preparing for the hearing, my Director at the time asked me if we needed to make an apology. I had gone through the thousands of records with a fine tooth comb and could see no evidence of illegal practices. That was hardly surprising, and even if practices weren't illegal then there were definitely ethical and moral failings. I was absolutely clear in my response that we needed to apologise. My Director was 100% behind my decision and drafted the apology.

We arrived at the hearing and sat before the panel ready to answer questions. When my Director read out the apology there was an audible gasp that went around the room; we were the first Agency, and some would say, the least likely Agency, to apologise for the practices of the past. Such was the surprise, we ended up being mentioned on the television program 'Good News Week' that night!

Whilst I was in that role I played a significant part in the drafting of the new Adoption Legislation; the NSW Adoption Act 2000. I have to give credit to the NSW Parliament for inviting those involved in adoption to be part of the process of developing the new legislation which replaced the NSW Adoption of Children Act (1965). I also chaired the committee which prepared the first ever standards for adoption practice.

My 15 years working in adoption provided a daily opportunity to work through ethical dilemmas. When I was on long service leave, my boss at the time called me with an issue that had arisen. She asked me if there was ever a week when nothing happens in adoption. My reply was no. What it did was really hone our skills in ethical decision making. Our North Star is always that the children are our primary clients. Whatever we do, when there are competing interests, is to ensure that decisions are always made in the best interests of the child.

What no one knew was that during that period of time, I was grappling with my own medical situation. I had always had intensely painful periods but one month, very early in my work within the Adoptions team, my menstrual cycle went a bit haywire. I saw my GP and she referred me to a gynaecologist who suggested I should have a laparoscopy for suspected endometriosis.

I will never forget that first laparoscopy. It was on the 11th November 1993; as I was being prepped for surgery the clock struck 11 and someone deep within the hospital started to play 'The Last Post'. I'm surprised I didn't jump off the gurney right there and then. I was already terrified of having surgery; now I was almost catatonic.

The gynaecologist was right; I had endometriosis and my whole internal pelvic area was a mess. On top of this my relevant hormone levels were through the floor. I was told that I would never be able to have children without medical intervention and even then there was a pretty remote chance of success. Bugger bugger shit!

Here I was; working with couples experiencing infertility whilst I was going through it myself. I had a choice; I could either leave the job I was

Bugger Bugger Shit!

beginning to really love or suck it up and get on with it. My stubborn nature meant that I was always going to suck it up. With hindsight I should absolutely have sought out some counselling at that point but to be honest I didn't even think about it. What it did do though was give me an insight into what our clients were experiencing; I could be completely authentic in my connection with them, whichever part of the adoption triangle they fell on.

I've lost count of the number of laparoscopes I've since had. I think I'm up to 6; along with what feels like a lifetime of hormone therapy to keep the symptoms at bay. When I was about 40 I needed to see a Gynaecologist again and I went to a new specialist, Dr Bill*. He had actually been part of my second laparoscopy when he was a registrar. He was so lovely and kind I cried in his office. He asked me what I did and when I told him where my career has been focussed, his mouth fell open. I think he misted up a bit at that point too as he realised how incredibly difficult that must have been for me.

I believe one of the keys, in this quest for resilience, is to have a multi-layered appreciation of the world we live in. I have a different core memory from the time in Greece in 1976. It was the following year, 1977. My family was driving across America; it was Christmas Day and we were in Alabama. Of course given where we were, we had to attend the church the Rev. Martin Luther-King had pastored. This family of red and blond haired children walked into the church and slipped into the back row.

I was in awe. Not only was every face black, something that I had not seen in the North West of England but the singing was magnificent. I hope you can imagine the voices, the harmonies, the joy, the clapping and celebration. After the service we were inundated with beautiful and kind men and women welcoming us and thanking us for visiting them. Stroking my hair; themselves in awe at the colour. That was it for me. The seed of

Bite Me!

the joy of music was sown. I was gifted with the capacity to sing and ever since, it has been my passion.

It has also been one of the ways I manage my vicarious trauma; along with regular massages; spending time with friends; reading; going to the theatre; concerts and movies. The arts are so very important in providing us with a way to, temporarily, escape the reality of this often challenging world and to recharge - as are appreciating the wonders and beauty of the natural world and the metaphysical. When we can step away from the horrible things happening in the world and appreciate some of the simple pleasures, it is an opportunity to build our resilience.

Mum Dad & Halina Exploring our new home Akuna Bay July 1987

Chapter 9

The Arena

It is not the critic who counts; nor the man who points out how the strong man stumbles, or where the doer of deeds could have done them better. The credit belongs to the man who is actually in the arena, whose face is marred by dust and sweat and blood; who strives valiantly; who errs, who comes short again and again, because there is no effort without error and shortcoming; but who does actually strive to do the deeds; who knows great enthusiasms, the great devotions; who spends himself in a worthy cause; who at the best knows in the end the triumph of high achievement, and who at the worst, if he fails, at least fails while daring greatly, so that his place shall never be with those cold and timid souls who neither know victory nor defeat."

Theodore Roosevelt
Speech at the Sorbonne Paris
23rd April 1910

I had been in my new job for two days and had been asked to attend a meeting with colleagues from three of our 'sister' agencies; I had absolutely no idea what I was doing or what the meeting was about. What transpired though was a request to develop, from scratch, a program for

The Arena

parents who are engaged in chronic conflict post separation. It was one of those scenarios where everyone takes responsibility for a task and the last person standing gets the hard job. I was the last person standing; so I was assigned the task of actually writing the program.

That meeting turned into one of the most satisfying projects of my entire career. We created a parenting program that is the only externally evaluated, multi-session course for separated parents; Keeping Kids in Mind (KKIM). The program is now internationally recognised and we have trained thousands of practitioners to deliver the program; countless parents have completed the program and we are continuing to train more practitioners today, 15 years later.

I needed to have a break from the intensity of the child protection and adoption work I had been doing, so, after 17 years in that particular sector, I took a step down from my statutory position. I became the manager of a very small parenting program, still within the same agency I had started with in 1991. The job changed within about 10 minutes of being in the role; I was informed that the Agency had been successful in being awarded a larger contract. Over the next 15 years, that little program became the provider of the largest number of parenting programs in NSW.

Alongside the new Keeping Kids in Mind (KKIM) program; my team and I quickly realised that we needed to develop a program for parents whose children have been removed into the child protection system. As soon as I had completed the development of KKIM; my team and I moved on to develop My Kids and Me (MKM) in partnership with another agency. Like KKIM, My Kids and Me was externally evaluated and the results were very positive and, like Keeping Kids in Mind, is now internationally recognised. In 2014 we even won an award for the program which was presented at Parliament House in Canberra.

There is an expectation by Governments that Community Services Agencies, (who are all Not for Profit organisations) will conduct evaluations of the work they do to ensure it is evidence based but they generally don't fund this part of the work. Parents whose children have been removed weren't, at the time, eligible to receive services from any state funded program. The fact that we were federally funded and mandated to work with the most vulnerable parents meant that my team was able to do work with this cohort of parents.

Prior to publishing and rolling out My Kids and Me though, we needed to raise money to pay for a thorough external evaluation of the course. Prior to the pandemic, the Agency held an Annual Charity Race Day to raise much needed funds to support the work we do. This particular year, the Executive made the decision to direct funds towards the external evaluation, to be undertaken by a major university, of MKM. We had a minor celebrity in attendance to encourage participants to give generously.

Before the event commenced, I was having a chat with her. She asked me why we were raising money for parents who have abused their children. I took a breath, looked at her and said, "I have never met a parent who wakes up one morning and chooses to abuse or neglect their child. Parents abuse and neglect their children because they were the abused and neglected children first." She looked at me with a dawning realisation that she had been judging these parents with absolutely no idea of their circumstances.

That simple sentence really helped her understand what I had known for years; the most vulnerable people we work with are the bravest and most resilient people I have ever met. They love their children but this society we live in has never effectively supported them to succeed.

The Arena

When we commenced the evaluation, my whole team and I were concerned about adding to the pressure of our most vulnerable clients by asking them to participate. To our incredible surprise, the overwhelming response was that they wanted to be involved in the evaluation because we cared enough to create a parenting program just for them and additionally, we cared for and respected them enough to seek out their thoughts and opinions.

The results of the evaluation indicated that by spending seven weeks with committed, caring, respectful and skilled professionals, parents could learn effective skills and become the best parents they can be. A significant number of parents, since completing the course, have had their children restored to their care and those who haven't, have been able to improve the relationship they have with caseworkers, foster carers and to support their children in ways they simply weren't able to do previously. There is no such thing as a perfect parent; we all just need to aspire to be good enough parents. As practitioners in the field, we are duty bound to support parents to be good enough.

The team that I was privileged to lead for another 15 years is fabulous. They are skilled, compassionate and knowledgeable professionals. Not long after we had developed My Kids and Me and Keeping Kids in Mind, along with my manager, I was invited to meet with a senior member of staff from the NSW Child Protection Department. As we were chatting, she asked me what my team did that was different from other agencies. I looked at her curiously; I hadn't really thought about any other agencies; my team and I were simply focussed on doing the best we could for our clients. She went on to explain that our service has better results than any other similar service and she wanted to know why. I struggled to think of an answer, so my manager helpfully filled the gap, whilst my brain went into overdrive. After a minute or so, I had my answer, "Circle of Security."

Bugger Bugger Shit!

Circle of Security Parenting is a program developed by an amazing team of committed and experienced professionals in the USA. Very early on in my tenure as Manager of the Parenting program, I had made a decision to spend some additional funds on training with my tiny team. I was aware of Circle of Security from my previous work in adoption and there was a two day training finally coming to Australia and New Zealand. We had a choice between Perth and Auckland; given Auckland is closer to Sydney than Perth, and cheaper to get to; three of us flew to New Zealand.

For two days, we sat in a lecture hall with dozens of other professionals watching and analysing 30 second clips of interactions between parents and infants, toddlers and pre-school aged children. It was fascinating. We were also introduced to the concept of the Circle of Security; the Circle is essentially an Attachment Based road map for parents to be able to understand the needs of their children.

A year or so later, the Circle of Security team had finalised the professional training so that other practitioners across the world could facilitate the program with the parents they are working with. We attended the four days of training at the first opportunity. Kent Hoffman delivered the training; he is one of the most insightful and committed professionals I have ever had the privilege of being in a room with.

I always say that during those four days, we were all taken apart and put back together again ever so slightly differently. I encourage everyone to seek out his Ted Talk on Infinite Worth. I hope it will transform you in the same way we were transformed. It is the fundamental reason why we do the work we do. During the training, Kent told us about his university professor; Frank Kimber, who transformed Kent's own life with the following sentence:

"Every person you will ever meet has infinite worth".

The Arena

Getting back to the meeting I was in with Child Protection; I explained to her that my team and I embody the principles of Circle of Security, irrespective of what parenting program we are actually running. The program's fundamental approach is that caregivers should be *"Bigger, Stronger, Wiser, Kind. Whenever possible they should follow their child's needs and whenever necessary take charge."* The second concept is that caregivers need to create a Secure Base and a Safe Haven for their children. My team and I, intuitively, internalised these concepts and used them with our clients.

My team are the caregivers for our clients whilst they are with us. We strive to be Bigger, Stronger, Wiser and Kind as practitioners. We are committed to creating a Secure Base and a Safe Haven for our clients. As the leader of the team, I committed to being Bigger, Stronger, Wiser and Kind and creating a Secure Base and a Safe Haven for my team and other colleagues. I lead and manage within a Circle of Security framework. I even presented this concept at our industry's major annual conference. Providing this explanation to the Child Protection staff member, she subsequently organised for a consultant to evaluate our program so that they could take the learnings from my program and apply them elsewhere.

I have worked in 'the Arena' with an amazingly dedicated army of professionals committed to the safety and wellbeing of others. We have all been "marred by dust and sweat and blood". To all of them I offer my genuine thanks and appreciation.

Some years ago, my Agency committed to understanding more about the impact of vicarious trauma (VT) on all of the staff members and arranged training for everyone. The only pre-determinant for vicarious trauma (VT) is to have witnessed someone else's trauma. In the community services sector, we all experience vicarious trauma (VT). The symptoms are varied and unique to each person but in caring so deeply about others, we risk the core of ourselves.

Bugger Bugger Shit!

The training was over two half days. On the morning of the first half day, my team and I had been attending a White Ribbon Day event. We had a bit of time to kill in between so we decided to get some lunch before we headed back to the office. On the other side of the road was a large Charity shop. My team loves to shop! Without saying anything, we all wandered over, had a look around the shop in silence and then wandered out and over the road for lunch. The only unusual thing was that we were silent until we'd ordered our lunch and then chatted as usual.

The trainer brought to our attention a significant piece of research and the following quote:

"Doing this work means bearing witness to atrocity, holding the pain of others and being an unwilling participant in traumatic re-enactments".

Saakvitne and Pearlman (1996)

In the training we were asked about the unusual things we do, sometimes to avoid things or situations or just in general. A few people answered about avoiding certain movies, books etc. Others talked about sleepless nights, others talked about the importance of exercising. I had a revelation; I put my hand up and said, "Well apparently my team don't do op shops." We all looked at each other and, somewhat inappropriately, burst out laughing.

I was right. I can't speak for my team but for me it's about two things; firstly there can be a musty smell in op shops which is very similar to the smell we have often experienced when we have done home visits, to see our most vulnerable clients who are trying to just keep their heads above water. It is said without any kind of judgement; it is simply a visceral reminder of the trauma we have observed when walking side by side with our clients. Because we have invariably walked with many clients over many years we have experienced it many more times than others.

The Arena

The second thing for me is that I have realised I don't want to "wear" anybody else's trauma. It is a completely inexplicable and irrational concept to anyone who doesn't understand the impact of vicarious trauma (VT). Of course, I don't specifically think there is anything wrong per se with wearing clothes with a history, it is simply one way I protect myself from "bearing witness to atrocity" when I don't know the history of the clothes.

I had no idea when I accepted that first job as Direct Care Counsellor that I was to be an 'unwilling participant in traumatic re-enactments' for the rest of my career. If I knew then what I know now, would I still accept the role or would I have pursued marketing? I like to think that I would have still said yes. That little girl in 1976 was so deeply impacted by what she had observed, she needed to make a difference.

There are many ways that we look after ourselves in order to minimise the impact of vicarious trauma (VT); for most of us we have developed a finely tuned sense of humour. With each other, in our private space, we endeavour to find the ridiculous in situations. Many people who work on the "front lines" develop a very dark sense of humour. There is no intention of disrespect or malice in it; in fact we feel very deeply about the distress our clients are facing, but in order to survive, and keep turning up, we have to be able to laugh at situations that other people would probably find distressing and, more often, laugh at ourselves.

Many years ago now, my Agency had a significant anniversary and so all of the organisations under its umbrella brought all the managers and leaders, across the country, together for a conference in Canberra so that we could share our work, our innovations and our struggles. The work we all do is hard but for some of our broader colleagues, working in remote areas of Australia, it is particularly tough. When you are listening to difficult stories intensively over a couple of days, it's really important you can find some time to switch off.

Bugger Bugger Shit!

My division within our Agency had a bit of a reputation for our excellence at creating and participating in Trivia Competitions. One of our colleagues was known as The Quizmaster, such was his skill in developing questions; both topical from the world, and personal within our division; his capacity to 'own the room' was second to none as he led the event. Of course we had to prepare one for this conference. They were always raucously funny and wildly competitive; this was no exception.

My colleagues, knowing I was allergic to wine, had ensured there were some alcoholic beverages on hand which I could imbibe in along with them, which was unusual for me. On this particular evening, whilst we were not inebriated, we were certainly relaxed. The quiz was well under way with its usual highly competitive spirit. I was confident I knew the answer to one of the questions; I shot up my hand with such vigour, I promptly fell off my chair with a loud breaking of wind and a dramatic bang - just as our CEO walked into the room. There are many things at work that I'm infamous for; this is just one of them!

Once we decide to step into the Arena, whatever our individual arena might be, we realise that the seed of resilience is sown. Resilience is a choice, a difficult choice but a choice nevertheless. We choose to be vulnerable and we can choose to rise. Very often, the act of seeking help from others is a commitment to our resilience.

There are other things that are essential if we are to stay resilient and to keep showing up. For a long time I sailed and raced yachts; being on the water keeps me focussed on the beauty of this world rather than the harshness I experience day after day. The ocean and the bush are a reminder for me to go gently in this world.

My work now, over 30 years later, is mainly spent in training practitioners and supporting their practice. Whenever possible I talk to them about the risks of vicarious trauma (VT) and the essential need to look

The Arena

after themselves if they are to have any longevity in the 'Arena'. Like many people, I heard Brene Brown talking about 'the man in the arena speech'. It resonated with me; as a mature manager, therapist and clinical supervisor, I was given permission to not listen to the many critics of those of us who choose daily to do the work we do.

It was my professional experience that saw me do something I couldn't do when I was nine years old outside that ancient monument in Greece. On this second occasion, I was in Macau with Dad. We were going around a museum and as often happens in a museum, we kept ending up in the same room as others who started their exploration at the same time as us. There was a particular couple who had an older toddler with them. The toddler was clearly bored and whinging a bit but nothing out of the ordinary and certainly nothing that impacted anyone else's experience of the museum. The mother, clearly aggravated by the whinging, grabbed her child by the ear and dragged him along so violently that he was airborne. I was apoplectic with fury.

Something within me welled up; that nine year old child who couldn't say anything in Greece; that 23 year old who heard the Archie Roach song; the Manager and Psychologist who listened to the celebrity dismiss the bravest people I have ever met. I walked straight up to the woman and I roared into her face, "Don't you ever do that again!" My Dad was completely shocked by the level of fury I displayed and quickly whisked me away. I think he was worried I was going to follow up by punching her in the nose; I wasn't. I had made my point. These two sets of parents were not in the same league as the vulnerable, brave and resilient parents I had worked with. They chose to be cruel.

Children are not the punching bags of adults. They are 'fearfully and wonderfully made'.

Chapter 10

I Carry Your Heart

I carry your heart with me
(i carry it in my heart) i am never without it
(anywhere i go you go, my dear; and whatever is done
by only me is your doing, my darling)

i fear no fate (for you are my fate, my sweet)
i want no world (for beautiful you are my world, my true)
and it's you are whatever a moon has always meant
and whatever a sun will always sing is you
here is the deepest secret nobody knows
(here is the root of the root and the bud of the bud
and the sky of the sky of a tree called life; which grows
higher than soul can hope or mind can hide)
and this is the wonder that's keeping the stars apart
i carry your heart (i carry it in my heart)

e.e. cummins
Liveright Publishing Inc 1991

I Carry Your Heart

I arrived at work and discovered a gift and a card sitting in front of my computer. Curious, I opened the card and discovered it was from my manager who was sitting in her office next door. I opened the box and discovered a Willow Tree Angel. I was incredibly touched and also somewhat surprised. My boss was a no nonsense woman with very little room for sentimentalities and as far as I could tell wasn't particularly spiritual.

I wandered into her office with the angel in hand and a questioning look on my face. She said, "I was at the shopping centre on the weekend and I saw this angel and thought of you." She went on to say, "I can't believe what the last few years have been like for you. It's almost every week you come in and tell me yet another friend or family member has been diagnosed with cancer or their cancer has returned. I saw the angel and thought of you so I bought it because I thought you'd like it." She was right, I do like Willow Tree figurines. I like their simplicity.

Looking back, I realise that every challenging experience in my life had been preparing me for the 2010-2020 decade. Earlier in this book I listed some of the qualities that make a person resilient. One of them was that a person had been through a hard time and had come out the other side. It seems like I had had my fair share of hard times but I needed to lean into the lessons I had learnt along the way in order to navigate the hardest decade of my life so far. If I thought I understood Bugger Bugger Shit before, I was just kidding myself!

On October 10th 2010 our beautiful friend Deb died from breast cancer. She left behind a husband and three young children who were bereft. She also left behind a sea of friends. Whilst relieved that she wasn't in pain anymore we were reeling from the death of such a young woman.

Bugger Bugger Shit!

Deb was filled with light and optimism. She was funny, generous, kind, gave encouragement to everyone and was incredibly wise. She recorded her own Eulogy that was played at her funeral. Her lovely face talking to us one last time was deeply meaningful. At her funeral, I wasn't to know it but she was just the first of many. I stopped counting when it got to 10 people close to me who all had cancer at the same time.

It's all a bit of a blur when I try to remember the order but I think I'm right when I say in the space of five years; Sarah* died after Deb, then Gill* died, then Penny died, then Chloe*, then Tim, my brother-in-law died, then Dad died. Deb and Sarah died from breast cancer. Penny, despite never having smoked a day in her life, died from lung cancer. Gill and Chloe died from ovarian cancer. Tim died from an esthesio-neuroblastoma (so rare there have been fewer than 1000 people in the world diagnosed with this type of tumour since it was discovered in the 1960s). Dad died from prostate cancer. Then of course there had been my sister who died from a malignant melanoma. My Grandpa and one of my 'Uncles' (really a cousin) had both died from pancreatic cancer in the 2000s. Apparently, we know how to 'do' cancer in our family.

Bugger bugger shit.

My grandmother also died in the middle of this decade, not long after my Dad. She was 100 when she died and our sadness was mixed in with relief. I was particularly relieved to experience the death, finally, of an elderly person where the surprise didn't come with her death but that she hadn't died earlier.

When Sarah was still well enough to travel, her sister had taken her to outback NSW. She loved the experience, and despite being very ill, she enthusiastically told us about it. There was one particular evening where she was sitting outside surveying the vast land before her. A beautiful sunset developed and it filled the skies with a technicolour array that you only ever

I Carry Your Heart

see in Australia. She commented to her sister, "That's just God showing off." Now, whenever I see a glorious sunset in front of me, I think of our dear Sarah and God "just showing off". It has given me an even deeper appreciation for our natural world.

When Sarah was dying she, along with my friend Cath and I, was watching the series Life on Mars; we had lots of animated conversations about it. After she died, I had the most awful realisation, which I spoke to Cath about; she wasn't going to see the final episode of the series and wouldn't ever know how it finished. We were so invested in the series it was ridiculous that those were my thoughts but it was important at the time.

Sarah's funeral was a standing room only event. There was a reasonable component of friends and family who walked up to the burial site. Our friend David is a funeral director and he had organised Sarah's funeral. As we were standing around the grave site, the cemetery employees started to lower the coffin into the grave, using a winch. All of a sudden in this sad and sombre moment, there was a little squeak, then a slightly louder squeak and then multitudes of squeaks coming from the winch.

There was a brief moment when I think all of us were slightly horrified but then I started to giggle silently to myself. I turned to look at Cath who was standing next to me; like me she was having difficulty controlling the mirth inside her. We were both trying very hard to hold onto a level of decorum for our dear friend; we failed. Our silent giggles soon became audible as our laughter infected each other. We tried so hard to hold onto ourselves but were hopeless. We each realised that had Sarah been there, she would have thought the whole episode was hilarious and would have been standing there laughing, snorting and crying with us both.

Penny developed a cough which just wouldn't clear; finally, scans revealed lung cancer. This was unbelievable for all of us who knew her. She had never smoked and never worked in smoky environments. We had no

Bugger Bugger Shit!

answers for why it had developed. I had met Penny reasonably soon after I migrated to Australia so we had been friends for a long time. She was an Occupational Therapist (OT) and very committed to her clients as well as her friends and her family; her husband and two teenage children as well as her siblings; her parents had died previously. Penny had been in hospital for a while and a musician friend of ours spent quiet hours with her and her visitors, playing his guitar and singing quietly. Her hospital room was so full of peace.

I received a phone call late one night from Suzie, a close mutual friend who also worked as Penny's PA. Penny had eventually died; her husband had left the hospital to tell the children and he called to ask her to go to the hospital to gather Penny's belongings. Suzie called me and asked me to go with her as she didn't want to go alone. I was honoured to be asked and we travelled in together.

The hospital was mostly in darkness and I remember the two of us feeling slightly awkward wandering the corridors in the middle of the night. Penny was still in her room when we arrived and as we collected her things, we were able to say our own goodbyes. Suzie told Penny it was the last PA thing she was going to do for her and she would need to find herself a new PA in Heaven. It was a very special time for us. Just like my sister, Penny's physical light had been extinguished but the gift she gave of herself to those who loved her, continues on.

Her husband asked me to deliver a Eulogy at her funeral on behalf of her friends; I compiled it from parts of conversations Penny and I had had on Messenger when she was ill, so it was very much Penny speaking through me. It was humorous and ironic, just like her. At the wake, I got asked by numerous friends to deliver the Eulogies at their funerals too. I didn't realise I had a hidden talent for performing at funerals - I'm not entirely sure I want to make a habit of it to be honest.

Gill was loud and funny and passionate. She often got on the wrong side of people; usually because she was standing up for someone, or being very direct when she felt there was an injustice. She took many people under her wing and many were devastated when she died. If you needed someone in your corner, Gill was the one to ask. She got things done and she wasn't afraid to go up against anyone in authority if she was advocating for someone. Her funeral was absolutely packed.

I sang at Chloe's funeral. The church was completely full at yet another young woman's premature demise. I arrived early and sat in the church to compose myself before everyone else came in. I couldn't bring myself to look at her coffin until right at the end because I knew it would undo me. Once everyone had left the room, I looked at her coffin, took a deep breath and dissolved.

When my brother-in-law was dying, my sister had been with him in hospital for weeks. On what was to be the last day of his life, she came home from the hospital in the middle of the afternoon, absolutely exhausted. She had reached the end of her fortitude and needed to spend some time with her children. I left her with them. I went home but I had this intuitive urgency to get to the hospital to see Tim. I grabbed something to eat and jumped in the car to get to the hospital. We had been told that Tim was near to death in May, it was now the 30th June.

Tim was asleep when I got to the hospital so I just quietly sat in a chair next to the bed. He woke up with a start and asked, "Has it started yet?" "Has what started?" I replied. "Masterchef" said Tim. I said, "Not yet, another 15 minutes." Tim dozed off briefly but woke up and I put Masterchef on the tv; Tim was a chef and an avid follower of the program. He tried valiantly to stay awake to watch the episode but he drifted in and out of sleep.

Bugger Bugger Shit!

As he woke up a little while later I reassured him that we 'had' the children and that they would be ok. I prayed a little prayer with Tim as he drifted back into sleep. I left about an hour later without Tim ever waking up. On my way out, I talked to one of the nurses. I reassured her that I knew she couldn't give me a definitive answer but my parents were in the UK and I wanted her advice on whether I should call them to come home. Her response was, "It's impossible to say, but given he's just been watching Masterchef, I doubt it will be today".

Tim died a few hours later. We have always found it very funny and apt that rather than anything deep and meaningful, his last word was "Masterchef" and that had he been slightly more organised he would have died on the 30th June not the 1st July; the 30th June being the last day of the Australian financial year.

I had seven other close friends who were diagnosed with cancer during this period; six with breast cancer and one with lymphoma. I rejoice that they survived and are well and healthy today but standing on the side lines as so many of my loved ones endured the roller coaster of cancer treatments, scans, breath holding check ups and getting to what I now know, in reality, is an arbitrary five years being clear, has taken its toll.

Of course the decade between 2010 and 2020 wasn't the only decade reserved for deaths of people close to me. Across the world, the beginning of the 2020s was the start of a wave of deaths with such huge numbers it was difficult to get our heads around. As a person with a seriously diminished immune system, I was very thankful to be living in Australia.

So many families experienced so many deaths in close succession I wonder how they could move forward. Isn't this the way of the world though? There have been so many natural disasters in my lifetime with so many families impacted by significant loss. My mum's nursing home has had many Covid-19 lockdowns, in fact they are in the middle of one as I

I Carry Your Heart

type, but they haven't lost a single resident to Covid-19. I was very lucky, in that no one I knew died from a Covid-19 related illness - until they did.

My beautiful friend Eileen was a Support Worker for adults with significant disabilities. She contracted Covid-19 from a client in 2022, after the worst of the pandemic was over. She had been vaccinated and had been particularly careful because of her vulnerable clients. Her initial Covid-19 infection didn't seem to be too bad in the scheme of things but one day she woke up unable to speak. Her movement and walking were also impaired. Initially it was thought that she had had a stroke but all of her scans came back clear and she was diagnosed with post Covid-19 Neurological Syndrome.

She struggled for a good 12 months but by mid 2023 she seemed to be on the mend and was doing really well. When she was able to drive again, we met for what ended up being a very long lunch and then made plans for coffee after I got back from a weekend in Tasmania.

I was on the plane in Launceston, returning to Sydney, and was about to turn my iPad's WIFI off ready for takeoff when her husband sent me a message. Eileen had died overnight. I sent him a quick message to let him know how utterly shocked I was and that I was about to fly to Sydney.

I spent that hour and a half on the plane with my brain whirling in total disbelief. I wondered for a minute whether it was a hoax and that someone had hacked her account but when I landed in Sydney, switched on my phone and it started to ping, reality hit. My beautiful, funny and vibrant friend had really died. It wasn't some sick hoax. Then I saw that she had sent me a funny message on Messenger the evening before she went to bed and never woke up. My head and heart were reeling.

The deaths of my friends and family previously had been expected; this side swiped all of us. I had had a bit of an argument with a friend a few days before and I sent him a message to let him know what had happened and to say our disagreement simply wasn't worth it. Yes everyone has arguments with people, we have disagreements about all sorts of things throughout our lifetimes but, if ever there was a wake up call to make sure we take responsibility to work to forgive and apologise when we need to, then this was it. Eileen's funeral was the most surreal I have ever been to. We were all in complete and absolute shock and I think, five months later, we're still processing it.

The thing about loving people is that we will inevitably lose them. When we love someone we choose to be vulnerable. We could in fact choose to go through our lives disconnected from everyone in order to protect ourselves from the intense pain associated with the loss of someone dear to us but that just exchanges one pain for another; the pain of loneliness and isolation.

Chapter 11

Tears Are The Rivers of Life

Connection is why we're here; it is what gives purpose and meaning to our lives. The power that connection holds in our lives was confirmed when the main concern about connection emerged as the fear of disconnection; the fear that something we have done or failed to do, something about who we are or where we come from, has made us unlovable and unworthy of connection.

Brene Brown
Daring Greatly: how the courage to be vulnerable transforms the way we live, love, parent and lead
2012, Avery

A few years after my sister died, I went to the movies with my fairly new Australian friends. None of them knew me when my sister died and only a couple of them were aware of her death. We went to watch Little Women. Despite having read Louisa May Alcott's books, I completely forgot that Beth dies in the novel. When it happened in the film I sobbed. I was inconsolable. The film finished and my friends were ready to leave

Bugger Bugger Shit!

but I couldn't move. The friends that knew quickly whispered to the others about my sister so that they comprehended that this wasn't just me having a deeply moving reaction to a movie but that it was personal. It took me right back into my own loss.

We cannot fear death or grief. We cannot protect ourselves from the pain. Many people try to pathologise grief and to label it as something else. I think they do that as a form of protection; 'if this person is displaying such intense emotions, then there must be something wrong with them. If there is something wrong with them, then it means when I am faced with a similar situation, I won't be that sad or distressed, or broken.' Grief is what it is. It isn't depression, it isn't mental illness. Grief is just an expression of love.

A colleague of mine wrote a guided reflection many years ago as we walked alongside people who were experiencing the grief of infertility. She wrote: *"Tears are the rivers of life that cleanse the heart and the soul. They are tears of sorrow but also of love."* When we understand this, then we can embrace grief, rather than run from it. We can step into someone's darkness and we can hold out a candle for them to see.

I was watching the BBC drama series 'Best Interests' recently. It is about a child with a life limiting illness. In the final episode the family have made the decision to switch off their daughter's life support machines. The nurse was explaining what would happen and said she would "pass". The mother said, "Can we just say it for what it is? She will die. It's not passing on or letting go. She'll just die." This is a contentious topic.

A few years after my sister died, I had been asked to give a guest lecture to nursing students about death. It was the last lecture in a series about the personal impacts of living with various medical conditions and the faculty wanted me to talk about the ongoing impact of death. I was asked to return a few years in a row to give the lecture to each cohort of nurses.

As I got to the end of my lecture I raised the topic of language. I said to them a similar thing to the mother in the television program. I said my sister wasn't 'late', she hadn't missed the bus. She had died. She hadn't passed away. She had died. She didn't pass on or pass. She died. I wanted them to know that when people are so worried about using the word 'died' it isn't actually helpful.

Even though people are trying to be kind and sensitive, the underlying message to the bereaved is that it is too uncomfortable for me to say the word death so I have to find a way to sanitise it so that I feel more comfortable. My experience is that this avoidance of the words dead or death or dying actually just isolates the bereaved even more. When someone has the inner strength to say very kindly and empathically, "I'm so sorry that your person died" it actually builds connection; it is authentic and it is vulnerable.

I firmly believe that every single one of us has a profound job to do, if we can. That is, to take the hands of our loved ones who are dying and walk them to the gates of eternity. To kiss them and give them permission to leave us.

None of us knows what happens when we die. For many, they have a faith in the after life; for many others they don't. Irrespective of our beliefs, we also have a responsibility to support those who are grieving in whatever way we can. Not by quoting trite sayings like, "They're in a better place now" or "God won't give you more than you can handle". These are offensive and completely unsupportive to someone who is grieving. What we need to do is hold on to our resilient selves and to step into the pit with someone. To be able to say to them, "I am in this with you. I am not going anywhere without you. When you're ready, we will step out of this pit together".

Just as I believe we need to walk our loved ones who are dying to the gates of eternity; we need to take the hand of the grieving and walk them to the gates of life. And when they are ready, to kiss them and give them permission to continue to live. They are not moving into a future without the person they loved; they are moving into a future with a changed relationship with their loved one. We carry their hearts with us. When we understand this and can embrace this, we are truly resilient.

Many people talk about resolving grief. When we understand grief as an expression of love, the inanity of this statement is realised. We're not called upon to resolve love so how can we resolve grief? What we do is accommodate it. We become slightly different versions of ourselves because of the grief, not in spite of the grief. We learn how to live without their physical presence. People thinking they've seen a loved one or who talk to a loved one are not crazy; they are grieving in a wholly authentic and healthy way.

We all grieve uniquely; there is no right or wrong way. Just because one person expresses grief through talking or crying, it is no more or less valid than someone who expresses their grief through exercise. In fact they are labelled by psychologists as intuitive or instrumental ways of grieving. Unfortunately however they are often misunderstood which can create all sorts of relationship issues and disconnection. Expressing our grief, however we demonstrate it, builds resilience. We all need to allow and support people who are grieving to do so in whatever way they like, as long as it's not harmful.

The most significant misappropriation of research around death and dying is the work of Elisabeth Kubler-Ross. You may not have heard of Kubler-Ross but I would be fairly confident in saying the vast majority of people are aware of the Five Stages of Loss and Grief; Denial, Anger, Bargaining, Depression and Acceptance. There are no stages of loss though.

Kubler-Ross talked about the Five Stages of Death and Dying which is very different to Loss and Grief. She was also clear that they were not a linear progression. This has been mis-reported on so many occasions it is now seen as being the 'truth'. The problem with this is that when we talk to a grieving person about the stages of grief, they cannot follow the 'rules' because the 'rules' don't exist.

When people don't follow the expected pattern of behaviour; they are commonly labelled, pathologically, as being depressed or in denial or at best not grieving as they should. These assumptions can do dreadful harm because the person then feels like a failure. How on earth can anyone "fail" at grieving? What these attitudes do is diminish resilience rather than build resilience.

The 'truth' about grief is that there is no right way or wrong way to grieve. What people need in the midst of grief is support. What that support looks like is different for everyone. As a Psychologist, it concerns me if someone isn't able to function at all and may need some additional support, but that doesn't make them depressed. They might also have depression but depression isn't the same as grief and we need to be careful not to conflate the two.

As a society, over time, we have become so intent on not being comfortable with experiencing or witnessing difficult emotions that whenever someone does have an emotion that challenges us, we seem to automatically assume it is more than it is. Emotions wax and wane and sometimes we can feel multiple emotions all at the same time. That is perfectly normal. When we don't allow ourselves or others to express difficult emotions then we impair resilience. Resilience is built when we are

Bugger Bugger Shit!

supported through our emotions; not when we squash them down or tell someone to "get over it".

When we allow someone to feel the full intensity of an emotion and we support them with it, rather than encouraging people to 'feel better', research shows that we get through the emotion and move to regulation faster. When we minimise people's emotional state then the research shows that the dysregulation lasts longer. That is not to say we do these things because we are being mean or unsupportive; we genuinely want to do what's best but so often people tell me that they don't know what to do and they want the other person to feel better.

What we do know is that when we Emotion Coach someone; that is, sit with their emotion, empathise with them and validate their experience, we build resilience and become much more able to manage our difficult emotions. The Circle of Security team calls it 'being with'. People who are grieving need others around them to 'be with them'.

David Kessler, a practitioner who worked with Kubler-Ross talks about an important element of grief; the concept of meaning making. Being able to make some meaning out of the death of a loved one or other loss is a significant aspect to being able to accommodate the associated grief.

The meaning I have made from my sister's death is that whilst I would never wish to go through that experience again, I believe it has made me a better human. It has certainly made me a better psychologist. I am unafraid to step into someone's grief with them and I believe it has improved my professional intuition into what will be more helpful than other things.

Her death has also been a warning to all young adults who decide not to wear sunscreen and to everyone to get their skin checked regularly. For many years though, it caused within me a certain level of healthy paranoia; given my red hair and very pale skin, to check moles and get anything vaguely suspicious checked. I'm not quite so paranoid now that I am in my 50s but I still get my skin checked regularly.

My experience of death at such a young age has also made me acutely aware of how grief works in the long term. I know that grief doesn't ever resolve, because my grief has never resolved. I understand that there is a fundamental part of me that is forever changed and that the triggers of grief continue long after the person has died.

A few years after the incident at the movies, I was driving behind my younger sister who was taking her car in to be serviced. We were coming up to an intersection when someone cut my sister off and drove into her lane ahead of her. We came to a stop at the traffic lights and it took all of my resolve not to get out of the car and yell at the woman. This was a very big reaction to what is a very commonplace experience in Sydney traffic. I thought for a moment about why I was so impacted and I realised that it was because I had already lost one sister and there was no way I was going to lose another one at the hands of a careless driver.

During my 41st year I felt ever so slightly less grounded than usual, yes my brother in law had been diagnosed with cancer and was going through treatment but it wasn't that. I couldn't put my finger on it until the anniversary of my sister's death. I realised at 41, I had now lived longer without my sister than with her.

Just last year I was back in the UK and visiting my home town. As I always do when I am there, I went to put some flowers on Halina's grave. I wept, as I always do.

There is nothing wrong with me. All I am doing is experiencing my grief. Do I experience it everyday? No. Am I able to get on with my day to day responsibilities? Yes. It waxes and wanes, just as it should. We talk about the people who have died. We joke about them, we complain about them, we tell funny stories so that they live in the minds of the people who never

Bugger Bugger Shit!

knew them. I am me because of the people in my life, the ones who have died and the ones who are still living.

Of course it is not just death that causes us to experience grief. Every single one of us experiences loss; it is a universal experience. The other significant loss I have walked is that of infertility. Infertility is an example of disenfranchised grief. It is silent and it is invisible. There is no funeral, no meals prepared by concerned neighbours and friends. No ritual and no acknowledgment.

There are unfortunately, insensitive people who make insensitive remarks like, "You better get a move on if you want a family" or, "If you're so focussed on your career it will pass you by." There are others who say nothing whatsoever even though they know what the situation is. One of the most insensitive remarks I have ever experienced came out of the blue one day. A friend made a comment about the nice dress I was wearing. I told her the shop I had bought it from (on sale). Her response to me was, "Oh it's alright for you, you don't have children so you can afford to shop there." The words impacted me like someone had whipped me. Sharp, cutting and unbelievably hurtful. I had no words to say to her.

The silence from others was deafening - and unsupportive. Being told, at age 25, you probably won't be able to have children was devastating. The dreams and assumptions that I carried about my future were shattered. I spent my 30s surrounded by friends who were having babies. I was invited to more baby showers than I care to remember and I was expected to smile through my pain. It was unbelievably isolating. Hardly anyone sat with me and allowed me to grieve; the expectation was that I would, "Just get on with it."

Eventually I said enough. When friends passed me their babies to hold, I declined. When I was invited to baby showers, I declined. I stopped buying presents for babies just born and I stopped going to children's birthday parties. I needed to look after myself because it was quite clear no one else was going to or be even vaguely compassionate. I could very easily have 'gone under' at this point in time but the words of my sister whispered in my ear, "The question is not why me, the question is why not me?" I believed I had a purpose; one of the keys to resilience.

It was through my experience of infertility however that my parents rose to do quite the loveliest and most supportive thing I think anyone has ever done for me. It was Christmas Eve one year and for some reason I was staying over at my parent's house. It was quiet before the throng of children arrived the next day for the festivities. Dad had made a lovely dinner, Mum had set the table. I arrived and wandered into the dining room to find two jewellery boxes sitting next to my plate. As Mum and Dad sat down they explained that they wanted to give me part of my Christmas present early when it was just us.

As I unwrapped the boxes, Dad said that he and Mum saw how much I helped my sister with her children and how involved I was in their lives. Then he went on to say, "We know how painful that must be for you so we just wanted you to know that we know and we appreciate you." Inside the boxes was a beautiful garnet bracelet and necklace. I had been to Prague in the late 1990s and had bought a lovely pair of garnet earrings for myself. The bracelet and necklace matched them. I was speechless.

In my own experience of grief, the most helpful and supportive environments are with people who connect with my experience and practise the art of 'being with'. I continue to strive towards 'being with'; none of us are perfect at it but the more we are open to fully experiencing our own loss and grief, the more we are able to support others. When people are genuinely supported, their resilience grows.

I medically retired from work six months ago. Prior to making the decision to finish up in permanent employment I thought it would be

Bugger Bugger Shit!

advisable to seek out some sessions with one of our Employee Assistance Counsellors. During our sessions, I filled her in on the multiple losses and challenging experiences I had been through. You know you've got a 'big' history when the counsellor takes multiple sharp intakes of breath as you outline everything you've been through.

One of the things I thought important to do was to lay down the fact that I couldn't have children so that I could move into my future without it. We mulled it over and she suggested I needed to do something symbolic to mark it. This is exactly the thing I have said to clients previously. I needed to give it form and shape. I thought about it and as I often do, I went to my closest friends for their thoughts. They agreed but we weren't entirely sure how to mark it. One of them half jokingly said, "I think it needs to involve jewellery". We all laughed and agreed.

A few days later it came to me. I remembered the garnet jewellery that Mum and Dad had given to me and I knew the answer was in finding a ring to match and make up the set. The ring was to be a physical symbol of what I had lost. I tried to find one online or in shops but none of them were quite right. Then one day as we were sorting through Mum's things I found her garnet ring. I realised this would match the set perfectly and the fact that it was Mum's was very fitting given the source of the other pieces. The ring itself can't be worn at the moment because it is too fragile but it is currently being re-designed and re-set to make it safe and when it is finished, I will wear it in remembrance of the babies I could never have.

My sister's death, when I was aged 20, was really the event which shaped the rest of my life. It felt like I was a million years apart from my peers in terms of life experience. I was grieving deeply and my family, despite their limitations, lived on the other side of the world. My very close friends were my support system but still they couldn't, as hard as they tried, understand what had happened for me.

Dan Siegel is a well known Trauma and Developmental Expert; uses the term 'feeling felt'. Every single person has a need to 'feel felt' and at this difficult period of time in my life there was no one who was able to step into my world and walk alongside me. Six months after my sister died, my beloved Grampa Hector also died; the day before my 21st birthday. I remember going to the room of one of my closest friends in our Halls of Residence, sitting on his bed and throwing my keys across the room. There were no words to describe how bereft I felt.

I have spent much of my career supporting and educating people through loss; helping them to contextualise their grief simply as an expression of their love. I loved my sister and my grampa and they had died. So many times I went to call them over the following months. I would get to the phone and then remember they weren't there to call. I couldn't have any conversations with them, I couldn't tell them what was happening in my life or ask what was happening in theirs.

Over thirty years later, looking back, I see how much they both influenced me. My grampa was an incredible storyteller, he was kind and funny. My sister was resilient and wise. Because of them, I am unafraid to step into the pit of despair with people and simply be with them in the mess. I truly understand that in order to heal, we need to 'feel felt'.

Whilst I would have dearly loved to have lived my adult life with my sister, I am able to see the positive influence she has had on me and I wouldn't change it. The experience of profound loss at such an early age has influenced me to appreciate the world, to appreciate the gift that people are to our lives. I have learned so much from the clients that I have worked with but I would never have been able to be the authentic psychologist that I am today without having lived through what I lived through. I would not be me.

Chapter 12

Boyfriend Trouble

It's no accident that the word "hysteria" originates from the Greek word for "uterus." There's still this pervasive belief in the medical community that anytime a woman complains about her health, it's either related to her hormones or all in her head. Female hysteria was once a common medical diagnosis for women, applied whenever women displayed "inappropriate" emotions such as anxiety, anger and even sexual desire. For centuries, it was believed that the uterus itself was the cause of a woman's "hysterical" symptoms.

And, unfortunately, these sorts of beliefs still carry on today. How often does a woman get angry, only to be asked if she's about to get her period? How often does a perimenopausal woman go to her doctor's office to complain about weight gain, only to be told that it's related to hormones? Our hormones aren't making us anxious or upset—these condescending attitudes are.

> **Dr Stephanie McNally**
> Gaslighting in Women's Health: No it's not just in your head
> Katz Institute for Women's Health
> https://www.northwell.edu/katz-institute-for-womens-health/articles/gaslighting-in-womens-health

Boyfriend Trouble

It was a reasonably typical northern hemisphere autumn day in 1990, except I was at St George's Hospital in Tooting, London, sitting in a neurologist's office who was telling me that, in his opinion, following a battery of tests that I had had a few weeks earlier, I had multiple sclerosis (MS). I needed to have a lumbar puncture to be 100% sure of the diagnosis, but he thought it would be inevitable. He further explained that a lumbar puncture isn't particularly pleasant and that a new machine had been developed called an MRI. This magical invention would be able to diagnose MS by doing a scan similar to a CAT scan, but a little bit noisier. Unfortunately, the National Health Service only had a few machines available in the United Kingdom at the time.

Given that he knew I was about to migrate to Australia, he suggested it would be much easier to have one in Sydney when I arrived. I asked him what my future was going to look like? He suggested it would be pretty normal, but I would probably find myself needing a wheelchair when I reached my 50s. Bugger bugger shit.

I was 23 years old and sitting in the hospital with my grandmother. My parents had migrated to Australia a few years before, so Grandma came to the appointment with me. My grandmother was not well known for her subtlety, either then or as she got older, but at that moment, she was everything I needed. She was practical and no-nonsense. She offered no sympathy or worried glances, but she did say she thought I should enjoy myself while I was young, give up my job as a Marketing Executive with Newsweek International, get a job that wouldn't give me too much stress, not worry about having children and get on with life for as long as I could.

I, of course, did none of those things.

Bugger Bugger Shit!

Unlike many people, I wasn't blindsided by the diagnosis. I had lived with MS since I was about nine years old because my mum had it. One of the most significant memories of my childhood is sitting in the car with my siblings as my mum and dad went into endless doctor's offices in search of an explanation for her weird neurological symptoms. She never got a diagnosis from these doctors. It was about 1978, and no one was willing to diagnose a young mum with four children with what they thought was a life sentence of an untreatable, debilitating and degenerative neurological disease.

It was my mum's cousin *Uncle* Jed, a GP, who, in the end, gave her the diagnosis every other doctor had been too paternalistic and weak to provide. My mum; a nurse, midwife and health visitor, thumbed her nose at those small-minded doctors and worked full time, getting her undergraduate degree, her master's degree and eventually her Doctor of Philosophy at the same time as raising four children while her husband travelled endlessly for his work. My mum has outlived my dad but is now in a nursing home, coming towards the end of her life with MS-related dementia. But no one could say she lived her life in the slow lane because of her MS.

No one could say I have either.

At about the same time as the weird neuropathy I was experiencing in 1987, I also suffered from excruciating pain in my lower back and my right arm, hand and wrist. My doctor organised x-rays and referred me to the Rheumatology Clinic. They were a little confused by my symptoms. Their confusion lay in the fact that my symptoms presented like rheumatoid arthritis (RA), but RA is a symmetrical disease, and my symptoms weren't.

They assumed that the pain in my arm, wrist and hand was carpal tunnel syndrome and they basically ignored the back pain; they splinted my wrist and advised me not to use that hand. They then sent me on my way with no further follow-up; I carried on trying to manage my painful back.

Boyfriend Trouble

My university organised scribes for me and when I graduated from my degree and joined the workforce, I tried to be careful not to aggravate anything.

I migrated to Sydney on Christmas Eve, 1990. Following the Christmas festivities, I made an appointment for an MRI at Royal North Shore Hospital in February 1991. I can still remember with a cold sweat that first MRI. Having since had a lumbar puncture, quite frankly, I would have taken one of those any day than lie in that insanely noisy coffin.

For the uninitiated, an MRI machine is a narrow tube that is only slightly wider than the average human. You lie on a patient table which recedes into the tube. If you are having an MRI of the lower half of your body you go in feet first, otherwise it's head first. The MRI machine is incredibly noisy with sequences of various lengths of different mechanical bangs and knocking. To alleviate this, the radiographers typically give the patient ear plugs and earmuffs or headphones. Sometimes, if you're lucky, they will play music through the headphones but I always find that useless because you've got ear plugs in and the music in no way minimises the racket of the machine.

Just to add to the hideousness of the situation, if you are having a brain MRI, you lie on the table and after the headphones are put on, a cage is put over your head and bolted to the table. I also have a cannula inserted into my arm before I go in; halfway through I am pulled out and contrast is injected into me. The contrast often gives you a weird metallic taste in your mouth and a slightly disconcerting warm feeling as it flows around your body's blood stream.

More recently MRIs have a mirror attached to the cage so that you can sort of see out. You then slide into the machine. I cannot open my eyes whilst I'm sliding into the machine or when I'm in it; otherwise the claustrophobia is impossible to manage. You are given a button you can

Bugger Bugger Shit!

press if you need to be pulled out and on one occasion I made the mistake of not closing my eyes before sliding into the machine. I pressed that button as hard and as frantically as I could.

The radiographer rushed into the room, ejected me fast and undid the bolts on the cage. I almost leapt off the table, such was my panic. He was brilliant though, we both knew I had to have this scan and whilst some people need to take Valium beforehand I really didn't want to. He talked me through my panic calmly and kindly, got me back onto the table, slid me into the machine and then went round to the back and touched my head so I knew I wasn't really in a long tunnel.

MRIs typically take up to half an hour, often shorter. For those of us with MS however, when both the brain and the spine is being imaged, they can take up to an hour. An hour of lying absolutely still when most of us have weird neuropathies is almost impossible but we all endure it; we know we have to. It can get quite hot in the tube so I always feel like my feet are freezing but my torso is on fire. I also itch mercilessly as part of my MS but you cannot move.

What I tend to do is use mindfulness to keep myself calm. I listen to the rhythm of the bangs and knocks and focus entirely on that. My mum tends to fall asleep in her MRIs; I thought she was nuts quite frankly, but last year having now had so many, I actually found myself drifting off as well. It probably helps that they are usually scheduled for the evening so I'm already really tired.

Following the MRI, I had my appointment with the neurologist. I expected it to be fairly straightforward, given the tests and preliminary diagnosis in London, but no. The neurologist said there was no evidence of demyelination, that my symptoms were most likely caused by *boyfriend trouble,* and that I should seek counselling with a psychiatrist.

Boyfriend Trouble

I was 23; I was in shock, and I was furious. I'm reasonably confident that if you were to scour the medical literature, there would be zero correlation between MS and 'boyfriend trouble'. But I was polite and respectful and went on my way with my tail between my legs; thinking I was a crazy hypochondriac whose weird neuropathy was all in her head.

Whilst I was writing this book, I found the letter the neurologist; a Registrar at the time, wrote to my GP following this appointment. If I was furious before, I have no words to describe the rage that this letter provoked in me. What was also appalling was that the letter, and a couple of letters from my UK doctors had clearly been released to my mother; without informing me, even though I was a 23-year-old, thoroughly independent adult at the time.

The letter referred to me as a "lass" and went on to say *"She has seen various neurologists and rheumatologists at many hospitals in England and presents to me distressed and upset by the fact that she is "continually being fobbed off by doctors who have been unable to find a physical cause for her complaint." She is reluctant to accept that this may be stress related or the results of psychological upheavals"*.

To clarify, I had been to two hospitals; the second was to have a barrage of MS-related tests because they weren't able to be done at my first hospital. The letter then went on to describe my symptoms; all of which are clearly related to psoriatic arthritis and MS; *"swelling of the arms, hands, wrist joints and fingers, constant neck and shoulder pain, intermittent problems with balance, intermittent weakness, she cannot manipulate objects and is always dropping things, problems with speech and is often lost for words and says she then stutters."* These are all symptoms that I currently experience and have been definitively aligned with my two major diagnoses.

Further, he wrote; *"As I had discussed with you on the phone, I had a long talk with this young lass and I mentioned I found no physical cause. I honestly*

Bugger Bugger Shit!

do not believe that I can justify any further investigations, in particular invasive tests such as lumbar puncture or even an MRI scan given the lack of physical signs and given the rather nebulous story." Nebulous story? Are you kidding me?!

This letter is in direct contrast to the letters written by my UK doctors which are generally respectful and clearly outline their suspicions of MS and state that my mother also has MS. The complete disrespect that he showed me is palpable. This was 1991, not 1941. I would like to say that things have changed but less than 10 years ago a friend of mine was fobbed off with her neuropathic symptoms being described as stress-related; she was later diagnosed with MS after she pushed for a second and third opinion.

My mother only discovered she had MS when the life insurance she had applied for was declined. Her neurologists had informed the life insurance company of her diagnosis but they didn't inform my Mum. My mum's cousin was the one who requested the information from the insurers. They released the information to him because he was a doctor, but they refused to release it to my mum; the actual patient. Mum's cousin was the one who gave her the diagnosis. This paternalistic and often misogynistic behaviour has to stop. It is, quite frankly, dangerous, if nothing else.

I have missed out on over twenty years of Disease Modifying Therapies as a direct result of this doctor. The internet now gives us access to so much more information than we had previously and there are a swathe of public complaints about him. Had I the confidence and personal power to make a complaint back then, perhaps this doctor might have been counselled to perform better and perhaps his subsequent patients would have received a much better service. He was, after all, only a 'baby' neurologist at the time and clearly needed much more supervision than he received.

My UK medical letters listed the name of the supervising consultant as well as the name of the registrars, not so, this letter. Since finding this

Boyfriend Trouble

correspondence, I have made a complaint to the Health Care Complaints Commission. Our complaints are one way to stop this outrageous behaviour. And when we complain we take back control of our lives which in turn builds our resilience. Every time we put in a boundary and speak truth to power; scary as it may be, we are taking a step towards a more resilient world. Unfortunately the commission responded that because of the length of time in between they aren't going to investigate the complaint. Unsurprisingly, I suggested to them that they might want to reconsider but I'm not hopeful.

Having re-read the letter, I am not entirely convinced that the doctor even bothered to check my MRI results so I am on a quest right now to find the original MRI and associated documentation to see what it actually found. My MRIs now clearly show a large patch of demyelination. Perhaps the MRIs of 1991 weren't sensitive enough to pick it up or perhaps the Neurology Registrar just didn't bother to check; preferring to dismiss, disregard and disrespect a 23 year old woman.

My first dramatic MS symptom happened in July 1987. My parents had just migrated to Sydney, and I had joined them for a holiday, as I had just finished the first year of my Psychology and Business Studies Degree in London. We were in Paddington in Sydney, having lunch with a colleague of my dad, who was welcoming us to Sydney.

As he went out to the kitchen to bring in the starters, the fingers on my right hand started to go numb. I told Mum quietly what was happening, but then our host came back into the room with the food, so I didn't say anything more. As he went out to take the plates and bring in the main course, I told Mum that my whole hand was now numb. Following the main course, he went out again, and I whispered my arm was now numb up to my elbow. After the coffee had been drunk and we said our goodbyes, my entire right arm was numb and felt cold. The only way I could describe

Bugger Bugger Shit!

it was that it felt like a refrigerated leg of lamb was hanging off my shoulder where my arm was meant to be.

The symptoms lasted for weeks as I dropped and smashed almost everything I picked up with my right hand. It reminded me that when I was 16; I had lifted a glass jar of sugar and couldn't work out how high the bench top was and smashed it as I rammed it accidentally into the side of the kitchen bench. It was a pretty dramatic incident as I sliced my hand and needed to go to the Emergency Department. We all put it down to me being clumsy, which was a reasonably common occurrence. Now, of course, I think that was when the demyelination started to grumble away.

Having been told I didn't have MS, the GP suggested my symptoms might be because of food allergies. She referred me to the Allergy Clinic at Royal Prince Alfred Hospital. Over the next few months, I underwent an 'Elimination Diet'; a truly unpleasant experience where you stop eating everything except boiled chicken, rice and parsley and then gradually introduce different potential allergens. I had a dramatic reaction to salicylates and later on to amines.

I found myself lying on the floor with the room spinning and the most atrocious headache I think I've ever experienced. Salicylates and amines are chemicals found basically in anything that tastes nice; most fruits; vegetables; flavourings; meat when it's browned; olives; the list is endless. This explained the daily headaches/migraines I had been experiencing and once I cut out salicylates, the headaches resolved. The dietician explained that because I had this underlying intolerance when I decided to become a vegetarian in my late teens, I had essentially poisoned myself. She further explained that a salicylate intolerance often presents with some neurological symptoms hence the GP's insightful hypothesis. I was a vomiting child when I was growing up; now I knew why.

Boyfriend Trouble

Managing a food intolerance is no easy feat; especially one that is as complex as mine. I can't eat most fruits and vegetables without having a reaction as varied as severe headaches that can't be eased by paracetamol; stomach upsets; swollen throat and swollen eyes. Anything containing aspirin is also on the banned list because aspirin is a salicylate.

Nevertheless, with the support of the allergy clinic, I just got on with it. I don't have anaphylaxis so I don't have to be quite as careful as others with true allergies but the risk is that my intolerance could predispose me to anaphylaxis. The way I manage my intolerances is to think about my environment and my schedule. I never eat things that cause headaches because I simply can't manage them, but with everything else, if I don't have anything planned I will be a little more relaxed.

When I have been at the Allergy clinic I am invariably asked by the dieticians to have a chat with parents whose children are newly diagnosed with intolerances and allergies. This is because I have been managing my food intolerances since 1991 and they tell me I have a positive attitude; essentially that I'm sensible and I don't let food rule my life. Sometimes it sucks that I can't eat a massive fruit salad and when I go to a restaurant I look at the menu for things that I can eat rather than the food I want to eat but basically it's just a way of life and I'm much less concerned about it than others are.

I ignored the multiple neuropathic symptoms I was experiencing because of the information that a salicylate allergy can cause neuropathic symptoms and of course, I had 'boyfriend trouble', not MS. I should state for the record that when I had the original MS episode I didn't even have a boyfriend. Had the neurologist been vaguely curious, he might have worked that out.

A year or so later, I went to a ball and early in the evening I went outside; there was a step which was deeper than I expected so I took a tumble. I swear I was not drunk! The friend I was with helped me hobble inside where

Bugger Bugger Shit!

I was tended to by a swathe of unexpectedly good-looking medical students who happened to be at the ball. I can't believe that with this cohort of educated, intelligent and good-looking young men I had to sit in the corner all night with my foot elevated on a chair.

I saw the doctor the next day who confirmed a sprained ankle so I implemented RICE and waited for it to heal. It recovered enough, but it was never quite right. About 10 years later, in 2002, my GP suggested I see an orthopaedic surgeon for his advice on the continuing swelling and pain. He opted to do an arthroscopy. At the follow-up appointment, he told me he wasn't happy with what he saw and referred me to a rheumatologist.

Between the ankle injury and this appointment, my younger sister had been diagnosed with inflammatory arthritis and a blood test revealed she was HLAB 27+. HLAB 27 is a genetic marker for inflammatory arthritis. This all added up with the damage to my ankle that the orthopod saw. My GP organised a blood test, and I too tested positive for HLAB 27. I had also very recently started to develop psoriasis on my head which my dermatologist had diagnosed at my annual skin check.

I had my first appointment with the rheumatologist who asked me endless questions about the pain that I had been experiencing for decades. When I thought about it, I realised my first symptom had been when I was about 16; the same time as the weird experience with the sugar jar. Finally, he asked me if I had psoriasis. "Yes," I said. He was suspicious and asked me how I knew it was psoriasis. I gave him a withering look, "Because my dermatologist told me". He had a look at my head and confirmed that yes indeed, I did have psoriasis.

He told me I had psoriatic arthritis. I was overjoyed to finally have a diagnosis, "You mean I'm not a hypochondriac, there really is something wrong?". His response was, "Well you might be a hypochondriac, I don't know, but you definitely have psoriatic arthritis".

I finally felt heard.

I saw this rheumatologist for years. I didn't particularly like him; he was somewhat dismissive of me, and when I complained in my appointments of chronic hip and lower back pain he showed limited interest and responded that I had psoriatic arthritis - so what did I expect? Unfortunately due to my allergies, there was no medication that would ease the symptoms.

In about 2006, I saw him and he had good news. There was a new medication he wanted me to try. When I asked him if I could take it with my salicylate allergy he checked. The drug company advised him that I couldn't. He was cross at this advice. The drug didn't contain any salicylates so he called them up and asked them why the drug was contra-indicated for people with salicylate allergies.

Their response was that it can cause stomach upsets and so can salicylates. He nearly hit the roof! He blasted them for being so cautious that they were denying a whole cohort of patients access to a drug that could relieve their symptoms due to the possibility that they might develop similar symptoms to a salicylate allergy.

He promptly prescribed me the medication. I started to take it and very rapidly my arthritis symptoms eased. I even ran up a flight of stairs at work which was a definite shock to the system; it's lucky I didn't have a stroke! It was short-lived, however. After about a month I got a call to say the drug company had recalled it because of the high incidence of heart attacks. I was back to square one.

I continued to complain about the chronic pain, I even suggested I have an X-ray or CT scan of my hip. He said there was no reason to because it was due to arthritis. Bear in mind, apart from the ankle arthroscopy and some x-rays years before, I hadn't had any imaging. It was about 2010 by now and at one appointment I complained again about the pain. When he replied that he wasn't really interested in my pain, just about how the joints were functioning, I knew it was time to find a new specialist.

Bugger Bugger Shit!

Coincidentally, the following Saturday morning I broke my ankle (the good ankle). I was living in a lovely villa with a laundry room downstairs in the garage. I was still in my pyjamas, and I decided to put a load of washing on. I popped it all into a laundry basket and walked down the outside stairs; except I didn't. I slipped. The washing basket levitated and all of the clothes flew out across the garden; I hurtled down the flight of stairs at a rate of knots, possibly even beating the land speed record, and came to a sudden and violent stop near the bottom. The world disappeared, and I came close to fainting. Bugger.

I sat there in so much pain I thought I was going to vomit. When the waves of nausea finally passed, I sat on the step taking in deep breaths and wondered what to do. I had left my mobile phone on the kitchen counter so I was stuck. I thought about calling out for help but given the neighbours I had at the time, I quickly discounted that as a possibility.

I decided there was nothing to do except try and make my way back up the steps. I stood up on one leg (the one with the already dodgy ankle); I surveyed the garden and saw all of the dirty washing strewn everywhere. I paused for a minute, and as any self-respecting woman in my position would have done, I thought, "Those clothes aren't going to wash themselves; now that I'm down here I might as well put them in the machine". I hopped around the garden, picked everything up, hopped to the washing machine, loaded it, switched it on and then tried to work out how to get back up the wooden stairs. I went down on my bum, I might as well go back up on it.

Whilst I may have broken the land speed record going down, getting up a flight of stairs with what turned out to be a broken ankle was a different matter entirely. Eventually, I got to the top, found my phone and rang a friend. When she answered the phone she assumed I was calling about the text conversation we had been having earlier and announced very firmly that she was not going to join a dating site! Instead in a fairly shaky voice I

Boyfriend Trouble

said, "No, I need you to take me to the ED." She came round immediately, helped me get dressed then took me off to the hospital.

I ended up in a boot, along with all the other would-be skiers who had come a cropper in the Snowy Mountains that winter. I was at the physio one day and in passing, told her that my hip didn't seem to be quite so painful now that I was wearing the boot. She immediately sent me for a leg-length CT scan. When the results came in, she put the images up on the light box and then called in one of her colleagues to have a look. They both looked at it and then, somewhat inappropriately, burst out laughing. Bugger Bugger Shit!

Her colleague asked me if I was standing on a slope when the scan was done. I thought this was a bizarre question and confirmed that I had in fact been lying down. My physio explained that my left leg was at least 3 or 4 cm shorter than my right leg, which totally explained my hip pain and why I was more comfortable in the boot. That was it; I needed no encouragement and asked my GP to refer me to a new rheumatologist.

I managed to get in to see Dr Lynda*, one of Sydney's leading Professors of Rheumatology. The first time I saw her, she spent two hours examining me. She confirmed the psoriatic arthritis but also said I had hypermobile joints, was a breach birth, had congenital left hip dysplasia, and as a result, my left leg was much shorter than my right. I was impressed. None of that had been in the referral, and she was correct on all counts. I thought this was the specialist for me, and I have been with her ever since.

When I told my mum I had congenital hip dysplasia she contradicted me; completely confident that when I was an infant her midwifery and obstetrician friends and colleagues had done the standard hip test for newborn babies. I must say, I took her protestations with a grain of salt. A few years earlier, in 2008, I had surprisingly caught whooping cough.

Whooping cough is known as the 100-day cough. They're right. I picked up mum and dad from the airport during this time and, as had

Bugger Bugger Shit!

become usual, was coughing like some sort of emphysemic seal. Dad expressed concern that I had a nasty cough. I rolled my eyes as I was driving, "Yes Dad, I've got whooping cough, I told you". As we were discussing the ins and outs of whooping cough, Mum seemed unnaturally quiet in the back of the car.

Dad, quite reasonably, was curious as to how I had contracted whooping cough after all, I had been vaccinated as a child. I said I wasn't sure, and then the quietness of Mum in the back of the car became deafening, "I was immunised wasn't I Mum?" (Knowing Dad would have had no clue, Mum was the holder of essential medical information). She paused; everything I needed to know was in the pause. "Well I thought you had but come to think of it, I remember that there was some issue with the vaccine, and so I couldn't get it done and then I think I forgot to follow up". My head exploded, as it so often does; and then Mum added, "But I didn't think it was with you, I thought it was one of the other kids".

As my sister and I were sorting out Mum and Dad's endless boxes of accumulated junk this summer, I found my vaccination information and sure enough, whooping cough/pertussis was not listed!

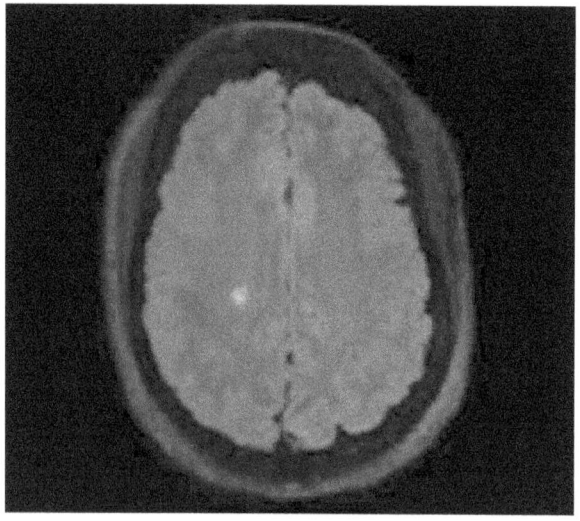

MS or Boyfriend Trouble

Chapter 13

You Have to Be Kidding Me!

We'll observe how the burdens braved by humankind
Are also the moments that make us humans kind;
Let every dawn find us courageous, brought closer;
Heeding the light before the fight is over.
When this ends, we'll smile sweetly, finally seeing
In testing times, we became the best of beings.

Amanda Gorman
The Miracle of Morning
Call Us What We Carry
2021
Random House

"You know I call you my famous patient". "No, I didn't know that", I replied to Dr Ervin*. Without looking at his notes, Ervin reeled off my complex medical history, including the ten years of chronic lower back and pelvic pain, which all other doctors had passed off as psoriatic arthritis or endometriosis. I'd only seen him in his rooms once before and

Bugger Bugger Shit!

then in theatre during a procedure. I was impressed. He told me he had presented me—anonymously—at Grand Rounds and a conference. He now tells me he uses my story as a teaching tool on how NOT to do medicine; about listening to and respecting your patients.

Having psoriatic arthritis is a pain, physically and metaphorically. It's a little understood disease. Most of the general population think of two things when the word arthritis is used; osteoarthritis and rheumatoid arthritis but this is a very simplistic view. There are hundreds of different types of arthritis. I like to describe psoriatic arthritis as a combination of osteoarthritis; rheumatoid arthritis; ankylosing spondylitis with a bit of psoriasis thrown in for good measure.

It isn't really any of these conditions but it is helpful in describing it. Psoriatic arthritis is known as seronegative arthritis. That means that the usual blood tests which show an elevated Rheumatoid Factor when there is rheumatoid arthritis, typically aren't abnormal or are very slightly elevated. It's also not symmetrical; as in if your left knee is impacted by rheumatoid arthritis, your right one will be as well. These two reasons are why a diagnosis of psoriatic arthritis is often missed; and certainly was in my case.

Psoriatic arthritis is a systemic disease so as well as the joints, it can affect the eyes, gastro-intestinal organs, the heart, the lungs, skin and blood vessels. Typically the Psoriasis comes first, but in a tiny percentage of cases the Psoriasis comes last; of course that had to be me didn't it.

My disease impacts my feet, hips, lumbar spine, cervical spine, wrists, elbows, shoulders, my hands and my fingers. I have never been able to find any pain medication which eases the symptoms. In terms of the fingers, it impacts the joints closest to the nails and the actual nails; whereas rheumatoid arthritis impacts the joints close to the knuckles. The top joints in most of my fingers have calcified. They are swollen, knobbly and painful; which makes day to day tasks pretty challenging.

The calcification looks on x-ray like osteoarthritis and is often described as such by Radiologists but as Dr Lynda told me; if a patient has psoriatic arthritis then what looks like osteoarthritis can be assumed to be psoriatic arthritis. The calcification doesn't just impact the fingers; it impacts the spine, hence the similarity to ankylosing spondylitis. Psoriatic arthritis specifically impacts the entheses which are the sites where tendons or ligaments attach to the bone. Enthesitis is the inflammation of the entheses; it is exceptionally painful and chronic and can impact any joint in the body.

It was psoriatic arthritis not carpal tunnel syndrome which impacted me when I was at University, but every doctor I saw in the 1980s missed it because they weren't looking for it. The erroneous assumption that there are only two types of arthritis; rheumatoid and osteo, means people who have other less common types are often disbelieved, misdiagnosed, misunderstood and unsupported.

Certainly with Australia's National Disability Insurance Scheme (NDIS) this is the case. Its current list of accepted diseases only lists rheumatoid arthritis which means that anyone with any other kind of arthritis has to fight really hard for it to be accepted. In my case, despite swathes of evidence, I have been accepted into the NDIS because of my MS diagnosis, not the psoriatic arthritis and there is definitely no understanding whatsoever about how the two diseases often co-occur and how hard it can be to manage the two of them together. Whilst my MS causes me many neuropathic and unusual symptoms, psoriatic arthritis is, by far, the most difficult disease to manage, simply because of the constant high level of pain it causes.

Dr Lynda, my rheumatologist has, along with Dr Jack*, my neurologist, been valiantly trying to find a drug that will help ease the severe symptoms

Bugger Bugger Shit!

I have been experiencing for the last few years. One of the problems is that a whole swathe of arthritis drugs are banned for patients who have co-occurring MS because they can cause brain lesions.

The only MS drug that is also effective for psoriatic arthritis has, very recently, been withdrawn for these patients because it has caused significant arthritis relapses. At a recent appointment with my neurologist, when it was apparent that, once again, the drug I was taking was not working, he told me I was at the end of the medication road and asked me what Dr Lynda was considering.

I was hopeful Lynda would perform some magic trick for me. Dr Jack decided CBD oil was called for and duly prescribed it. I started to take it as prescribed and found myself with a chronic headache for a week, which wouldn't respond to paracetamol. It dawned on me that the headache started when I commenced the CBD oil. I rang the drug company to ask what oil the CBD was suspended in. Coconut oil was the answer. Of course it was. Coconut is high in salicylates. The rep confirmed that all of the Australian companies manufacturing CBD oil use coconut oil. CBD oil was now also removed as an option for pain relief.

I had my follow-up appointment with Dr Lynda mid-last year, and sure enough, she had pulled a rabbit out of a hat. Tremfya had just been approved in Australia for use with psoriatic arthritis patients. Tremfya is an injection administered every eight weeks. I started it in July 2023 and its effects are being closely monitored by the drug company, which means I have to complete a very long and detailed form every time I see Lynda. At my visit in December 2023, she said she thought my disease activity had fallen from 80% to about 50%. I'm not quite that optimistic but we're both hopeful that Tremfya will finally halt its progress.

As this book was getting ready for publication I had check-ups with all of my specialists. When I saw Lynda, she confirmed that my recent blood tests were all normal so everything is finally heading in the right direction.

Along the way, the pain from endometriosis ebbed and flowed. I had seen my current gynaecologist, Dr Bill, for the first time when I was about 40. In that appointment, through tears, I said I couldn't go through yet another Laparoscopy. He ever so kindly said he wasn't going to do one and simply amended my hormone therapy and referred me for a pelvic ultrasound.

A few years later I went back to see him and this time, through tears, told him I needed to have a Laparoscopy because I couldn't handle the pain anymore. He agreed and scheduled me for the operation. As I was coming round in the recovery ward, I heard Bill speaking to the woman in the next bed to me, telling her it was good news. He then came to me, opened the curtains a crack and popped his head through, holding it together just under his chin, "And it's good news for you too" he announced, as I laughed at this unexpected and comical site from my surgeon. "No way!" I exclaimed, "Yes way," he replied, "there's no sign of endometriosis" he said as his body followed his head into my cubicle.

"What we did find though," he stated in a very conspiratorial way, "was a fucking massive varicose vein wrapped around your left ovary". I looked at him in total shock, not least because of his unexpected expletive and promptly asked, "Did you get a photo of it?". "Absolutely!" he replied. "When the camera picked it up, everyone stopped what they were doing, came and crowded around and said, what the hell is that?"

Talk about feeling like an alien being. I asked him if he'd fixed it but he told me he couldn't but not to worry, he had a mate that could. When I saw him for my follow-up appointment he showed me the photos; one ovary looked like a very smooth hard-boiled egg; the other looked like a

Bugger Bugger Shit!

plate of sausages. It's known as Pelvic Congestion Syndrome (PCS) and is one of the least-diagnosed causes of chronic pain in women.

Bill referred me to Dr Ervin, an interventional radiologist who embolised my dodgy vein a couple of months later. I was awake for the procedure, which was fascinating. These two doctors have been incredible and I cannot express how thankful I am to have them in my camp. They are the very embodiment of what a doctor should be. They are kind, considerate, curious and respectful.

Having experienced these two doctors, I realised quite how bad some of the doctors I had previously seen actually were. Now, I will not tolerate doctors who do not see me as a whole human; who do not discuss my treatment with me; who do not listen to me. If a doctor is writing a referral about me, then I want to read it first and likewise, if one of my specialists writes back to my GP I want to know what has been written.

Women who complain of chronic pelvic pain are routinely told it's just period pain and to take an analgesic. What was really good about my diagnosis was that two of my friends had also been experiencing considerable pain that had been dismissed by their doctors; after follow-up, they were both diagnosed with pelvic congestion syndrome (PSC) which meant that their chronic pain could be fixed with a simple day stay procedure.

I had experienced 10 years of chronic pain which was fixed in about half an hour during a procedure I was awake for. What a waste of time, money and my quality of life. For anyone who, having read this account, might think they have PCS, the key is to have a pelvic ultrasound, with a vascular sonographer, on a table that tilts so that your feet are towards the floor; otherwise, they can't see the blood flow as it actually is when standing.

Just to help make me feel even more like an alien being, about five years later I had gone in for a routine colonoscopy. Well I say routine; in an effort to manage my psoriatic arthritis pain, I had been taking a particular medication which caused me to develop an ulcer so was having a follow up procedure to check everything was ok. As the anaesthetist came around to see me, prior to the procedure, he looked at me, back at my name on the notes then back at me. "I know you," he said, "I was the anaesthetist for your laparoscopy when they found the ovarian vein." Yes he was, I had recognised him straight away!

A few months later, in mid 2007, I was still experiencing some lower back pain, so I went back to see Ervin, who organised for an MRI. He found lower back disc issues, typical of psoriatic arthritis, so he arranged for me to have a guided cortisone injection into the L5/S1 joint. I duly arrived for my appointment. I changed into the hospital gown and lay face down on the patient table that moves in and out of the machine. I trusted Ervin implicitly so I wasn't at all nervous.

I was moved back into the scanner so that Ervin could line up the injection, he brought me back out, and gave me a local anaesthetic which took a few minutes to take effect. Ervin then slid me back in to check the exact placement, slid me out and marked it with a texter then slid me back in to double check. He slid me out then put the needle into my spine and slid me back in so that he could triple-check it was in the right spot before injecting me with the cortisone; I was starting to feel like a yoyo with all this in and out of the scanner.

He checked the needle placement and pressed the button to slide me out. Nothing. He pressed again. Nothing. I was stuck in a CT machine with a great big needle sticking into my spine. I really don't go looking for medical disasters, I promise. Bugger Bugger Shit!

The lovely nurse whom I had met when I had the procedure on my vein leaned right into my face and said, "Don't move". I wasn't going to. He disappeared out of my line of sight. I could hear lots of increasingly

Bugger Bugger Shit!

panicked voices. He leaned back in again, "Don't move. You've got a needle stuck in your spine, and the bed won't move". I'd worked that one out. He went away again and then came back a minute or so later, "Don't move". "Not going to", I reassured him. He went away and came back; yes you guessed it, "Don't move", "Not going to" I replied, my voice slightly wavering with the length of time this was starting to take. "Are you ok?" He asked me. I wasn't entirely sure how to answer that one; I hadn't actually planned to get stuck in a CT machine with a gigantic needle stuck in my spine but I suppose there are worse places you could be; like with my head stuck in the mouth of a lion, or I don't know, maybe swimming naked in a river full of piranhas.

It took about 20 minutes - no I'm not exaggerating. Twenty minutes, lying face down stuck in a CT machine with a massive needle in one's spine is not something you usually forget! Every two minutes the lovely nurse came and checked on me; every time I reassured him, through gritted teeth and a withering smile that I was ok under the circumstances. I wondered if I should take the opportunity to have a nap but the table was a bit uncomfortable so I gave up on that idea.

Thank God I went to the loo before getting into this position. I should have asked for a gin and tonic with a straw and one of those little cocktail umbrellas in retrospect. Finally, they somehow managed to do a factory reset on the machine; either that or they just switched it off and on again. Maybe that was actually it? Maybe someone had pulled out the cord to plug in the coffee machine! Ervin eventually completed the procedure and they pulled me out. I have never seen so many green and terrified faces in a hospital; well not on the medical staff at least.

About a year later, I needed another injection so, not to be phased; after all the worst had happened hadn't it? I went back to see Ervin. I got changed and discovered the same nurse waiting for me. He looked at me; all the

You Have to Be Kidding Me!

blood drained from his face, clearly he had been scarred for life by that previous experience. "I'm so sorry," he said earnestly, "it won't happen today. I promise you". I laughed, confident with him that it couldn't happen twice. We were both right; it didn't.

What did happen however, was that once I had slid into the machine for the first check, prior to the gigantic needle being inserted I hasten to add, there was an almighty ringing of sirens, and everyone disappeared from the room I was in. I was stuck in the CT machine AGAIN! Bugger Bugger Shit! I could get a complex if I wasn't so resilient. After about 10 minutes, "Hello," I called out pathetically, "is anyone there?". Silence. YOU HAVE TO BE KIDDING ME!!!!!!!!

A further 10 minutes later everyone came back in, chattering animatedly. The lovely nurse, who probably went home and curled up into the foetal position at the end of his shift, came up to me as I was pulled out of the machine. "I am so sorry. I can't believe that happened to you", he said in a completely shocked and apologetic tone. He explained that someone had 'coded' whilst having a scan hence the alarms and the hospital policy dictates that everyone drops what they're doing and attends.

I do wonder though whether it was just some sort of ruse and it was actually someone's birthday so they were in the tea room with birthday cake, hats and party blowers having a lovely time. I have been back to the same hospital for a cortisone injection into my cervical spine but it was in a completely different part of the hospital with a different team and a different machine. I'm delighted to report that it went smoothly.

In 2016, I was back in Ervin's office to see my gynaecologist, Bill, with whom he now shared rooms. As I came out of Bill's office into the waiting room, Ervin bumped into me. He looked worried and delighted at the same time. He was deeply concerned there was something wrong. I reassured him I was fine and just needed Bill's medical opinion. He looked at me suspiciously until his colleague reassured him I had just come in for a chat and a catch-up. Satisfied, he gave me a big hug and asked me to come into his room because he wanted to show me something. Curiously, I followed him in.

He showed me multiple posters and hundreds of brochures about pelvic congestion syndrome. He pointed to everything and said, "This is because of you". I looked a bit taken aback as he went on, "I decided after treating you and using you as a case study to train other doctors, I was not going to allow another woman to be treated like you were. So, we created all of this information; for patients, for surgery waiting rooms, for doctors, nurses, clinics, to be distributed everywhere". Ervin and Bill are two of my amazing doctors. I have referred countless friends and other women to them. I am 1000% confident that patients will be listened to and respected by these doctors.

Chapter 14

Would You Like Fries With That

> *"I live my life at full capacity, because that's the way I've always lived. I walk slowly, sure, but I carry a big stick. I travel the globe teaching the craft of writing comedy... I'm making TV, books, live shows, a movie, and sweet love to a woman whose beauty and brains are way outta my league. I just do it at my own quirky pace.*
>
> *People with any disability know they have 2 choices: laugh or cry. The wise ones feel free to do both, with as much optimism and tenacity as possible.*
>
> *If anyone wants to see the way I live as an example for their own life, I can't stop them. But I'm sure they've learnt to rely on their own inner-strength. That's the gift of a disability – it's a good teacher."*
>
> Tim Ferguson
> *https://carlyfindlay.com.au/2012/05/31/tim-ferguson-interview/*

In 2016, I complained to my rheumatologist, Lynda, of consistent numb toes over a period of months. She sent me for an MRI on a much-

Bugger Bugger Shit!

improved machine than the 1991 debacle. The results indicated a hot spot in my cervical spine at C2/3. She wasn't worried, my GP wasn't worried, and neither was my physio, so I wasn't worried either. She just said we should repeat the MRI in 12 months. The numb toes continued into 2017, and true to her word, she organised a referral for a follow-up MRI. As I was walking out of her room, she called me back and amended the referral from a cervical spine to a full spine and full brain MRI.

I duly got into the noisy coffin again for nearly an hour and went off to see Lynda with the results a week later. There it was in black and white. Probable MS lesion at C2/3 and multiple lesions in my brain. As a bonus, they also found a meningioma, a type of benign tumour of the meninges, the gloopy cling-wrap-like covering of the brain. I wasn't thrown by the MS diagnosis, but I was a bit surprised by the meningioma.

With hindsight, if ever there was a way to downplay an MS diagnosis, simultaneously having a brain tumour diagnosis, is it. I felt like those offers on tv where you get a free set of steak knives or at the McDonald's drive through when they ask if you want fries with that.

Fortunately, I'm a psychologist, so I understand the brain and knew cognitively that if you are going to have a brain tumour, a meningioma is the one to have. As if by magic, or at the very least, some sort of weird conspiracy theory, meningiomas were everywhere—on *24 Hours in Emergency* that night on television, on that week's episode of *Grey's Anatomy* and on some other random television shows. Bugger bugger shit, indeed.

Multiple sclerosis (MS) is a disease of the central nervous system. It can impact both the brain and the spinal cord. If you imagine electrical wires within the tube of insulation it's a pretty good metaphor for what happens within the brain with our neural pathways. With MS, the tube of insulation gets damaged and forms scars or lesions. This means that the messaging from the brain to the body is disrupted.

Every single person who has MS has a different experience of it because no two people have scars in exactly the same place. I have a large MS lesion at C2/3 which means it impacts all of the nerves below it - so my hands/arms/spine/legs as well as some aspects of my general functioning that is controlled by the part of the brain just above it. I also have a couple of lesions in my right parietal lobe which is the part of the brain which, amongst other things impacts what is called proprioception.

Proprioception is the process that helps the brain understand where the body is in space. It's also why I fall over so much. I have discovered, whilst doing Pilates, that my left leg is a bit of a rebel. If you ask it to do anything without its matching right leg, it will choose its own adventure or just stubbornly refuse to play the game. Likewise if I am particularly hot or fatigued it goes on strike and won't move.

Lynda referred me to Dr Jack, yet another brilliant doctor I have in my camp. At my first appointment, he asked me to give him my history of symptoms. I said it spans a really long time, and I have no idea what are just normal things and what are abnormal things. He said give me everything, and I'll work it out.

It took a long time. It turns out they were all MS symptoms. A quietly spoken man, he was horrified when I told him about my 1991 appointment, and I could tell he was outraged. He told me that my 1987 symptoms correspond exactly with quite a large area of old demyelination in my brain. He organised for me to have several other tests, including a lumbar puncture to test my cerebro-spinal fluid (CSF).

The MS lesion had always been there. The 1991 MRI apparently wasn't developed enough to pick it up; although having read the letter from the

Bugger Bugger Shit!

original Neurological Registrar, I'm wondering whether he even read the MRI report.

Before I go on, for anyone who is wondering what on earth happened about the meningioma, the short answer is nothing. Upon seeing the scans, my neurologist presented my case at the weekly Local Area Health District Neurology meeting. The group of neurologists and neurosurgeons decided that because of the awkward location of it; right underneath my brain, it would be very difficult to remove. Their advice was to watch and wait.

Meningiomas are typically quite slow growing but because we didn't know when it had developed we had no way of knowing how fast it was growing. If it was rapidly developing then that would be a different matter and it would need to be removed. My neurologist organised bi-monthly MRI scans, then quarterly and in the last 12 months they have dropped to twice a year, thank goodness! The meningioma has never grown so it's still there.

Since the early 1990s, there has been an amendment to the way neurologists classify neuropathic events. Now, if someone had an experience similar to mine, they would no doubt be diagnosed with clinically isolated syndrome (CIS). CIS essentially means that a person has experienced something weird, neurologically speaking, and should be followed up to see if it happens again.

MS is diagnosed using the now updated McDonald Criteria where two of the following conditions need to be met. At least one year of disease progression; a positive brain or spinal cord MRI for lesions; a positive lumbar puncture showing 2 or more oligoclonal bands in the CSF. In brief, this is described as Space and Time. My results came in; confirmed lesions in my brain and spine over multiple periods of time and in different spaces and two oligoclonal bands in my CSF. I met all of the McDonald Criteria and was finally formally diagnosed with MS.

I had actually been experiencing MS symptoms since my bout of whooping cough towards the end of 2008 but since I had 'boyfriend trouble' and not MS and food allergies that give you neurological symptoms, I had actually been ignoring them. In fact my dear friend Cath and I had a conversation one day where she told me she was concerned she had MS but had been told that it was stress, and proceeded to rattle off the neurological symptoms she had. My response was to tell her I was sure it wasn't MS because I have the same symptoms and I didn't have MS. She was diagnosed a few months later but I still didn't twig.

I know I'm a psychologist, I understand the brain. Apparently I'm also intelligent - clearly not. I'm also not one of those people who go to Dr Google for its diagnostic capabilities. I tend to wait until an actual qualified person has given me a diagnosis and then I go and scour the pages of Dr Google; I only used trusted medical sites and proper peer reviewed evidence based research papers.

I had been at a Christmas Party in 2008; I hadn't drunk any alcohol; not because I'm opposed to it, but because I'm allergic to grapes and therefore wine. My preferred alternative is a gin and tonic but they don't tend to be served at your average party. Anyway, getting back to where I was, I came home and was suddenly, and out of the blue, hit by the worst vertigo I've ever experienced in my life.

I went to see my GP a few days later, when it didn't resolve. Unfortunately, she wasn't available so I saw a very young and inexperienced doctor. She said she thought I had benign positional vertigo and showed me how to move my head to flick the crystals back into my ear. It sounded very 'new age' but I'm told by others that yes, lying on your bed, hanging your head over the side and moving your head does in fact do what it's supposed to do. I came home and tried to stop the world spinning. I failed. The GP rang me up later that evening and said she wanted me to get a brain

Bugger Bugger Shit!

CT. Talk about anxiety - my panic went through the roof. Note to any doctors out there - don't do that, it freaks non-medically trained people out; wait until the next day when they can actually do something about it.

The CT didn't show anything, so she felt that confirmed the simple vertigo diagnosis. Had she done an MRI though, she would have seen the new MS lesions that had formed. The vertigo was the start of a relapse. I started to get lots of weird neuropathies; fizzy legs, my thumb was permanently numb, burning sensations in my feet and a sensation I couldn't find the words to describe until I told my neurologist. At various points I actually thought that it was the ground shaking whilst they were boring for the new train line that was going underneath my house; until I stayed at a friend's house and experienced it there as well.

Again, apparently I'm an intelligent human being. When I gave my neurologist this whole garbled explanation of symptoms he looked at me with a curious expression and said, "A tremor?". "Yes!" I exclaimed. Seriously, I couldn't come up with that word myself? It's an internal tremor. A lot of neuropathic symptoms are really weird and very difficult to describe because they're not everyday sensations that you learn labels for as a child.

Two years after the Christmas Party and the episode of vertigo, I experienced the "MS Hug". Nothing could prepare me for that. It sounds lovely, doesn't it? A hug gives you an impression of warmth and comfort. Yeah. No. I woke up one Saturday morning in the Spring of 2010 and was smacked with the worst pain of my entire life. It started in my back and radiated around to the front. It was so extreme it took my breath away and made me nauseous. It went away after about half an hour as suddenly as it came.

I woke up the next day and it happened again; what the actual heck? Then the next day, except on that day - the Monday - it happened a few times throughout the day. I rang to make an appointment with my GP. I saw her on Tuesday and she told me to take myself immediately to the Emergency Department right then and there and definitely no passing go and stopping to collect $200.

I was seen by the RAT (Rapid Assessment Team - seriously, who thinks of these acronyms?). Whilst I was there, another wave of pain hit me. This was the time I discovered that Endone is a completely useless drug for me. It didn't even touch the sides. I told the consultant that I had endometriosis and psoriatic arthritis and thought I knew what 10/10 pain was but I was kidding myself. This was a thousand times worse. Their hunch was a twisted ovary "What is it with my ovaries?" I thought.

The ultrasound was clear. They told me that if it happened again to call an ambulance. I woke up on Wednesday morning and it happened again. I called an ambulance. The paramedics arrived and said they would take me to my local hospital emergency rather than the main trauma centre. I protested. There was no way I was going to my small local hospital and besides which the larger hospital was where I'd been the day before.

They explained that they would need to take a bit of a circuitous route to get there and I would likely be waiting all day because North Shore's ED was really busy. I asked why, "Because a meth lab blew up at the other end of your road in the early hours of the morning". A meth lab? On my suburban street? They had to be kidding! They weren't. Bugger Bugger Shit!! I saw the house later that day - it looked like a bomb had exploded and the place was flattened. Both drug chemists died; allegedly the second one died running back into the house to grab the stashes of cash but I admit, I have no actual evidence of that and it might just be an urban myth.

This time at the hospital they sent me for a CT scan. It showed a small kidney stone but it was high up in my kidney where it was minding its own business. So they sent me home. The pain happened every day for a week and then stopped as unexpectedly as it started. Until a few weeks later when it happened again; for exactly a week; but the 30 minute spasms were becoming more frequent and when it happened again a few weeks later I knew I was in trouble and there was something going on. I had an attack of this pain one day whilst I was at the chemist. She got me to describe it as it was hitting me. My description went something like this, "Imagine you've got a vice tightening around your torso and twisting at the same time and then just for fun, someone is stabbing you in the back with a kitchen knife". My pharmacist said that sounded like nerve pain to her.

Off I went back to the doctor, who referred me to a neurologist. She's quite a well-known and respected local neurologist; after examining me, she told me she didn't know what it was but it wasn't neurological and sent me on my way. I'm not sure where she got her qualifications from but it certainly wasn't the University of the Bleeding Obvious given she was a neurologist and later I discovered this phenomena is a very common MS symptom.

This excruciating pain came and went for years; sometimes at the most inopportune moments - for example when driving over the Harbour Bridge in peak hour traffic! Fortunately after a few years, the episodes started to come less frequently and, touch wood, I haven't had one for about 6 years. I asked Jack, my brilliant neurologist at my second or third appointment about this pain; quick as a flash he told me it was the MS hug. That was when it was confirmed to me, once again, that not all neurologists, or doctors generally, are created equal.

There are a couple of other common MS symptoms that I experience; the first is heat intolerance. Not great when you live in Australia. My OT told me that apparently 27 degrees is the cut off point for people with MS to be able to regulate their temperature. When we built our house, our architect assured us that we wouldn't need air conditioning because it's an eco-designed house. That's probably true if you don't have MS.

Fortunately the NDIS funded me for an air conditioning unit in my first plan so we at least have one room in the house where I can cool down. They also funded an Ooler - which is like an electric blanket except, like underfloor heating, it has water that flows through the pipes. This water can be heated or cooled. In summer I have it on its lowest setting every night to stop me overheating. It's very effective. Other people with MS also purchase cooling vests which is something I'm seriously considering given how hot Australia is becoming.

When you're heat intolerant, all of your MS symptoms temporarily exacerbate which can be hugely worrying for people who are newly diagnosed because it seems like you're having a relapse. There are other people with MS who are cold intolerant and are impacted in the same way as I am by the heat. It basically boils down to your body not being able to thermoregulate whichever direction that is.

The second major symptom is fatigue. Fatigue is a major issue with all auto-immune diseases and unless you've experienced it, it's very difficult to comprehend. I think people generally think about fatigue as just being extra tired. It isn't. It's like your whole body is encased in a cement block; even your face is exhausted. Some people are able to sleep but it does nothing to alleviate the symptoms; other people, like me, aren't able to sleep. I don't really think it makes much difference which camp you fall into, the exhaustion just follows you. My neurologist has seen me fatigued first hand. He has seen me so utterly exhausted that I can't string two words together.

Fatigue really is the thing that has done me in and changed my life. I used to be like the Energiser Bunny; not any more. This is hugely frustrating, there is so much I want to be able to do with my life, but the reality is, I just can't anymore. It is the single biggest contributor to me deciding to take medical retirement.

Bugger Bugger Shit!

I also experience word finding difficulties. This is not like the 'tip of the tongue' situation that everyone experiences. I described it to my speech therapist as me hurtling along and then suddenly my speech hits a brick wall. I have absolutely no warning that it's going to happen and because I speak publicly for a living, it was causing me some consternation.

I was prompted to do something about it when I was facilitating a very easy two hour seminar about neuroscience and child development - something I could do whilst standing on my head and counting backwards from 50. I was explaining that the brain develops from the bottom up so I started by explaining the function of the brainstem. In neuroscience there are no alternate words for parts of the brain, so when I lost the term brainstem I was stuck. I'm not entirely sure how I got around it but it was so disconcerting that I spoke to Jack about it and made an appointment with the Speech and Language Clinic at Macquarie University.

One of the other things that happens is that I have a tendency to choke on water or my own saliva. It's not attractive and tends to worry the people around me - except of course my family; they're so used to it that they just carry on as if nothing happens when I'm stuck in a paroxysm of coughing. The management of it is complex and difficult; I have to use a straw. Seriously that's it; no Physio, no speech therapy, just a straw. The speech issue though saw me spend 18 months with fortnightly speech therapy appointments (via zoom thank goodness).

The speech therapists were fantastic. When I started, I spent most of the 30 minute sessions trying to think of half a dozen objects starting with a particular letter. By the time I was discharged I was finding words that the speech therapists didn't even know the meaning of. They taught me techniques to find words and gave me ways to feel less conspicuous when it happens.

Would You Like Fries With That

I remember the first time I was out and about after I had been taught Semantic Feature Analysis. We had just been released from Covid-19 lockdown and I had met with two friends and our kids in a park that overlapped each of the 5km we were allowed to move within. I went to the local bakery to get some sausage rolls for the children. It was my turn to order and I lost the words "sausage rolls". I panicked initially about how I was going to explain what I needed without appearing like some kind of weirdo. Then I remembered one of the tricks; where can you find the word? I realised the word would be on the chalkboard with the prices. I looked up and there it was, "Six sausage rolls", I said confidently.

Now when it happens I just buy some time by making a joke about having MS and by now I'm so practised at Semantic Feature Analysis I can find the word and carry on. If I don't, who cares? It happened yesterday in the Apple Store. Do you think I could find the words for Magic Keyboard or Apple Pencil? Of course I couldn't, so I said iPad and mimed the actions whilst nodding my head towards where they were. The sales assistant wasn't phased and just went with me and knew exactly what I was talking about.

I now do Wordle everyday and other language exercises to keep that part of my brain from deteriorating again. And yes, writing a book has definitely helped. There have been times when I have lost words whilst I am writing, and so I just pause, take a moment and know that the word will come if I give it time. One of the most infuriating and unhelpful things though is when people try to helpfully provide me with the word. What that does is interrupt my process of finding the word for myself and stresses me out so it takes longer. I just need people to wait patiently; it won't take long.

I also experience a set of irritating neurological symptoms that involve sensations within my head and brain - things that feel like flashes of electricity across my brain; very, very quiet sounds sometimes feel like

Bugger Bugger Shit!

explosions in my ears; it feels like there are tiny little pixies inside my ear canals tickling them. I find it very difficult to process accents (please accept my apologies if you ever experience me saying I'm sorry I didn't understand) - this has been one of my most upsetting symptoms having grown up in a family of linguists and interacted with people from all over the globe since being a very young child.

The neurologists and pain specialists are very committed to trying to find ways to alleviate these invisible symptoms. One of my friends described the Pulsed Radio Frequency that I had last year as "intense acupuncture" because essentially, the pain specialist sticks a very long needle into your brain and then heats it up to damage the nerve fibres causing the symptoms.

There are so many things to understand with MS. One of them is to understand that there are various types. Traditionally they have been categorised as; Relapsing Remitting; Primary Progressive and Secondary Progressive but there is more and more evidence coming to light that this is too simplistic. I have relapsing remitting but this doesn't accurately explain the disease. There is an assumption that when you are in the remitting phase you return to baseline. This is not the case; the disease has already caused damage and that damage continues to cause symptoms even when the disease isn't active.

I was probably in remission for about 15 years, with very few symptoms for which I'm very grateful. I then relapsed after the whooping cough and am technically in remission again but now I have constant symptoms. My neurologist describes my MS as grumbling. He explained it to me by saying with any auto-immune disease there is inflammation which causes symptoms but there is also a type of inflammation that causes damage. I've got the first; it just hasn't grumbled away badly enough to cause damage - yet. Research is continually being done around MS and one of the studies I am involved in involves providing blood samples so that the researchers can test Neurofilament light chain to see if it is a biomarker for what is being described as grumbling MS.

You may be thinking, this woman has had really bad luck with her health. Can one person really have so many things go wrong? The answer is actually yes, very easily in fact. What I have learnt is that when you have one auto-immune disease you have a significantly increased risk of developing others. I also learnt that MS and psoriatic arthritis are frequent bedfellows. I have also learnt that whilst endometriosis isn't officially an auto-immune disease it is certainly a disease of inflammation and is often a precursor to developing an auto-immune disease.

It is also no coincidence that the psoriatic arthritis and MS started to eat away at my body at about the same time and the endometriosis shortly after, if not at the same time; we'll never know on that one. We also know that asthma and allergies often go hand in hand with endometriosis and psoriasis. It's also no surprise when you take into account the fact that I have red hair, blue eyes and very fair skin which are all recessive genes.

The real clincher though is the research published by Harvard University in January 2022. This was a total breakthrough in understanding what was necessary for MS to flourish. The Harvard research was groundbreaking. The team retrospectively examined the medical records of 10,000 US service men and women. They chose the Armed Services because, unlike any other cohort, personnel are required to have annual physicals, including blood tests. They wanted to see if there was a common denominator; and they found one.

The Epstein Barr Virus (EBV) is a common virus and about 90% of the world's population have been infected with it at some point or another. It is the same virus that causes glandular fever, but it also causes a number of other respiratory infections. When I was in high school I developed chronic pharyngitis. I lost my voice a lot and when I coughed, I once again sounded like a seal. Pharyngitis is caused by EBV.

The Harvard University research clearly demonstrated that despite 90% of the general population having the Epstein Barr virus in their systems, 100% of people with MS had been infected with EBV. There has been a long standing theory that MS is linked with EBV and now they have the evidence. Of course there is more to it than that; there has to be something else that triggers MS to develop and scientists haven't quite nailed that down.

What we do know though, is if scientists can come up with a vaccination for EBV; MS will be prevented. There will become a time when MS is relegated to the history books and I don't think it's that far away. I have my own theory related to EBV; I have a hunch that at some point in the future, further research will be completed which will demonstrate that all auto-immune diseases will somehow be linked to EBV infections.

I've had frequent MRIs since 2018 to monitor the development of the MS and the meningioma. In my December 2019 appointment, my neurologist was pleased to report that my MS and meningioma continued to be stable. But I had developed a significant disc rupture at C5/6, which had forced all the spinal fluid out of that disc space, explaining the increase in neurological symptoms I had been getting. Dr Jack was clearly worried so he called his *neurosurgeon mate*, Peter*, and chatted with him over the phone while I was with him.

I saw Dr Peter four days later. He looked at my scans again, examined me, and told me I needed to have surgery. I suggested January; given it was two weeks before Christmas and January's much quieter at work. Peter looked at me as if I was slightly bonkers. He said, "Let me put it this way, I am booking into April, but you can't wait that long. We're doing it on Monday." As I left his room, reeling, he called out down the corridor after me, "Don't let anyone touch your neck". I didn't need that reminder, quite frankly. Bugger Bugger Shit!

The following week, I underwent an anterior cervical discectomy and fusion (ACDF). This procedure basically involves horizontally slicing your throat open at the front, removing the disc, inserting a cage where the disc was and fusing the whole thing together. Whilst completing the procedure, Peter discovered I had, as he put it, "A big chunk of bone" where it shouldn't be. He said I had Ossification of the Posterior Longitudinal Ligament (OPLL), which he had removed. When the anaesthetist came into the ICU to check on me he told me exactly the same thing. Both of them seemed quite excited by the discovery. There's nothing like an additional piece of drama to add spice to your life and having a massive great big scar across the front of my neck made me want to add bolts on either side so that I looked like Frankenstein and could have made some money on the side. My x-ray is amazing!

Apparently it's not everyday that a neurosurgeon is surprised by a chunk of bone that isn't supposed to be there and has to be removed. He told me he was quite surprised by the finding because usually "old Japanese men" are the ones who experience an OPLL. I asked my rheumatologist, Lynda later on about the OPLL and she confirmed that it was actually linked with my psoriatic arthritis. The psoriatic arthritis is now causing issues at C4/5 and C6/7 so along with the original problem at C5/6 and the MS lesion at C2/3 my cervical spine is not happy.

At my post-op check, I asked Peter how long it would take for the bruising on my spinal cord to heal. He looked at me and simply said, "It doesn't." "Bugger bugger shit, AGAIN", I thought. On the bright side though, the scar across my throat has healed nicely and Peter did such a good job you would never know it was there. If you're ever in the same

Bugger Bugger Shit!

position, I can thoroughly recommend silicone strips which aid healing brilliantly.

If anyone reading this is facing a similar procedure, all I can say is in my experience it was a really easy recovery. I spent a planned 24 hours in the ICU and then went to a ward. I was on some reasonably heavy duty pain relief for a couple of days but then just had regular paracetamol for a few more days. I spent less than a week in the hospital.

Of course it was the week before Christmas so we needed to finish the Christmas shopping and besides I'd seen a pair of shoes online that I wanted. I went with my sister and borrowed one of the mobility scooters at the shopping centre. Come to think of it, I did scare a few children who saw the big dressing across my throat, apologies to any parents in North West Sydney whose children went on to have nightmares. I wasn't allowed to drive for a few weeks and was quite tired from the anaesthetic but I was back at work a couple of weeks after the Christmas break - just in time for Covid-19 to hit.

Despite all of these medical dramas, I still look at the world optimistically. My body is a bit broken but with the right aids and supports in place I am still just as effective and connected as I ever was. I'm certainly no Pollyanna and I will rage at anyone who tries to tell me not to do something or that I can't do something or I shouldn't do something.

There are genuinely a whole host of other diseases which are way worse than the conditions I have been diagnosed with. After all, if it isn't me, it's going to be someone else so why not me? I mean that. Really, why not me? I am not special; I don't have some sort of entitlement to be healthier than anyone else. It happens to thousands of people around the world everyday. What keeps me resilient and bouncing back is the possibility that my experience might help someone else.

Would You Like Fries With That

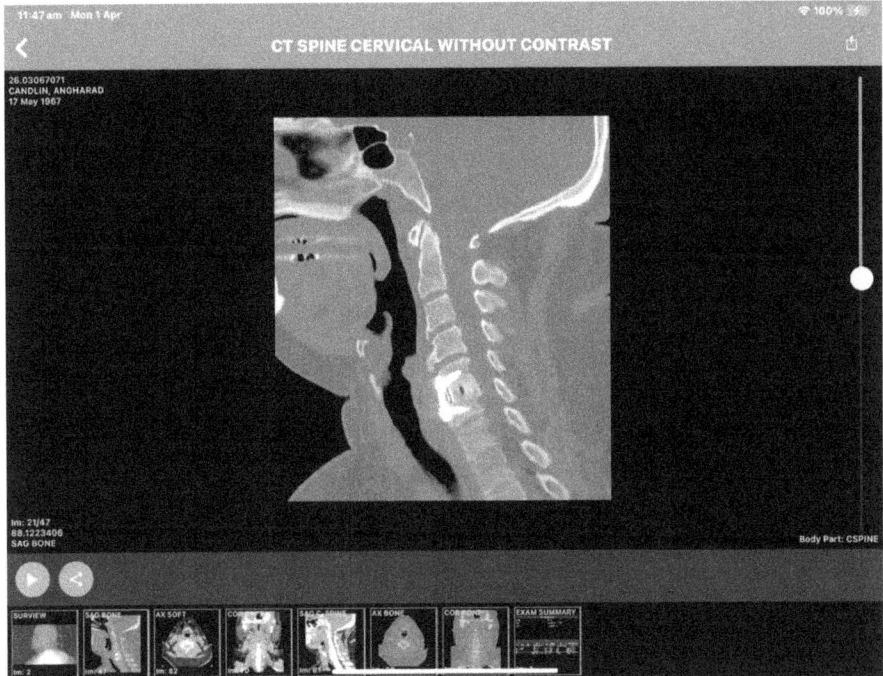

Bugger Bugger Shit!

Chapter 15

WTF!!!!

I am a feminist because to be one seems perfectly obvious and reasonable to me. I am a feminist because it bothers me that women are more than 50 per cent of the population and more than 60 per cent of university graduates but somehow only 3 per cent of chief executives. I am a feminist because it bothers me that a woman gets killed by her male partner every single week, and somehow that doesn't qualify as a tools-down national crisis even though if a man got killed by a shark every week we'd probably arrange to have the ocean drained. I am a feminist because it bugs me that "working Mum" is a phrase I hear every day but I never hear "working Dad".

Annabel Crabb
6th March 2015
Sydney Morning Herald

It was 1987; Mum, Dad and my younger siblings had just migrated to Australia and my older sister and I had joined them for the Northern Hemisphere summer holidays. Dad was employed at Macquarie University and Mum had been employed by Western Sydney University in a

WTF!!!!

permanent position as a lecturer in the Department of Nursing. She needed to buy a car and I went with her.

She chose a second hand Ford Laser but needed to apply for a small loan with the car dealership. The salesman explained that she needed her husband to guarantee the loan. Mum and I looked at each other and our heads exploded simultaneously! It was 1987 not 1937; a woman in her forties with a permanent academic job had to ask her husband to guarantee the loan?

In fact it was only a few years previously that women hadn't required their husbands to approve a credit card application. Australia had a long way to come. I wondered if I had unknowingly got into the TARDIS with Dr Who; rather than a Singapore Airlines jumbo jet, and accidentally arrived in a parallel universe.

When I eventually migrated to Australia it was a new decade; the 1990s. Nothing had changed. I remember going for a job interview in a marketing role. I arrived and was welcomed by the receptionist and then walked through a huge open plan room to the office at the back. The receptionist was the only female; I would have been the second. I don't think so.

I had come from the UK where even though I'd grown up in the North of England in the 1980s women were treated equally. I had been raised in a family where my father was a feminist and my grandfathers championed their granddaughters. I had gone to a university where there were more women than men and if the men even thought of treating a woman poorly or metaphorically beating their chests, they were very quickly chastised by the female student population. I had worked in the marketing department of a very well respected international news magazine where there were just as many women as men and we all generally treated each other with respect

Bugger Bugger Shit!

even if there were some hot tempered outbursts which were never gender based.

My decision to migrate to Australia was done with little planning due to the impending expiration of my permanent residency visa. I was in a reasonably lengthy relationship at the time and we hurriedly decided that I would leave in time for Christmas and he would follow in the new year. We would spend a year in Australia and then return to the UK.

I was 23 and in all likelihood had I not moved to Australia this would have been a permanent relationship. Moving to the other side of the world when you're 23 was a challenge. To be honest it would have been a challenge at any age but it came when I was just establishing myself as an independent adult. We tried to maintain our relationship but in the end he wasn't comfortable about moving to the other side of the world and I couldn't return to the UK for a while. I was also annoyed that he didn't appear to have enough 'backbone' to come over for a 12 month adventure. Whilst we attempted to maintain our relationship, in the end it wasn't feasible.

What kept me going in Australia in those early years were my friends from the UK who were having adventures travelling the world on their post university gap year. At several points I had five at a time living in my little two bedroom flat. I had a wonderful time exploring Sydney and its surrounds with different friends and it bridged the gap until I made my own Australian friends.

I had started to work in adolescent residential care and gradually the desire to return to the UK dissipated as I started to genuinely fall in love with this country. I have never forgotten one of the most quintessentially Australian conversations of this time, and it was such an example of how I had so quickly settled into life here.

WTF!!!!

I arrived home from work one day and the friends who were staying with me expressed their relief that I was finally home. They had heard this loud electrical static noise and couldn't work out where it was coming from. They asked me about the noise. "What noise?" I asked. "That noise," they said. "What noise? I can't hear anything" I replied. They looked at me in absolute disbelief and I think were about to tell me I needed to go and get a hearing test. "How can you not hear that noise? It's so loud" they said, with concerned looks on their faces. I listened carefully. "The only noise I can hear is the noise of the cicadas" I replied. They looked at me with curious expressions on their faces as I realised the electrical static noise they could hear was in fact the crescendo of cicadas on a hot summer's day. This was something so utterly Sydney that no local even hears it anymore.

Once my friends all returned to their lives in the UK, I decided to embark on my psychologist's registration and my Masters' Degree. By the time I was 30, I had successfully got them both under my belt and I was soon successful in my application into a management role at work. Here I was, a successful, highly-educated woman in a country with a long way to go to reach gender parity both in employment and attitude.

My parents were having a lunch party one day and the University's Vice Chancellor (VC) and her husband were both in attendance. The VC's husband was talking to me and I must have mentioned finishing work early one day. Bear in mind that in such a complex industry I would often support my team from 9-5, ensure they all left on time, and then I would commence my Principal Officer work for another two hours, leaving the office most days at 7pm.

The VC's husband made a comment along the lines that if I took time off work it showed that I lacked commitment and I would never get to the top in my chosen field. I looked at him in amazement and replied, "I'm already at the top of my field, in a statutory position covering the whole of

Bugger Bugger Shit!

NSW. You can't get any higher than that and that's precisely why I can leave work early when I need to." I will admit that I have always looked about 10 years younger than I actually am but even so, his assumption that a 'slip of a girl' wasn't committed to her work; when he knew nothing about what I did, or my qualifications, was not only insulting but fairly typical. When I was working in adolescent residential care I even had a male practitioner from community services ask where the adult was when I answered the door.

It was about this time that I had started sailing. There were very few females who sailed regularly and even fewer who raced. The long-standing members however knew me and there was a great camaraderie amongst us. They were mostly older men and they just treated me like everyone else on the crew (albeit for the first couple of years I was terrified when the wind was gusting and would often jump below and 'woman the winches' from the safety of the cabin). Even through my fear, I knew that I wanted to be out on the water in a boat. I could have very easily quit but I didn't because my desire to sail was larger than my fear of being overturned into the water. Being able to grit my teeth and keep going was a significant element in embedding resilience within me.

It was after I had been racing for a couple of years that I discovered I could get very competitive and was just as likely as any of the male crew to use some creative language when I yelled at someone on another boat who wasn't doing the right thing. On one occasion I was skippering the boat, we were coming towards the end of the race being chased down by the large multi hulls. Our very experienced, male crew member; our usual skipper who was teaching me the ropes, very firmly said don't look behind. I didn't. I'm glad I didn't because out of nowhere this massive catamaran skimmed past us with only a couple of inches between us.

On another occasion, a couple of guys in a little 'tinny' were at anchor, fishing in the middle of the race course. It's not like this was a surprise and it's not like there wasn't a whole vast waterway that they could have chosen to lower anchor in instead. The local twilight race took place every Monday evening during summer and easily 50-100 yachts participated. Being on a smaller 24 foot yacht, we were in the first groups to start and we were often on our way back to the finish line whilst the large, and very fast multi hulls were on their way up the course.

We looked in horror at what was unfolding before us. People on other yachts were yelling at the guys to get out of the way but their backs were turned so they didn't see the dozens of very large and very fast catamarans and trimarans approaching at a hell of a lick. There was no time for the skipper of the catamaran to take evasive action so sure enough it sailed right over the top of the tinny which sat precisely between the two hulls. I'm sure there was more than bugger bugger shit that got yelled from the members of the crew that night! Absolute expert skippering as the tinny emerged out the back of the larger boat, completely unscathed. I'm not entirely sure what happened to the guys on the tinny but I bet they've never done that again!

Of course regularly there were new (mainly) men who joined the club and they would come out on a boat with me and the men I regularly crewed with. It was so predictable. These inexperienced blokes saw a woman on the boat and assumed I knew nothing and needed their help whilst generally following the instructions of the men on the boat. We would all let it go and waited to see how it would play out. Invariably he would not follow some instruction and I would step in and quietly fix it so that he was clear that in fact I did know what I was doing and wasn't a woman who needed to be rescued.

In fact I remember one particular race where I got a work phone call. There had been an unpleasant interchange in the federal parliament which

Bugger Bugger Shit!

could have potentially impacted my program. A colleague was calling to give me the heads up but also wanted to understand how it could impact us. I explained that I was involved in a yacht race in the middle of Pittwater just in case we lost the mobile connection.

I went below whilst I took the call to be out of everyone's way but could still handle the winches if necessary as we rounded the mark. I filled her in on how we would handle it whilst still being able to back up the rest of the crew during the race. I could definitely multi-task and stay focused on two completely different matters simultaneously.

The only time I have ever been injured whilst sailing was when an inexperienced man attempted to display his questionable skills around me. We had decided to implement a tricky manoeuvre aimed at keeping the yacht moving in very light wind. His job was simple, to lean hard against the boom at the mast to stop it swinging. My job was to hang somewhat precariously over the side of the boat whilst holding out the sail to try and gather what little breeze there was.

He was instructed to yell very loudly if he felt the boom starting to move, so I could duck. He failed entirely, was scared when the boom started to shift and he stepped to the side of the mast without saying anything. The boom swung around without anyone having any warning and smacked me in the back of the head. We were all very lucky I wasn't knocked unconscious and didn't fall overboard. I hope he learned from this event and hasn't continued to over inflate his sense of skill or underestimate a woman's.

I have dated numerous men over the years who have all commented at one point or another that my intelligence is 'intimidating'. This has been echoed by the husbands of my friends with whom I get on well. Here we are back in the 1930s when women could not be more intelligent or successful than men. I have always refused to diminish myself to make

WTF!!!!

someone else feel comfortable. If there is no equity or genuine respect both ways in any relationship it is destined for failure. It takes a certain level of resilience to not compromise one's sense of worth.

Of course by now you just know there's some disastrous story coming. I had been on a date with a South American man - I only mention his cultural heritage so you can imagine the accent that goes along with the conversation I am about to describe. He seemed to be quite nice, was divorced, no children and in fact explained that there had been infertility issues with his former wife which was partly why their relationship had failed. Fair enough, I could empathise with this. We decided to see each other the following weekend.

A friend of mine sang in a gospel choir and they were having a concert. I hadn't been able to see any of the choir's previous performances so, ever practical, I thought I could kill two birds with one stone and see the guy and the concert at the same time. I asked him if he would like to go and he said yes. During the week he bombarded me with text messages so, by Saturday night, I was feeling more than a trifle apprehensive.

I arranged to meet him early, near where the concert was, so we could have a bite to eat beforehand. We had dinner and he was fine; we chatted away about our lives and his experiences in South America. We duly went along to the concert. As the concert was about to start, I saw my then CEO sitting in the audience and was mortified.

Sure enough, at the interval, he turned around, saw me and came up to say hello. He had a camera in his hand and was enthusiastically taking lots of photos - it turns out his wife was in the choir as well. I introduced him to my date and he asked if we wanted a photo. "No thanks," I said firmly as we wandered off to get a drink. My former CEO continued taking photos throughout the interval and on numerous occasions, whilst the following conversation was taking place, he interrupted us, stuck the camera in our

Bugger Bugger Shit!

faces and asked if we wanted a photo. Keep that vision in mind whilst you read along.

Once we had our drinks, my date announced, apropos of nothing, "I don't believe in God." "Oh really?" I replied. He went on to explain, "I died once and so I know there's nothing there." "Oh right." I said, not really knowing where this was heading but, ever curious, I couldn't help myself and asked him how.

He told me a story about being in the first gulf war; he had told me over dinner that he had been in the US Navy. He said he got grazed by shrapnel and slowly bled out over a number of hours, died and was then resuscitated. I wondered how this had happened given he was in the Navy. He explained that Navy personnel had been brought in to 'clean up' after the conflict. Apparently, he was in a village and one of the residents, overcome by grief, had taken an AK47 which he waved around and fired in the air. My date was in the firing line. I thought to myself, "If you're in the middle of the desert, straight after a war, I'm fairly confident that if you get shot, bleed out and die you're not coming back from that one", so I was somewhat dubious about the story.

Nevertheless, curious once more - I really should have taken on board the old saying that 'curiosity killed the cat' but I couldn't stop myself. "You know you said you and your wife had experienced infertility, do you think it could have been because you were exposed to the chemicals you were cleaning up?" His response was something I could never have predicted.

"No, just the opposite," he said, "I saw the doctor and he told me I had *too much*." As he said this, his hands dipped out from his crotch in a forward motion, just in case I needed further clarification. I was dumbfounded and just at this moment, my former CEO ducked in between us, "Would you like a photo?" "No," I squeaked with a somewhat alarmed look on my face. My date carried on as if there had been no interruption, "My doctor told

WTF!!!!

me that if I didn't expel it regularly then it would calcify." I nearly died, there and then, open-mouthed in horror. Then he said he needed to go to the bathroom. I wanted to run and have a shower as I envisaged him in the bathroom expelling whatever needed to be expelled so that it didn't calcify.

I don't know why I didn't make my escape there and then. Well I do, women have been raised to be polite and not to offend people. I didn't care about offending him but I did care about offending my friend who I was ostensibly there to see, so I stayed for the second half. At the end of the evening the audience were invited to stand and hold hands with the person next to them whilst the choir sang their last song. Bugger Bugger Shit!!!!!! You want me to hold hands with someone who has just been in the bathroom expelling whatever he needed to expel so that it doesn't calcify and turn him into a stalactite???? I was physically repulsed and had to stop myself running, screaming from the room, trying to not chop my hands off simultaneously!

I went out on another date once with a man who talked about his passion for cycling, didn't once ask me anything about myself and then told me a story about a woman who went out on a date with him, excused herself to go to the bathroom and never returned. I could understand why.

The last fifteen years of my career have, amongst other things, been spent working with couples who have separated; not with the majority of the population who separate respectfully with minimal professional support but with couples where there are high levels of acrimony and often significant levels of violence. I have also experienced numerous friends in this situation.

Having stood on the sidelines of dysfunctional and often abusive relationships, and lived through my own parents' relationship issues; power and control are the common thread. It's a complex topic that deserves its own book but speaking generally; power and control tends to surface when

Bugger Bugger Shit!

one person feels 'less' than the other and uses coercion and control by systematically annihilating, isolating, diminishing and gaslighting them. I was not going to slide into a relationship that was not truly equitable and respectful.

Australia has had a reckoning of sorts around violence towards women with the appointment of Rosie Batty in 2015 and then Grace Tame in 2021 as Australians of the Year but there is a very long way to go. Rosie Batty started the public conversation about Domestic and Family Violence and Grace Tame followed her; raising issues around sexual violence and child abuse.

We have had numerous scandals in parliament around toxic masculinity, sexual assault and misogyny as well as the seemingly endless circus of Sports Stars in particular, caught up in violent behaviour towards women. In March 2024, the Principal of one of the country's most elite private boys' schools; Cranbrook resigned over his complete failure to deal with abusive male staff and entitled and misogynistic boys.

Just over one woman a week is murdered in Australia by a current or former intimate partner. In the first 10 weeks of 2024, 17 women were killed due to domestic violence and one woman was murdered whilst she was jogging one morning. Two men were murdered by the former intimate partner of one of the couple. All of the perpetrators, bar one, were male.

Many years ago, my program had a matter being heard in the Supreme Court in Sydney. On this particular day, my male team member and I had driven into the court together. The closest car park to the court is very dark and dingy. It feels unsafe. I was driving around looking for a parking spot and my young, male colleague pointed one out. I explained to him that I was looking for a parking spot close to the lift. He jokingly called me lazy. I, very seriously, explained that at the end of the day he would be getting the train home so I would be coming back to the car park by myself, in the dark; for safety, I didn't want to walk through the car park to my car alone.

He looked at me in amazement and asked me if all women thought like that. I told him that every single woman not only thinks like that, but walks to her car with her keys in hand, alert and risk assessing the whole time. It had simply never occurred to him that this is what it is like for half the population because of the behaviour of the other half of the population, albeit a small proportion of the other half of the population.

For a time, in the very recent past, it seemed that almost every private boys school was in the news because of the outrageous sexist and violent behaviour of groups of boys and young men. Elite, faith-based university colleges had story after story after story in the news about the male students' atrocious behaviour towards women. We have endured the public downfall of well-known male religious and political leaders due to their unacceptable behaviour towards women. We have had Parliamentary Inquiries and Royal Commissions and still the appalling behaviour and attitudes of men towards women is pervasive.

Australia has a problem. This is not a women's issue, and as the inimitable Annabel Crabb would say; every day we don't 'drain the oceans' to change this, we are perpetuating the status quo that men have power over women. Whilst I have some amusing anecdotes about dating in Australia; the reality is that, for women, dating could very well mean risking their lives.

I cannot fathom this happening with the group of boys and young men I grew up with and went to university with. Maybe I'm lucky but maybe my peers at school and university learnt early on that men and women are equal. Yes absolutely it happens all over the world, but when children are raised to respect everyone; when adults kindly challenge children and young people to attempt things that cause them to feel anxious; when children, young people and adults challenge values, beliefs and behaviour; when we talk about the difficult things that make us feel uncomfortable; we are setting the stage for respectful relationships into the future, irrespective of gender.

It's not however just violence against women that is pervasive in Australia. Women still haven't reached parity in their salaries, there is still an overwhelming discrepancy in the numbers of women in executive positions in comparison to men and we have seen how women have been treated in parliament; both with the experiences of Julia Gillard, Australia's first female Prime Minister, the woeful lack of female members of cabinet, specifically in the Liberal Party that was in power for so long. Then we consider the treatment of the female CEO of Australia Post who was summarily dismissed on the floor of the parliament by the then Prime Minister. It feels like Australia is still about 30 years behind the rest of the world when it comes to its treatment of women.

If we think about the Health Care system; women continue to be dismissed by the medical profession. In 1991, I was described by my initial Neurological Registrar as a 'lass' with 'nebulous' symptoms due to 'boyfriend trouble' which are so clearly indicative of both MS and psoriatic arthritis that it would be laughable if it wasn't so serious. Thirty years later, nothing has changed.

My Interventional Radiologist uses me as an example of how NOT to do medicine, specifically around the treatment of women. It takes so long for a woman to be diagnosed with Endometriosis that the current government has attempted to redress this by funding specialist Endometriosis clinics. Women are still not equally represented in medical research and female heart attacks have been ignored for decades because they present differently to the heart attacks of men. Choosing to be resilient, for a woman in Australia, is exhausting.

In amongst this however, I have seen countless examples of resilient women and men stand up and challenge the behaviour of others, often despite being vilified in the media. We desperately need all of our young people; male and female, to develop the resilience and grit and the confidence to say, privately and publicly - enough. This ends now.

Chapter 16

I'm Not Disabled I'm Just Bloody Stubborn

> *I really think that this lie that we've been sold about disability is the greatest injustice. It makes life hard for us. And that quote, "The only disability in life is a bad attitude, "the reason that that's bullshit is because it's just not true, because of the social media of disability. No amount of smiling at a flight of stairs has ever made it turn into a ramp. Never. Smiling at a television isn't going to make closed captions appear for people who are deaf. No amount of standing in the middle of a bookshop and radiating a positive attitude is going to turn all those books into braille. It's just not going to happen."*
>
> **Stella Young**
> Ted Talk
> 2014
> "I'm Not Your Inspiration, Thank You Very Much"

As a result of MS; Mum started using a wheelchair about 10 years ago but it was about five years previously that she organised a mobility parking sticker. We had all pushed her to get one but she stubbornly refused; that would be some sort of weird admission of failure. In the end she did and oh how we celebrated as a family. Finally, we could get a parking spot in the shopping centre at Christmas!

One day, not that long ago but prior to the worsening of her dementia, I took Mum shoe shopping. We went into a shop that sells very expensive shoes designed by podiatrists. I was pushing her slowly around as she looked at the shoes. The shop assistant asked me if there was anything she could help with. Initially I thought she asked me because Mum was engrossed in a shoe; it turned out she wasn't. I said, "Mum's just looking for some new shoes". The assistant asked me, "What size is she?". I said, "I don't know, why don't you ask her?" The woman looked slightly taken aback as Mum answered, "size 36".

Eventually Mum found a couple of pairs she liked and she asked the assistant to grab her the correct sizes. I pushed her over to the trying-on bench and Mum got out of her chair and sat on the seat. The assistant brought them to Mum and once again spoke to me, "How are they, does she want to try on any others?" I looked at Mum and could see how furious she was; so was I. Once again I very firmly said, "Why don't you ask her?" Mum and I needed no second bidding, we left without purchasing anything.

The term disabled is a vexing one. Are people who have issues with mobility; sight; hearing; neuro-diversities; psychiatric or genetic conditions, disabled? Or is it the world around them that causes them to be disabled? Does having an aid to assist someone manage their lives make them disabled? I would imagine that every single person with a 'disability' has a different emotional response to the word and conceptualises it differently.

Bugger Bugger Shit!

All I can authentically do between the pages of this book is to explain my perceptions and experiences and help build a greater understanding for people without 'disabilities'. Gone are the days, thankfully, when infants born with down syndrome, cerebral palsy or any other obvious physical impairment are banished to institutions but there are still visceral responses to people with an obvious disability. People with invisible disabilities can struggle even more in a world designed for the fit and healthy.

I live in a family of people with disabilities. My sister and her children are all neuro-diverse because they have Irlen syndrome; a type of dyslexia which in itself is a simplistic way of describing this particular visual processing disorder. People with Irlen syndrome tend to wear coloured glasses to assist their processing complexities. When her youngest son tried on his Irlen lenses for the first time it was profound; I was with him as he put them on. He looked around him with his mouth wide open and declared, "Oh wow, where have all the colours gone?"

As someone without Irlen syndrome I had no idea what he meant, so I asked him. He took the glasses off and started pointing in the air, "There's a yellow line, and a pink one and red and blue". I was completely gobsmacked. I had no idea he had been experiencing the world through a mass of coloured lines and shapes. How frustrating; he had no idea however that not everyone experienced the world like this. I tried to imagine what it would be like as a little boy navigating that amount of visual 'noise'. I failed.

I failed partly because I have a different type of visual processing issue. I have a condition called aphantasia. Like dyslexia, millions of people have aphantasia but, like me, until a few years ago, would have no idea. Aphantasia is a condition of the "mind's eye". Whereas some people can close their eyes and see an image; people with Aphantasia don't see anything.

I'm Not Disabled I'm Just Bloody Stubborn

I remember the first time I realised that I might have a difference. I was at university in a Philosophy of Psychology lecture. The lecturer was talking about visual dreams. I put my hand up, somewhat confused and said, "I don't see pictures when I dream". His response was, "Yes you do." "No I don't" I said, "Yes you do" he said, "No, I don't" I insisted. I could have burst into a song from Annie Get Your Gun - you know the one that starts "I can do anything better than you", in hindsight maybe I should have because his less than insightful response was "Well you must be dead then". What a ridiculous, ignorant statement and yes; "I can do anything better than you. No you can't, yes I can, no you can't. Yes I can, Yes I can, Yes I can" - c'mon sing it aloud and with gusto everybody. Sorry, I got carried away. Apologies for the earworm.

If he had been curious, he might just have discovered this phenomenon and grown his professional career. Instead 25 years later, academics from Essex University came across someone whose mind's eye changed as a result of a brain injury. They decided to put a call out across the world to see if anyone else had this experience; they were inundated with responses. They completed a swathe of research, published their findings and got to add their names into the neuroscience history books. In the meantime I can't even remember the name of my arrogant and ignorant lecturer.

I will be the first person to admit that I am reasonably new to the disability world; the last 30 plus years for me have been focussed on keeping women and children safe; not on supporting people with disabilities. What I have very rapidly become aware of is the utter lack of understanding from many of the bureaucrats and some practitioners who work within the disability sector.

It is infuriating and over the last three years I have found myself using my voice and my experience to hold people to account; to question the policies; to question the attitudes and hold up a mirror to the people who

Bugger Bugger Shit!

discount, dismiss or disrespect people with disabilities. Actually, come to think of it, maybe I should have sung to them too and that would have got some swifter action.

The National Disability Insurance Scheme (NDIS) is a world-leading concept and piece of legislation. It is utterly brilliant. The rest of the world needs to take note of what Australia is doing. There is however a lot of misunderstanding within the general community about the NDIS. All people see is the dollar signs of expenditure. What they fail to comprehend is the financial contribution to the budget bottom line. What the NDIS has done is provide people with a disability the opportunity of joining the workforce and paying taxes rather than drawing on social support to live, in many cases, a very limited life.

The NDIS also means that parents of children and adults with a disability who have been informal and unpaid carers for their child's life have an opportunity to get back into the workforce; and pay taxes. The current Minister and Architect of the NDIS, Bill Shorten, has said publicly on many occasions that for every dollar spent on the NDIS, the NDIS provides two dollars back into the budget. Not only that but it has created millions of jobs for otherwise unemployed or underemployed Australians. Support workers, allied health practitioners; NDIS employees to name but a few. If people could only open their eyes and think laterally they would understand just how amazing this social support structure is.

Unfortunately however, once the NDIS was enacted the Liberals took over the government and the architects of the scheme had to leave it in the hands of a government who had not conceived it and did not see it as a priority. The NDIS has many structural issues; quite frankly if I were to outline them all we would die of boredom so I won't. What I will do however, is give you my experience of it.

I woke up one random Saturday morning in September 2020 and when I got out of bed, I was hit with the most excruciating pain; it felt like every bone in my body was not just broken but smashed into a thousand pieces. It felt like the MS, Psoriatic Arthritis and Spinal Cord injury had all plotted together and bitten me on the bum, but it was actually a flare of the Psoriatic Arthritis. Bugger Bugger Shit!

Due to the pandemic, all medical appointments were by telehealth so I had various phone appointments with my rheumatologist and neurologist. Both of them were quite surprised to see and hear how ill I was because their usual experience of me was of a buoyant, optimistic patient. My resilience was definitely tested during this period of time but because of the pandemic there was no way I could just curl up in my bed. My team and I were smashed for over 12 months, trying to support individuals, couples and families struggling to keep their heads above water.

I was extremely thankful for the ability to work from home which meant that I could hobble from my bedroom to my living room in order to continue working. My specialists were focussed on trying to get this beast back under control but despite their valiant efforts they just couldn't find a drug to control the rampant inflammation in my body. Either they didn't work for me, or the side effects were too severe to manage.

On the advice and encouragement of Cath; my partner in crime, red hair and MS, I approached the MS Society to register for employment support. I was linked with a physio who has been my employment caseworker ever since. He organised a bunch of physical support so that I could continue to work and he encouraged me to apply for the NDIS. I just couldn't bring myself to do it. I had heard such negative feedback about the process that I couldn't find any kind of brain space to consider it. We were in the grips of the pandemic; my team and I were working all hours of the

Bugger Bugger Shit!

day and into the evenings and my sister and I were managing a mum with dementia and home schooling the boys.

A few months later, I bit the bullet and agreed to work with the MS Society to put in an application. Of course we still couldn't have any face to face meetings so we did everything by phone. Their NDIS application support person was amazing. She took the Access Request Form (ARF) and grilled me about the answers over several long phone calls.

My sister and I had decided to brave IKEA because, hallelujah, Sydney had come out of lockdown. The first roll out of vaccinations had come through and those who weren't vaccinated were still locked down. As someone who is immune compromised, I felt reasonably safe venturing out, so of course, rather than go to the beach or a park, we decided IKEA was the best possible venue for our new found freedom.

As we walked through the doors, my phone rang and it was the practitioner from the MS Society with the next section of the ARF to complete. Mobility impairments. Everything is exact with the ARF, it really isn't designed for humans to complete. It requires precision responses that only a robot could confidently provide. One of the questions was along the lines of how far you can walk. This is the question on pretty much any assessment of physical disability. I have no idea how far I can walk. I failed maths twice before I finally scraped through a pass. What on earth does 20 metres look like anyway?

I was deliberating about how far in metres I could walk. Apparently it's as far as the picture frames if you take the shortcut. My foot dropped (a common MS symptom where it basically becomes impossible to lift your foot off the floor and walk properly). My right foot started to slide rather than walk along the floor so I found a stool to sit down on. Thinking about it, I'm not sure which was more dangerous, wandering around IKEA with foot drop or sitting on a stool. I interrupted whatever she was saying; "How long have we been talking?" I asked. "I'm not sure", came the reply, "Why?" "Because you rang me as I walked through the doors and I've just now got foot drop". It was just shy of 10 minutes. I might not have been able to work out what 20 metres looks like but I can still tell the time.

A few days later, in another call, we got to the section on communication and I told her I didn't have any issues with communication. She said, "Really? Because I've heard you talk about needing to use voice to text because your hands are too painful to type and write. I've heard you talking about word finding difficulties, speech difficulties and swallowing difficulties. They're all communication".

She made me really think about everything I could and couldn't do. For someone who has always worked in a strengths based way, this was confronting and challenging. The ARF impacted me emotionally in a way nothing had before. I realised just how much I had lost and compromised due to my health.

Completing the form in such a detailed way made me face the fact that I was now in fact, disabled, rather than just having a couple of autoimmune diseases that, somewhat annoyingly, slowed me down. Her attention to detail paid off and my application was approved straight away.

So here I was, a participant in the greatest disability reform scheme in the entire world. My first planning meeting was a hugely positive experience. I asked the MS worker to join me on the call. Afterwards she said that it was the most positive planning meeting she had ever attended, something I was still, in my naivety, to learn.

Bugger Bugger Shit!

Having Ruby means total freedom - even just doing the mundane things is a joy

Yes Ruby can go in the hold of a plane and with the chain on the back I can hook on my bags and travel completely independently

Chapter 17

Entitlement is Not a Disability

"You never really understand a person until you consider things from his point of view… until you climb inside of his skin and walk around in it"

Harper Lee
To Kill A Mockingbird
1960
JB Lippincott & Co

I met a friend for lunch at a lovely cafe in a precinct owned by NSW Health. It's full of historic buildings which have been rejuvenated and brought back to life. It was a Monday so it wasn't particularly busy but as I drove in I discovered the one disability space was taken up by a very large and very new Ute. I looked and there was no sign of a mobility sticker or any signs at all that the driver or occupant had a disability. I had promised myself that next time someone parked in a mobility parking space I would just park them in. I was sorely tempted but, unusually for me I have to admit, my courage failed me and I drove to the other side of the precinct, parked and rolled back to the cafe on my wheelchair.

I needn't have worried because two hours later when I came out, the ute was still there. Simultaneously another diner was leaving. This customer had an amputated leg and was on crutches. I watched him and his friends hobble out of the precinct and down the street to their car which was parked some significant distance away. I was really cross now, so I scrambled around for a piece of paper and a pen and wrote "Seriously? This was the choice you made this morning? You've taken my parking spot, would you like my disability too? As a result of your decision, a man with an amputated leg was forced to hobble on crutches to his car parked on the street. I am in a wheelchair and I had to park across the precinct. Do better."

My sister and I have often talked about the selfishness of people without a mobility parking sticker parking in the disabled spot and we've thought of lots of sarcastic comments we could write. We talked about this one later and I decided to get some bright yellow A4 stickers made up with the words "entitlement is not a disability" emblazoned across them and stick them right in the middle of the windscreen of drivers who really should know better.

The first thing to know about the NDIS is that it is full of ridiculous acronyms and if you are to have any kind of vague idea about what's going on you have to get your head around them. My first Local Area Coordinator (LAC) was a social worker whose career had always been in the disability sector. She started by apologising that she didn't know very much about MS but she wanted to learn from me. How respectful.

Following that meeting, I requested the MS Society Occupational Therapist to conduct a functional assessment. That was when I met Alison*.

Entitlement is Not a Disability

Her professional history had been working in a neuro ward in a large hospital and then with the MS Society. She thoroughly understood MS. She also saw a gazillion hazards in my home and had incredibly creative ways to deal with a variety of challenges I was facing, not least, the surprising capacity of my left leg to choose its own adventure.

Alison decided I needed a new bed due to my frequent capacity to get out of it and promptly fall over because my leg and brain had clearly had an argument and weren't talking to each other. I just saw it as an opportunity to get creative in falls management and I was becoming an expert. She also decided that I needed what has become known as my throne. It's a shower seat that, wait for it, lowers into the bath with the press of a button! I feel like Cleopatra!! I just need it to have a little shelf for my gin and tonic and I'm set. Then came the biggie; she said I needed to start thinking about a wheelchair. Oooph, if I had a wheelchair I really would be disabled... It took me a while to get my head around that concept. Deep inside I knew she was right. Walking was becoming increasingly difficult and my capacity to fall over dramatically was second to none.

Walking with MS is an interesting concept. Most people when they walk don't actually think about it; they just put one foot in front of another. When you have MS, you're never entirely sure what's going to happen. Sometimes it feels like I'm walking on a trampoline; sometimes it feels like I'm standing or walking on a slope; sometimes it feels like my legs are made of jelly. Almost all of the time it feels like my right leg is wrapped in a lead blanket, my left leg is off with fairies and my right foot has an annoying tendency to drop like clockwork after 6-10 minutes of walking; yes, I know this because the MS Society worker timed it when she was putting my NDIS application together. All of this means that walking, for me, feels like what other people would experience after running a marathon.

Bugger Bugger Shit!

There have been many dramatic falls. On a particular evening, I was picking up one of the kids from a friend's house. They lived in a complex of villas with no visitor parking. I had temporarily parked in a neighbour's drive but before I could get out of the car they arrived home so I needed to move. I moved my car to the side and got out, I would like to say jumped out but let's be realistic, it was more like the slow lumbering of an elephant.

As I was putting my feet on the ground, I realised I was alighting into a garden bed. This was a risky move and sure enough as both feet planted on the floor I lost my balance and sank to the ground. I narrowly avoided a rose bush! All I could think about were the neighbours who were sitting in their car with their headlights pointing towards me. I could imagine them watching this middle aged woman getting out of her car and then disappearing. As I so often do, I sat on the ground and snorted with laughter.

My capacity to fall up the outside steps of our house is second to none. There have been so many incidents, my family now do a cursory check that I haven't killed myself and then get on with whatever they were doing. The first time though was a classic. It was dark, there were no outside lights because the staircase was newly built and we hadn't thought about them; Lewis and I were racing out to pick up the take away we had ordered. The clue is in the term racing. What on earth was I thinking? I was ahead of Lewis and I heard him yell, I turned around without stopping myself, and saw that he had tripped. I asked him if he was alright and then I suddenly hit the deck too.

I had forgotten that we had put a large planter box between the deck at the top of the stairs and the driveway, ostensibly to stop me tripping on the side of the deck. I didn't, but I should have foreseen the possibility of me falling over the planter box and through the bush contained in it. Bang! I smacked down onto the driveway, narrowly missing hitting my head on the front of my car.

There I was, face planted into the driveway with my legs, somewhat awkwardly, caught in the Moraya bush, dangling in mid air. I managed to scratch my brand new glasses, and my face. I yelled for my sister and the whole family rushed out to check I was ok. Lewis, in the meantime, was still slightly behind me, lying prone on the steps from where he had fallen.

Ever practical and focussed on the things that really matter, I yelled to my sister, "Quick, go and get the takeaway it's going to get cold". She, equally practical, jumped in the car whilst calling out to Seb to check I was ok. Seb wandered over, asked me if I was ok. When I replied, "Yes", he nonchalantly wandered off, leaving me still lying on the ground unable to get up; partly because I was laughing so much, partly because it really hurt and partly because I was stuck in the bloody bush. He was somewhat surprised when I called for him to come back and help me up, "You said you were ok", he replied.

Following this episode I thought it prudent to update my Apple watch to the new one that has a falls detection setting. This piece of technology has proven invaluable to the MS community. The next time I fell up the stairs, the family once again heard my yell as I was heading down and rushed out to check I was ok. Not to worry, Siri was already on it. A message appeared on my watch, "You appear to have fallen over". "No shit Sherlock" I thought to myself. 'Are you ok?' Siri followed up; then she gave me a list to choose from 1. Yes I have fallen over but I am ok or 2. Yes I have fallen over and I need help. I presumed 3 was when you're dead and can't select either one. I selected the first one. "Are you sure you're ok?" came Siri's helpful reply. "Yes I'm sure" I thought to myself as I hauled myself up and applied the ice pack Bryn had helpfully brought out for my fast developing black eye.

Bugger Bugger Shit!

I feel like I ought to pay Siri overtime rates for the number of times she's checked in on me. I was getting a bit irritated by her voice a few months ago so I changed it to the Irish female setting. She seems to be so much more supportive now that she's Irish, although I do feel a bit disappointed that Siri is more helpful than my family when I'm lying prostrate on the ground.

When I was in the UK in 2019, I met up with a group of school friends for dinner. The restaurant they chose had a private room upstairs so that we could be noisy and not disturb the other diners. As I arrived and saw the steep flight, I thought, "This could be a challenge". I was fine going up but once we had finished dinner and were going off to the pub, the reality of getting down the stairs hit. Two of my friends were behind me as I held onto the wall and gingerly took each step one by one. "Sorry," I called out behind me, "not pissed, MS".

I had forgotten that I hadn't told them that I had been diagnosed with MS so it took them by surprise. One of them then messaged my friend Laura, who I talked about in the Introduction, to clarify the situation. She casually said, "Oh yes, she's got MS and a brain tumour too". He freaked out a little bit at that news so I had to reassure him the tumour was benign and the doctors were keeping a close eye on it. It was a reminder that whilst I take my health challenges in my stride, a lot of people don't and they genuinely worry about me. They don't need to, I've got it in hand. There are way worse things that I could have been diagnosed with and I'm genuinely thankful it's only MS and psoriatic arthritis.

The additional complexity I face is the impact of psoriatic arthritis. Psoriatic arthritis truly is the gift that keeps on giving. When you feel like one issue has been resolved another one pops up; it's like whack-a-mole on steroids. Whilst my feet were dreadfully impacted 5 years ago; the last few years it has been my hands and my fingers. In all seriousness, whilst I can

Entitlement is Not a Disability

laugh at my amazing capacity to fall over, the one thing I find difficult is the excruciating pain in my fingers.

I don't feel particularly resilient when it comes to my hands. Having arthritis eat away at the joints in your fingers is nasty. It means writing, typing, holding a walking stick, managing a wheelchair - joystick or self propelled, cutting my food, opening anything - particularly plastic packets, is either a chore or completely impossible.

Alison realised that the impact of my hands was going to cause me a bit of a challenge when it came to mobility devices. Almost all of them require the user to manipulate a joystick the whole time they are using it. My hands simply weren't up to the task and the pain would have been unbearable. I started to do some research. I needed something that I could use without my hands; that I could use at work, particularly when facilitating training sessions; that didn't make the kids feel embarrassed to be around me and that gave me total independence and I could use if I needed to fly to remote communities to conduct training; something I had been doing regularly prior to the pandemic grounding everyone.

Literally the only thing that met this criteria was a personal mobility device called the Omeo. I think Alison would agree when I say she was dubious. This is a relatively new machine which is essentially a sitting down Segway. It was designed and built in New Zealand by a man who became a paraplegic and his friend who are both engineers. It is an amazing piece of tech and it has revolutionised mobility devices.

I now see other companies that are starting to use similar technology but none will work as well as the Omeo for me because they still require the user to manipulate a joystick. Whilst the Omeo does have a joystick, it's only for left and right and with the flick of a switch it can move to what is called 'active seat' mode which makes the joystick redundant.

Bugger Bugger Shit!

I wanted to see this machine for myself. Due to the pandemic it took a few months to be able to organise a trial of it. I took to it like the proverbial duck to water. Last year I had a coffee with the UK distributor of Omeo; someone who uses one himself. He told me that they have found that people who intuitively understand the Omeo are people who used to ride horses or people who used to sail. I grew up riding horses and of course I sailed and raced yachts for years.

I completed the trial and Alison was impressed but she said that we really needed to trial other machines. She organised a trial at a distributor of a variety of mobility devices. She wanted me to try a mobility scooter. I felt they were too bulky and awkward for my needs but I genuinely gave it a try. It was immediately apparent they weren't going to work. Not only did the joystick cause almost immediate pain, I couldn't grip it enough to be safe and as my arms are unusually short I needed to bring the handlebars right up to me in order to reach safely which meant I was pinned into the seat. They were definitely not going to work. Alison duly wrote her report for the NDIS and sent it off, along with the evidence for the bed and an outside stairlift.

I had also been diagnosed with an MS related sensory-neural hearing impairment and requested funding for a low level laser pain management device which cost about $1,200 (think Tens machine but more effective). Everything was sent with the required evidence and quotes. Everything was declined. I couldn't believe it. The NDIS, this innovative, world first social support system declined everything explaining they didn't meet the 'reasonable and necessary criteria'. You have to be kidding me I thought, quickly followed by a very frustrated bugger bugger shit!

That was the start of an almost two year battle in the Administrative Appeals Tribunal (AAT) with the NDIS and their eye-wateringly expensive lawyers. I had no representation or support because there had been a 400%

Entitlement is Not a Disability

increase in applications to the AAT for services the NDIS refused to fund. I was furious, not least because I was concerned for all the other people who didn't have my education, my experience in the Supreme Court with work-related matters or even English as a first language. It was shameful and the Liberal Government of the day, in my opinion, should hang their heads for what they put vulnerable people with disabilities through.

This two year battle nearly did me in on several occasions. The ineptitude of bureaucrats who haven't got a clue about disability is totally offensive. There were a myriad of obscene conversations during this period. Too many to recount here, so I will just provide the edited highlights.

My first dubious conversation was with my new LAC. Alas my respectful, engaged and thoughtful LAC had moved onto other clients when it came time for me to apply for my second round of funding. I spoke to a lovely man. Whilst we were on the phone and he was filling in forms etc, I asked him how he came to work for the NDIS. He explained that he had been an IT consultant until six months previously but his son had a disability and so he decided he wanted to work where he could make a difference in the lives of people with a disability. It was a noble sentiment.

The NDIS desperately needs good IT consultants because their IT system is impossible to navigate. This lovely man wasn't actually working as an IT consultant where he really could make a difference; he was working as an LAC, directly supporting people with a disability to access support. Except he didn't have a clue about disability.

When we got to the sensory-neural hearing impairment; he said, "You don't have a hearing loss listed as a secondary disability". "That's because it isn't a secondary disability". "Yes it is" he replied - I had visions of my old university professor and the argument about visual dreams. I took a deep breath, "No it isn't, it's part of the MS". "No it isn't", he replied, "it's a secondary disability". I asked him if he had any experience with MS. "No", he replied.

I offered an explanation as simply as I could; "The sensory-neural hearing impairment is exactly the same as my legs being impacted. The lesions in my brain impact my capacity to walk properly and they also impact my capacity to process sounds". He replied, "But your hearing loss isn't significant enough to warrant hearing aids". I said, "That's because it's not a hearing loss per se, it's an issue with processing sounds". "So it is a secondary disability" he said. I'm not entirely sure how I managed my composure; probably because it was just the first of what was to become many ridiculous and nonsensical conversations with people who have no clue.

He changed tack. "Why does your quote say $7,000, when I just looked up hearing aids online, it states a hearing aid costs $3,000?" I said, "Because not all hearing aids are the same and you are looking at the price for one hearing aid and not two which is what I need". Then he said, "You haven't provided any evidence that it is related to MS". I said, "I've given you the report from the audiologist which clearly states that it's related to MS. And I've given you a report from my Neurologist which states that it's a well known phenomenon related to MS".

The letter I eventually got back from the NDIS confirming the rejection of the hearing aids said that there was no evidence to suggest that the hearing impairment was related to MS. I followed up and reiterated that I had a report from the audiologist and one from my neurologist saying that it is. The lawyer who responded to this said but the letter doesn't say that it's the cause of your specific hearing impairment. I once again pointed out that there are two reasons for this type of impairment; a tumour and MS. I didn't have a tumour but I do have MS, ergo it had to be MS; as my neurologist and audiologist had both stated.

Entitlement is Not a Disability

This conversation with the lawyer happened about 2 weeks before Christmas in 2022; as part of a conciliation meeting. I had already provided them with 50 pages of evidence; in two separate documents, point by point refuting their claims. None of the NDIS objections, or their expert witnesses, were supported by any evidence, just the opinions of NDIS employees. My years of work in adoption was paying off; even though I had no advocate, legal or otherwise, I knew exactly what I was doing in a court process. I think the NDIS and their lawyers completely underestimated me.

The second insane conversation in that meeting referred to the stair lift that had been rejected. The AAT member asked what I would do if it rained. I was somewhat taken aback by this question, it was after all, a weather proof stairlift manufactured specifically to be used outside. I paused, somewhat confused that this seemingly intelligent person had asked such a stupid question, "Umm, I'll wear a raincoat," I replied, then I had an inspired thought; "or use an umbrella". She looked aghast, "Oh gosh no, please don't use an umbrella, it might blow inside out if there's a gust of wind".

I have no idea what my face was doing but I do know I could not believe what had just come out of her mouth. I think at that point the NDIS representative, who had been absolutely silent until then, realised the ridiculous nature of the statement and she intervened, "Well I think she will do whatever everyone else does in that circumstance. Wait in the car or in the house until the rain eases or stops". I mean, I know Sydney has some extreme weather at times but seriously?

The final discussion of that meeting enraged me. We came to the Low Level Laser. My physio had provided the NDIS with five peer reviewed research papers about the efficacy of low level laser in the management of pain. She had also offered to send them the links for 3000 more. The NDIS' independent 'expert' had indicated, despite being offered the research and being provided with the five peer reviewed published papers, that there

Bugger Bugger Shit!

wasn't any evidence to support the use of low level lasers at the same time as admitting he didn't know anything about it. The lawyer, in that meeting said, "I don't care if everything else is approved, we will take you to a full hearing before we'll approve the laser". I saw red. I could not believe the utter waste of taxpayers money on a full hearing to deny me a $1200 piece of evidence based technology.

I went around the room and, rhetorically, asked each person what they earned. I said, "As a taxpayer, I find it offensive that you would waste an exorbitant amount of taxpayer money on a full hearing rather than fund a piece of assistive technology that costs just over a thousand dollars".

I came out of that meeting and immediately rang Minister Bill Shorten's office. As I explained what had gone on, I found myself crying. I explained that I wasn't crying because I was upset, I was crying because I was absolutely furious at what the NDIS and its lawyers were choosing to put participants through. I said that I found it almost impossible and I am educated, experienced in working alongside a large bureaucracy and the legal system. If I couldn't cope, how on earth were people with psychosocial disabilities, learning delays or migrants with little English supposed to manage this system, just to get the most fundamental support to assist them in being productive members of our society. What has our country become? I was disgusted.

Due to the election result in 2022, Minister Bill Shorten was now back in charge of the Scheme and he had been pulling his hair out at the absolute shambles the Liberal Government had made of the NDIS during their nine years in government. His office was inundated with complaints from people just like me who had been banging their heads against a brick wall just to get the most basic of support.

Every time I felt my resilience wane during this period, I thought about the people who were worse off than me; that gave me a new resolve to battle on. I had a responsibility to do everything I could to make this incredible department provide what Bill Shorten and the Labor Party had envisaged.

A week later we were on holiday in Port Macquarie, it was Christmas week. On Monday afternoon it was reported that the new Labor Attorney General was dismantling the AAT. It had become an organisation stacked with Liberal Party cronies and was the antithesis of what it had been created to be; an independent body developed to mediate disputes with government departments. I, along with hundreds of others I'm sure, celebrated.

First thing the following morning, I participated in my fortnightly Zoom speech therapy session. When I finished, I checked my emails. At 9.30am an email from the NDIS was sent to me. Despite the promise of the NDIS lawyer to see me at a full hearing, all of my assistive technology requests had been approved. I was over the moon but I was also incredibly angry. The NDIS had put me through almost two years of hell, arguing against me every step of the way; causing me to waste hours researching and putting together evidence and reports to refute their completely illogical and unfounded claims. More importantly, I couldn't even comprehend how much taxpayer money had been wasted.

At every meeting there were two lawyers, an NDIS representative and at least one person from the AAT. On top of all the work they did behind the scenes to prevent me accessing the fundamental supports I needed. It must have racked up hundreds of thousands of dollars; and I was just one of hundreds of participants engaged in disputes with the NDIS to access vital support. Whilst I was in the middle of my matter, there was a much publicised case of one young man who died because the NDIS refused to provide him with the funds to purchase a mattress equipped with an alarm to alert his parents when he stopped breathing. It was hardly going to break the public purse but it certainly broke that family.

Bugger Bugger Shit!

When ignorant people argue about the wastage in the NDIS, hardly anyone talks about the fundamental waste of money spent on high end lawyers pitted against participants. The statistics demonstrate that about 90% of matters that go to the AAT are eventually approved because they are, in fact, reasonable and necessary support. What an utter waste; it disgusts me and I hope it disgusts you. That fact alone gives me the resolve and resilience to continue.

A couple of days after my new plan and funding were confirmed I received the following message on Facebook. I had been posting updates of my AAT battle in our, not so little, supportive MS group and so of course I posted when everything was approved and thanked them for their support through the experience. When I received the following message on Facebook, I knew my battle had been worth it.

"I am absolutely ecstatic for you (secretly for me too) 💃 💃 💃. It's YOU I wish to thank! It was heartbreaking reading your posts these past two years but I truly thank you for sharing! I've been following your fight (especially for the Omeo) and I'm truly sorry you had to go through this saga. Personally for me, you have now given me and my team (OT/SC) the precedent and the confidence for when we're ready to put in my request! I've trialled the Omeo and out of everything that I'm grateful to receive through NDIS, the Omeo has been #1 on my needs list so I can have the ability, dignity, freedom and independence to access places I have not been able to go to since my decline. I'm not expecting smooth sailing but I now have the confidence through you to go ahead now……thank you 🥺 You've fought so long and hard and even though I don't know you personally, I am so so proud of you! You're a bloody inspiration on not giving up!!!!!!"

When I reflect on what kept me going and built my resilience through this ordeal, it is my fellow NDIS travellers. People who totally get it. I met Ben and Deb through Facebook; we've actually never met in real life. Ben

Entitlement is Not a Disability

and I were put in contact with each other through our Omeo representative who thought we might be able to support each other. Deb and I met because she kept showing up on Facebook groups I was part of; MS, Omeo and Tamaruke (our breed of dog) groups. Ben, Deb and I were all in the AAT at the same time fighting for our Omeos so we formed a little Messenger group.

Ben and I were a few months ahead of Deb and we were also in opposition with the same NDIS lawyer so we'd been messaging back and forth for a while and then Deb joined in. I can honestly say the conversations between the three of us; particularly between Ben and I raging about the lawyers, were what kept my head above water. Being in community with like minded people, calling on friendships and the support of others in our worlds is a significant aspect of building resilience.

I am forever grateful that we met, even though it was through such a shared horrible experience. Our Omeos were approved a few months apart; Ben first, then Deb, then me - even though I had been in the AAT the longest. In 2022, Omeo brought out a limited edition red Omeo; there were only five in the world. Ben got the last, and only, red one in Australia. When my Omeo was eventually approved, my Omeo Rep asked me what colour I wanted. "Red," I said, "but I know Ben got the last one so if they can't do an extra red one it will have to be black".

I don't know what magic Katrina did but I got my wish; the sixth red Omeo in the world. I named her Ruby. She goes faster than all the other Omeos because she's red. Ben, Deb and I still message each other; sometimes with Omeo adventures, epic failures on our Omeos and new NDIS battles. We will meet as soon as I can get up to Queensland; so watch out for three slightly crazy individuals on the best and sexiest personal mobility devices in the world; two red and one black.

Chapter 18

Ruby

"The plain fact is that the planet does not need more successful people. But it does desperately need more peacemakers, healers, restorers, storytellers, and lovers of every kind. It needs people who live well in their places. It needs people of moral courage willing to join the fight to make the world habitable and humane. And these qualities have little to do with success as we have defined it."

David W. Orr
Earth in Mind: On Education, Environment and the Human Prospect
2004, Island Press

We had set up the training room and were waiting for the participants to arrive, so my colleague Sam and I were having a chat; as we commonly do, about gender roles. We had been facilitating a Domestic Violence Training Course together for about two years and we loved it. Sam told me that she had been talking with her partner about the way men are treated in public compared to women.

She recounted the conversation to me; that when men walk down the street alone, other men get out of each other's way. When women walk down the street alone, men don't even see them, and as a result men bump into women all the time. Sam's partner was completely oblivious to this so she set up a random experiment with him. He walked down the street ahead of her, no one bumped into him. She then went ahead of him and was bumped and jostled by men on numerous occasions. He was shocked. Sam is an attractive young woman in her late 20s. The situation is even more pronounced for older women and if you have a disability you are either completely invisible or an oddity to be gaped at.

In January 2023, my new NDIS budget was released and I had enough money in the 'capital items' line to pay for all of the assistive technology I had applied for. I went about ordering all the things I needed; new hearing aids to counteract the sensorineural hearing impairment, a new mechanical bed so that I could raise and, more importantly, lower it so I didn't fall out of bed and I could raise the head and foot so I could sit on the bed, support my legs and finally be able to do up my shoes without asking someone else.

I bought the low level laser to manage my chronic pain so that I wouldn't need to constantly attend my physio for her to do it and I finally ordered my Omeo. The Omeo was going to take up to six months to arrive; they are purpose built with the controls placed according to each individual and some of the parts were taking a while to arrive because of global supply chain issues following the pandemic.

I had started to consider medically retiring in October 2022. My dear friend and colleague Andree could see how fatigued I was which was impacting my capacity to work and live my life. One day she said, "You know you have income protection insurance don't you?" I had completely forgotten. I was focussed on paying off the mortgage and then attempting

Bugger Bugger Shit!

to apply for the Disability Support Pension whilst I waited for my Super to be released.

I spoke to my MS Employment Caseworker about it and he agreed that the timing was appropriate. He put me in touch with an employment lawyer who offers his services to the MS Society. He checked my policy and confirmed that I could apply for five years salary continuance and also Total and Permanent Disability payment. What an unexpected Godsend. I then spoke to my neurologist who was completely supportive and told me he had thought for a while that I should finish work but he didn't want to push me into it, preferring to wait until I was ready and brought the subject up with him.

I also decided that I wanted to have a trip back to the UK to catch up with my extended family and friends. I decided to finish working on the 17th March 2023 and booked my flight the following day. I knew that if I finished work and just stayed at home I would struggle with the sudden change and probably end up regretting it.

I spent the next few months preparing everything to transfer over to whoever was going to take my place, preparing myself for the change and preparing my team. It was really hard. I loved my work, I loved my team. I couldn't envisage not seeing them every day. I couldn't envisage not grappling with complex clinical issues and supporting our clients. I knew though that it was time. I wasn't doing my life well and I wasn't doing work well. I decided I could either work or have a life; not both. Life won out. As much as the passion had sustained me for over 30 years, I couldn't keep going.

I started planning my trip. A big aspect of my thinking was around my mobility. I had been using a manual chair part-time for about 18 months but I needed someone to push me in it; something I detested. When someone needs to push you in a wheelchair all independence is totally eliminated. You are confined to the whims and timetable of someone else. You cannot just jump in the car to go to the shopping centre. I had missed dozens and dozens of events because I couldn't walk the distance required; or expect someone to push me; or be available.

One of the things that used to drive me up the wall was when I was shopping; whoever was pushing me would push me past what I was looking at so they could see it, which meant I couldn't see it or I had to crane my neck to see it (not good when one has a cervical spine injury); or when we got to a check out they would push me through so I couldn't reach the eftpos machine. There are only so many times you can instruct someone on the basics of wheelchair assistance. I decided I would need to hire a power chair.

In all honesty, I could have hired a power chair at any point, but it is a huge psychological adjustment in going from being independently mobile using your legs, to admitting you need to use a power chair. I also had to grapple with the question of whether I was 'disabled' enough to warrant a chair. I process things by considering the aspects of the issue, then talking them through with trusted people. When I had asked friends and my GP about a mobility parking sticker a few years previously, they all looked at me as if I was a bit mad. Of course you should have a mobility parking sticker was the consensus. So I got one.

A few years after that, I went to Melbourne for work with one of my colleagues who is over 10 years older than me. After the training, we would hurry to jump on a tram to go into central Melbourne to do some shopping in our favourite spots. People would offer to give up their seats for my colleague; she would invariably accept them and then stand aside for me to sit down. She was quite capable of standing on a tram; I wasn't. I didn't look like I wasn't though. I looked like a healthy forty something year old. Little did they know about my rogue legs and challenging hands.

Bugger Bugger Shit!

A wheelchair though, especially a big awkward ugly one; that's a whole different kettle of fish. The Omeo is different, it's like a Ferrari. A standard powered chair in comparison is like a slow and lumbering tank. I really didn't want to be riding around in an ugly tank. I also decided that I needed time to adjust to being an obviously 'disabled' person and it seemed like doing this in the UK away from my friends and workplace was a good idea.

The wheelchair I had hired was delivered to my aunt and uncle's house and I was taught the basics. The next day I took it for a spin around their village; not bad, it gave me the freedom to get out and about and the weather was pretty bad so there weren't very many people around to see me. The big test came a few days later.

I was going into central London to meet up with my uni friends. I rode down to the train station and my aunt came with me to make sure it all went smoothly. Honestly it couldn't have been easier. The UK and - I'm told, Europe in general - is light years ahead of Australia when it comes to accessibility. When I say this to people in Australia and the UK, the overwhelming response is surprise.

Yes the UK has many hazards for wheelchair users; like narrow pavements for one thing and very old buildings with steps to get inside for a second. In Australia though, by and large, the pavements are completely atrocious and downright dangerous unless they are brand new. Even when they are new, it's a lottery as to how safe they will be, and even the most minor of adjustments for someone with a mobility impairment seems to be beyond the reach of the majority of people with any level of decision making power; despite the strong legislation we have and the existence of the NDIS for goodness sake.

The rail staff in the UK were brilliant; there is a passenger assistance app and call centre. The London Underground map is detailed with its mobility information; tube trains are easy to get on and off and there are dozens of

Ruby

staff to assist. I had lived in London in the mid 80s until I migrated to Australia so it's much easier for me than the average tourist. I got off at Bond Street and decided to roll down to London Bridge where I was meeting my friends. It was fantastic. When I lived in London, I got the tube everywhere; this wandering above ground was marvellous.

I met up with my friends. I was nervous about them seeing me in a wheelchair. I was the last to arrive, and we all burst into tears of joy to see each other after years of being apart. Who cared whether I was in a wheelchair or not.

I hired a wheelchair accessible vehicle for part of the time; I went to the Minack Theatre in Cornwall with a friend. It was freezing and the wheelchair clearly didn't like it so it was a bit hairy when we couldn't restart it; but once again staff were brilliant and offered to push this beast of a machine up the significant hill back to the car park. Fortunately I got it started!!

Then the enormous emotional test came. I was going back up to Lancaster to meet up with my school friends. Whilst there was no option other than use the wheelchair in London and my uni friends were completely fine with it; my school friends were a different matter; for some reason I still haven't fully been able to grasp. I hasten to add they would have been totally fine with it, I was the one with the problem. I used my walking stick. I just couldn't bring myself to look so disabled when we had all grown up together.

Becoming visibly disabled is a process. I have to say that every person I met, every person I rolled past were respectful and kind; except for one woman. On Easter Sunday I had gone out for a bit of a ride and was making my way back to my aunt and uncle's house. I was a bit stressed because the charge light was flashing so I knew I had to get back asap. I passed this family walking in the opposite direction; they had to move to single file

Bugger Bugger Shit!

because of the narrow pavements. The mother looked right at me with a look of utter pity on her face. It wasn't subtle; there was no way I misread it.

I have spoken to dozens of wheelchair users; not a single one feels hard done by because they use a mobility device. Every single one has enthusiastically embraced their wheelchair because it brings them freedom. Our wheelchairs are like anyone else's legs. You don't pity anyone with legs; don't pity anyone in a wheelchair. Yes, if we have become 'disabled' then we need to adjust to our new identity but not for one minute do we need sympathy or pity. I am disabled when I need to use my legs; not when I'm using a chair.

That day was also a bit of a lesson in battery management. I had completely underestimated how long the battery would last. It started flashing yellow for a while. Not to worry, I had been told there was still some juice left when it was yellow - but pretty quickly yellow turned to red. I decided that if necessary I would detour into a pub, call my aunt and ask her to bring me the charging cables which I had stupidly left behind.

Eventually I made it to their road. It's a long road. The battery was still flashing red and by now had started to slow down. Could I make it? My aunt came out of the house and was standing there anxiously waiting for me and watching me crawl up the road. I got to their driveway and the battery gave up the ghost. I switched the wheelchair into manual mode and pushed it into the garage to be charged. Note to self, if you're going anywhere take the blooming charging cable with you!!

I arrived back in Australia at the end of April and less than two weeks later my Omeo arrived; a few days before my birthday! I was notified of the approval just before Christmas; what a Christmas present. For my Omeo to arrive in time for my birthday was perfect. Katrina and Neil brought it down from Queensland for me and gave me a half day training session at our local oval.

A couple of friends came with me, as did Bryn who was 13 at the time. One friend is a Professor of Occupational Therapy so I wanted her to come and see it for herself so she could talk about it with her students. The second friend is an MS buddy who lives near me and is considering whether the Omeo would be right for her. Words cannot describe those few hours; well actually there are two; liberating is the first and fun is the second.

After I re-acquainted myself with the machine; after all it had been over two years since I had originally trialled it, I took off at a rate of knots. It felt like I was flying across the oval. As I was racing Katrina turned to Neil and said, "If she brakes suddenly going at that speed will she come off?". "Yes" said Neil just as I braked and flew off the back. Well flew off is possibly a slight exaggeration. The Omeo has a safety mechanism; it will tip backwards whilst it cradles you so you end up in the slightly undignified position of lying backwards on the ground; still cradled within the seat with your legs up in the air.

Come to think of it, Siri completely failed me with that crash; she didn't even bother checking in with me, how rude! I couldn't move. Not because I was hurt in any way, but because I was laughing so much. Katrina, Neil and my friends ran across the oval to make sure I was ok. I was completely fine, my stomach hurt because I was laughing so much but apart from that nothing.

I can't go on any fairground rides because I get motion sickness and I regularly get car sick if I'm not driving (although not on boats which is a bit weird). Having the Omeo meant I had my own personal fairground ride!! What a hoot. Here was this fifty something woman hurtling across the oval, crashing and howling with laughter. Like I said; liberating and fun!

Bugger Bugger Shit!

I didn't know whether Katrina had managed to persuade Omeo to build a 6th red one until it arrived - I got my wish, and she definitely goes faster because of it! I named her Ruby and she's now an additional member of the family; "Is Ruby in the car?", "Can someone grab Ruby?", "Hang on don't forget Ruby", "Don't worry, you can use the car, I'll get the Metro into the city with Ruby". The Omeo has extended life batteries so I have never been in a position that I was in the previous month. The Omeo can manage about 50km on a single charge although I'm sure it would be longer.

There are numerous modes of public transport in Sydney; buses some of which have automatic ramps and some don't. I'm never entirely sure which I'm going to get so I tend not to get a bus anywhere; partly because of the ramp issue, partly because I get motion sickness on a bus and partly because the Omeo doesn't do well on a bus because of the frequent stops and starts in Sydney traffic.

Then we have the usual heavy trains. The platforms around the Sydney rail network are particularly dangerous because of the completely inconsistent gap between the platform and the train; both in terms of width but also height. There are multiple hair-raising videos circulating on social media of people falling between the platform and train. If travelling on the train network, wheelchair passengers have to ask a station staff member to put out the ramp for them; that of course relies on a staff member actually being around which is fine at the larger stations but at the suburban stations it's sheer luck.

The light rail is often colloquially referred to by Sydneysiders as a tram but sometimes not; a generally excellent and reasonably new service which sometimes requires a ramp and sometimes doesn't but the light rail trains only have a couple of carriages and the driver will see you on the platform, jump out and drop the ramp for you. Are you confused yet?

Ruby

Finally, is the Metro. A brand new piece of infrastructure that is completely accessible which is good because the Metros are driverless and go unbelievably fast. Until later this year, the Metro system has been limited in the area it covers but it's in the final throes of being expanded and when it does, I will be able to get from my suburb into the city and beyond without needing any assistance at all. True independence, I have recently discovered, is a priority for people with disabilities and something I actually didn't think about in any great detail until my legs let me down.

The first outing I had on Ruby was to the hospital for a specialist appointment and an MRI. I persuaded almost 18 year old Elliott to come with me, just in case anything went wrong. My sister dropped us off at the Metro station. I had never actually been on the Metro. It opened just before the pandemic and there was no way I was going to go on public transport at the time, so it was my first time and I was on Ruby having only had her for a matter of days. Getting on the Metro was as easy as pie but I discovered an immediate problem; there was a woman sitting in the wheelchair space, so I had to ask her to move before I could park. Foolishly I thought the Metro would be like the train and I would have time to sort myself out before it took off. Apparently not. There was just enough time for me to *not* put the stabilising legs down before the Metro hurtled away.

Ruby and I went flying a few feet down the carriage; I managed to grab onto the pole to stop me zooming down the whole length of it. The train stopped five minutes later at the next station and I quickly dropped the legs, slightly nervous about what might happen. Not to worry, she was completely stable and didn't move an inch. Elliott was more relieved than me I think because if anything untoward had happened he was going to have to be the one to get me out of the pickle. I've never paused again getting onto the Metro. Having frequently got on to discover people unnecessarily sitting in the wheelchair spot, despite there being dozens of

Bugger Bugger Shit!

empty seats in the carriage, I'm now pretty direct: "You need to move" is what I usually bark at people, in fear of being sent hurtling down the carriage again.

The Metro takes us almost to the hospital but not quite so we alighted at Chatswood, crossed the platform and waited for the train to go the last two stops, which required a guard to put a ramp down. Fortunately this station is a large interchange so there are staff on the platform all the time.

We alighted at St Leonards and as we wandered up the hill to the hospital we were stopped by a young woman in a manual chair with a power assist attachment. She had seen videos on YouTube of the Omeo and thought they were too good to be true. I reassured her that even though I'd only had my Omeo for four days it was already life changing. I gave her the business card for Katrina and Neil. I hope she's gone ahead and trialled it for herself.

The outpatients department is quite a walk from the main entrance to the hospital; for the first time in ages I had no problem getting to it. I saw my rheumatologist; it's not an overstatement to say she was amazed at the machine, particularly because it's balance based; it only has two wheels. I am constantly using my core rather than being passive in the chair. Every time I use Ruby, I do a core workout and it is now the part of me that is the strongest.

After the appointment, we got back on the train, went up to Chatswood to check out a shop and then back to St Leonards for the MRI. Once the MRI was done, we went back up to the train station and retraced our route but instead of going home we stayed on the Metro and went to our local shopping centre where we spent an hour or so before finally going home.

I was on Ruby for about 9 hours that day and her battery was only half depleted. There is no way prior to having Ruby that I would have been able to manage such a long day. My exhaustion would have set in after about 2 hours and I would have had to go to bed for a couple of days to recover. Whilst I have had some hugely fatigued days since having Ruby, they have been minimal in comparison to the pre-Omeo struggles and have mostly been because of the heat of an Australian summer.

As those of us who live in Australia know, it has been getting increasingly warm here over the decades. Twenty years ago, in Sydney at least, we shook our heads in disbelief if the temperature gauge hit 40 degrees. Now it's so common we have just come to expect it as part of summer. Whilst 40+ degrees is no joke for anyone, for people with MS it's a serious issue. People with MS frequently can't thermo regulate properly. Once the temperature hits 27 degrees celsius, our bodies stop being able to regulate our internal temperature which leads to a 'pseudo exacerbation' of our symptoms. That means all of our MS symptoms get worse until we can cool down. It's not just the heat though, we can struggle to thermo-regulate in the cold as well. For me one of my significant symptoms is fatigue so when it's hot, I am completely and utterly exhausted.

My friends fall into one of two camps. The first camp is mainly made up of my female friends who encourage me from the sidelines and who would willingly race me if they had an Omeo. It's probably no surprise that our dog is a female because she goes bonkers when we go to a certain park because she knows we're going to race.

The second camp is mainly made up of my male friends who worry about me hurting myself or damaging Ruby; especially when they realise quite how fast she can go. Fair enough probably, if I'm being honest. What they don't grasp though is the pure excitement that having the freedom to do what I want, when I want provides; except for going up or down a flight of steps, but I'm sure with time and a few tweaks the next generation of Omeos will get there; after all, the Daleks did!

Bugger Bugger Shit!

Bryn is probably the most concerned person about Ruby. Bryn himself has a disability; he was diagnosed with an extremely rare genetic disorder; so rare in fact that he's the only known person in the world with his disorder and only one of 30 people in the world with something close to his. He 'gets' it. He worries about Ruby; not so much about me. He was at the training I had so he knows how she works and that a high end, expensive piece of technology needs to be looked after. Whenever she does something slightly unusual, Bryn gets very concerned. Much more concerned than I do.

The Omeo has a warning mechanism to let the rider know it's not happy. The mechanism makes a noise and shakes. If the rider doesn't adjust what they're doing immediately, it will go into safety/shut down mode and tip backwards, even if they're not travelling at light speed. This happened to me a few times in the first couple of months of having Ruby. Usually because I banged into things whilst trying to reach something. This is when I realised quite how disability unfriendly Australia is. And just to clarify, in case anyone wants to report me for speeding; light speed is a slight exaggeration - anything vaguely faster than someone pushing a heavy manual chair and the lumbering of a tank feels like light speed but it's quite safe.

One of my scariest incidents was when I was on my own, trying to push the button on a pedestrian crossing. They are usually set too close to the edge of the pavement and the incline down to the road to be able to safely stay upright, reach forward and sideways to press the button. People in wheelchairs simply can't reach far enough forward while remaining on the flat. Slight inclines and wheelchairs facing forward are generally fine; inclines sideways are disastrous. A little forethought from town planners would transform the experience of people with mobility aids.

Speaking of inclines, our house is built on the side of a hill. To say the driveway is steep would be an understatement. How to get Ruby up and down it? After the session on the oval we adjourned to our house so that Katrina and Neil could best understand the topography and how I could manage it. Fortunately I don't need to use Ruby in the house but I do need to plug her in whenever I'm not out and about with her.

Neil gave it a go first. The brake on the Omeo is, like virtually everything else, managed by the rider adjusting their body weight. Neil leant backwards and easily managed a controlled roll down the hill, then I did. It was freaky but I succeeded in understanding exactly how much I needed to lean back to find the sweet spot of not engaging the safety backwards tip mechanism, or putting her into reverse and being able to slowly descend the hill. I felt like an olympic skier flying down the giant ski jump; trying not to hurtle towards the house and, given my propensity for unplanned stops, not hit the balcony railing and catapult over it into Elliott's bedroom. I navigated the descent like a pro.

Now to try and go up the hill - Neil gave it a go forward and failed. The incline was just too steep to manage the lean of the chair without scraping the foot plate, so he turned around and went up backwards, like the professional he is. My turn. I failed. I just could not work out the incline going up, but I did manage to perfect the art of 360 degree turns. I was like one of those jewellery box ballet dancers, pirouetting around and around and around. I gave up. That was in May. I tried a few other times, equally disappointingly until for some reason on New Year's Eve, I decided to give it a go so that I could take the dog for a walk.

My sister had the car so if I was going to get out of the house I had to get Ruby up the drive. Skye came out and held onto the dog and cheered me on. Well that's possibly an exaggeration; she looked at me with the bemused expression of the average 16 year old when an adult is attempting

Bugger Bugger Shit!

to do something they really should know better about; and with the fear they will be mortally embarrassed by said adult. She didn't have anything to worry about. During the previous six months of riding Ruby, something had clearly clicked in my brain; I rode it up the hill backwards, first time - woohoo I cheered. Skye looked at me as if I was a bit sad, getting so excited about getting up a driveway that she could easily run up. Ahhh the naivety of the young. Now I can do it just as easily as Neil did that first time.

I am now so expert at managing hills that I traverse up and down travelators in shopping centres - thanks to another Omeo user's helpful videos and advice. I'm waiting for the day a security guard stops me and tells me off for playing on the travelators.

I did have a slight, how shall we say, accident, one day when I was coming down the drive. I had been on the Metro somewhere and as I got off at our local station I saw the threatening clouds and could hear the rolls of thunder. I really didn't want to be out in what can often be a fairly dangerous Sydney storm. I hurried home ahead of the threatening weather and got to the top of the drive. I put the chair into joystick and turtle mode, lined myself up and started to slowly descend the drive.

The wind suddenly started to gust; then a massive gust hit and I felt myself getting knocked off balance and Ruby started to wobble. I kept my head and leaned back to instigate a safety tip, all good, very controlled and slow. I forgot about the incline though, and this physics thing called gravity. As I gently landed backwards, Ruby started to slide down the hill. Oh my God, would she stop in time, I wondered as I was lying back looking at the sky. Cradled in the seat I was completely unable to do anything as I waited for the impact. Nothing, Ruby came to a stop of her own accord. I had lined her up so that the trajectory of the slide moved towards the flat part of the drive at the side rather than the continuing incline down to the house. Phew!

Ruby

Poor Ruby needed a new seat cover though. I had wanted to keep Ruby looking pristine but she has a number of little scratches on her now from the arguments I've had with pavements, bushes or pedestrian crossings. I look at them with pride. Ruby is looking worn because she has been used. Ruby being used means I have been out and about, regaining my independence and having fun. She and I have navigated the Metro, trams, trains, planes, ferries and the bus from Melbourne airport into the city. Yesterday she even went on a historic steam train. She's been to Tasmania and Melbourne. I'm hoping to take her up to the Gold Coast soon so she can meet Ben and Deb's Omeos and later in the year, a big trip to the UK and Europe.

Omeos have two sets of tyres; on road and (drum roll please) off road. That means she can go on the beach, in the snow as well and 'trekking'. I would like to say bush walking but as I have mentioned, Australia is simply not set up for people with mobility impairments. There is virtually no information about whether a bush track has steps, what the grade of the incline is or the width of the track. There is completely unhelpful advice that a path is 'wheelchair accessible'. This tells us nothing. Not all wheelchairs are created equal and 'wheelchair accessible' generally means manual wheelchair or stroller. I don't want to be restricted to paved paths over a short distance. I want to be able to go on long 'walks' and explore nature with my friends.

Once again, the UK and Europe are much more set up with information about accessibility. Whilst country tracks do have styles to be climbed over; local councils and the National Parks are systematically working to eliminate them and put in other types of gates. They also have detailed information about the accessibility of the track. We really need to start doing this in Australia. For too long it's been left up to individuals to make that information available on apps which means, although very

Bugger Bugger Shit!

helpful, it's not consistent. Yes, it's a mammoth task but if we don't make a start, we'll never get there.

So far, I have plans to do the Cotswold Way, the Thames Path, walk along the bottom of the UK and do a number of treks in Italy. My number one on my Omeo bucket list though is to ascend Clougha Pike. This is a hill near where I grew up. As a child and adolescent, I walked Clougha many times, as well as other tracks in the Lake District. I loved it. I want to do it again.

I contacted a well known travel firm in Australia about one of the Italian guided treks they offer. I asked them about wheelchair accessibility and told them all about the capacity of the Omeo so they knew I wasn't talking about a standard wheelchair. They immediately came back with a no. Not to be deterred, I emailed them again and asked them why it was a no and that I would be much better placed to assess the task if they told me the reasons. They explained it was because the accommodation along the way isn't accessible. I reassured them (again) that I can walk and so don't need the accommodation to be wheelchair accessible. I just needed to know if there were steps on the track. They came back to me and said they'd ask their local guide. They hadn't even spoken to the local guide when they said no. They didn't ask any clarifying questions and assumed I couldn't do it. This is not helping people with impairments; this is the attitude that makes us disabled.

After talking to their local guide, they came back to me with a yes. The local guide wasn't at all thrown by the idea of someone in a wheelchair doing the walk. He suggested there might be a couple of short sections which could be challenging but there were alternatives. This is the type of attitude that breaks down the barriers of disability and makes the world accessible. It seems to be the fundamental difference between the

Ruby

UK/Europe and Australia, which is really weird when most people think of Australia as a kind of 'can do' country.

I was warned before Ruby arrived that it would take me twice as long to get anywhere. Not because it actually takes twice as long to get somewhere but because you are stopped constantly by people in awe of the machine that she is. I am invisible, all people see is the wheelchair. How brilliant is that. I have met so many wonderful people because they are so curious about the kind of machine she is. They start by staring at Ruby and then because Ruby looks like a Ferrari with two wheels, they ask about her, and then we have a conversation about how she works and then we get talking about disability and, one conversation at a time, Ruby is breaking down barriers.

I am in no way disabled when I am riding Ruby. I was at the Disability Expo last year with my sister and I felt a tad guilty because of the looks of envy from others. We were there much longer than I had anticipated because of the number of conversations we had. I looked at my watch and realised the time. I was due at a medical appointment in 20 minutes. I rushed out so I could load Ruby into the car and then drive to my sister who was somewhat disabled herself, because she was walking. I sped down to the car and loaded Ruby; when my sister eventually arrived, she commented that several people got whiplash as I sped past and they turned to watch open mouthed!

It's not just getting out and about that Ruby helps me with. As a trainer I was finding it increasingly difficult to do my job. Despite medically retiring from my permanent job, I have continued to speak at events and run training. Having Ruby means I can still do part of what I love to do. Facilitating full single or multiple days of training takes some stamina. I have been doing it for years so I'm used to it but having unreliable legs makes it challenging.

Bugger Bugger Shit!

I found myself being slightly less focussed on the participants because I was constantly working out how I could sit down, whether I could hold on to the whiteboard whilst I was writing on it, and how I could involve the people at the back of the room without walking to them. The first session I conducted with Ruby was nothing short of transformational. Not only could I catch the train, so I wasn't stuck in the endless traffic jams of Sydney, I swanned into the room like some sort of Queen on a chariot! I was facilitating with Sam so I felt confident this first time. Ruby did exactly what I envisaged she would do when I was fighting so hard for her.

Just like people don't think about using their legs when they're moving about, I don't think about how I'm moving when I'm using Ruby. I just slightly adjust my body as I move; just as you do when you're walking or standing. I could move around the room and involve those people at the back of the room just as effectively as those at the front. The only thing I struggle to do on Ruby is write on a whiteboard. Mind you, because I'm short, I have always struggled to write on a whiteboard. Being able to sit on Ruby for the majority of the session, means I have the strength and stamina to stand up for the parts of the session when I need to write on the board, or I ask my co-facilitator to do it if I have one, or I ask the participants to write on butchers' paper, stick it up at the front of the room and speak to it.

Having Ruby means I am a better facilitator, trainer, speaker - I can wholly focus on the presentation and it forces me to think laterally when I need to adjust something because I can't do it quite as easily on Ruby as I would have liked. I have discovered however, that I can't sit on Ruby and rock slightly, as I like to do, engaging my core for a bit of incidental exercise; whilst looking at my phone.

I did this at the training with Sam when the participants were in small groups. I felt a wave of nausea and thought I was going to vomit. For a

Ruby

minute I thought I'd got food poisoning from my lunch but then I realised it was motion sickness. Lesson - no looking at my phone unless the stabilising legs are well and truly planted on the ground.

Something that really needs some awareness raising is able bodied people 'helping' people in wheelchairs and then getting offended if the response is no. We had a conversation about this recently in my writing group; which is half and half people with disabilities who use mobility aids and people who are not. I explained that I couldn't have anyone touch the Omeo whilst I am riding it because it is balance based; if someone holds onto the back, especially when I'm not expecting it, and I don't have time to adjust my position, the whole chair can tip over.

The other thing that regularly happens is that people offer to help. The motivation is kind. Often I don't need help, but sometimes I do and I'm not averse to asking if I need it, but I also need to learn how to navigate the world from my Omeo. Yes I am perfectly capable of standing up and opening a door at the moment, but I may not always be, so I have to build up the skills now.

I've had many experiences of being asked if I need help and when I say no the person is usually completely fine and gives me a wave and a smile. Others aren't quite so laid back. I was in the Opera House not that long ago, waiting to go into the accessible toilet. The toilet door is an automatic sliding door so really not a problem at all. A woman walked out of the toilet, looked slightly embarrassed (I assume because she was using the 'disabled' toilet rather than the standard women's toilets next door). She offered to help me, I said, "No thanks I'm all good" in a cheery voice; she responded in a very huffy voice, "Well I was only offering to help" and stalked off. Don't be that person.

I had an even more disconcerting experience in Melbourne a few months ago. I was facilitating training with the older colleague previously

Bugger Bugger Shit!

mentioned. After the training one day, we did our usual thing of racing into the laneways to check out our favourite shops. She went by tram but I nipped down on the Omeo. I got a phone call whilst we were there so my colleague wandered off ahead of me, whilst I moseyed around on Ruby talking to a child protection caseworker on the phone.

All of a sudden, out of nowhere, a young man swiftly approached me and threw his arms around me in a vice-like hug. Any ideas I had about feeling safe on the Omeo if I was going to be assaulted on the street, dropped out of my brain. I had always assumed if a man was going to try and assault me, I'd just move my body and the Omeo into full throttle and get away.

I hadn't considered someone hurling themselves at me from the front. I was not only pinned to my seat; the seat was tipping backwards dangerously with his weight and my weight combined. "Back off!" I loudly and firmly stated. He didn't. "Back off!" I yelled. The child protection caseworker I was talking to on the phone asked me if I was ok. I told her that a man had grabbed me. She was in Sydney and completely unable to do anything but she stayed on the phone with me. "Back off!" I yelled even louder, as I attempted to push him off me.

By now my colleague, who was some way away, had heard, turned round and was racing back to help me. Another man got there first and yanked and prised the first man off me. The first man was hanging on to me for dear life; the caseworker was asking me if I was ok and I was trying to get this bloke off me whilst trying to make sure Ruby didn't tip backwards and I ended up lying on the ground with this guy on top of me. Bugger bugger shit!

I can usually see with hindsight the funny side of random events, but this one remains unfunny. Eventually, the second man was successful in hauling the first man off me. The caseworker was still checking in if I was ok and I heard the second man speak to my colleague and ask her if he

Ruby

should flatten the first man. "No," she calmly replied, "I don't think that will be necessary." Then as quickly as he had arrived, he disappeared, as did the second man. My colleague and I looked at each other in complete disbelief. The caseworker carried on checking I was ok. I reassured her I was fine, as we continued on a really important conversation about the ongoing safety of a child. She said she couldn't believe how calm I was. I'm not entirely sure how calm I actually was. Completely and utterly shocked was a better description.

My teammate had given me some space again to complete the phone call so I sped up to her when I finished. We looked in another shop but we were both somewhat dazed by the event. She said, "Right, I'm going to say to you exactly what you would say to me if it had been the other way round; you're not ok, no matter how you feel. You're in shock. Let's go up to Hardware Lane and get some dinner." I agreed and decided a gin and tonic was much needed for its medicinal qualities.

As we had dinner, we were quiet, still shaken from the ordeal and we tried to work out exactly what the man was doing. I'm very used to working with people who have psychiatric disorders and drug or alcohol addictions. It didn't seem like this was the case with this man, but it's the only logical conclusion I can come to. I still have no idea if he was trying to express his compassion for a woman in a wheelchair; whether he was expressing his amazement at Ruby; or whether he actually wanted to hurt me. Was this an assault? I came to the conclusion that it was.

We finished dinner and headed back to our hotel, aware we had another full day's training the next day. I got to my room and started to shake. Shock had set in. Women navigate unwelcome advances and assaults from men every single day. I had never felt unsafe in central Melbourne; especially during daylight hours, but having Ruby had made me feel much safer than I usually would. It was a learning experience; just because I have a mobility device that is fast, doesn't mean I'm invincible. It does mean however that I have now thought through how I might be able to get out of a situation if someone comes at me from the front.

The only Assistive Technology I haven't yet acquired is the stair lift - not because I'm worried it might rain whilst I'm using it, but because to have an outside stair lift built is a huge process with my local council. I'm serious! Yet another bureaucratic nonsense that people without disabilities put in the way of people with disabilities. People with disabilities are not disabled until people without disabilities put a spanner in the works. I live in a newly-built house that council approved. They have all the plans, reports and surveys. You cannot tell me that our whole site needed to be surveyed in order to install a stairlift at the back of the house, completely out of sight of the street and the neighbours.

I have had a meeting with the council about the appalling state of our pavements and that I cannot in fact get to our local train station because there is no way to get from our little street onto the main thoroughfare because there's no pavement at all and no way to cross the busy road. Apparently the fact that one person can't access their community isn't a breach of legislation - hint, yes it is - but bureaucracies rely on people with disabilities not being able to afford the fight in court and there is only so much the Human Rights Commission can do. Besides which, it isn't just me; parents with strollers and other people in wheelchairs also can't get to the main road.

Australia has a fundamental problem with disability access because Australia, generally speaking, fundamentally has a problem with people with disabilities; despite the fact that we have the most innovative legislation and support system in the world. I am not disabled, my world makes me disabled. The resilience that I have developed across my lifetime however, gives me the capacity and stubbornness to fight for a less disabled world.

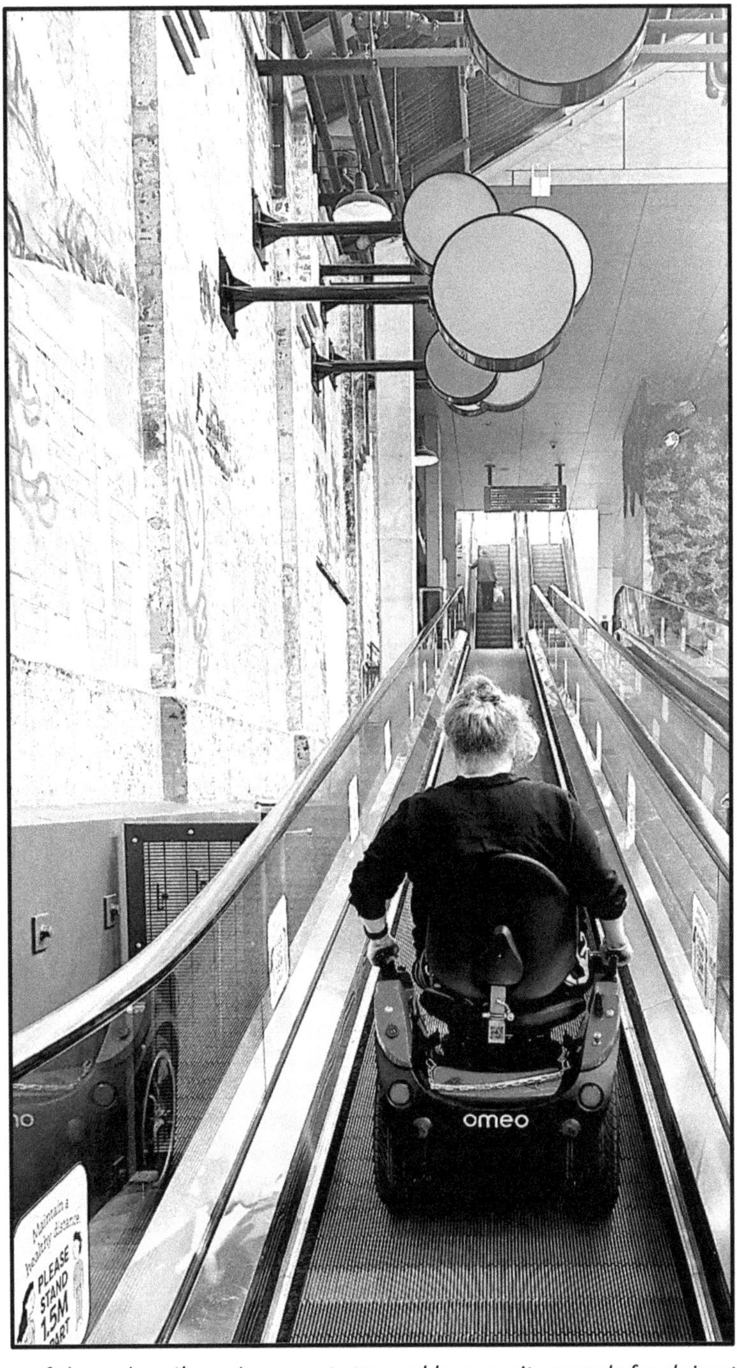

Ruby

One of these days I'm going to get stopped by security guards for doing this

Bugger Bugger Shit!

Ruby - my Ferrari

Ruby with her off road tyres easily managing a rocky partially built drive

Chapter 19

Anxiety Is Just An Emotion

I'd ask her, 'So you're afraid of everything? Don't you ever get thirsty? Don't you ever get hungry? You say you're afraid of everything? That includes water? Good food?' And I'd put her in a position of knowing she had exaggerated and misinformed me. And she's going to be—start checking everything she says and she's going to start doubting the all-inclusiveness of her fears. And when she starts doubting those, then you can give her faith in this, in that, until she knows that she likes to be alone at times. And she does like the scenery. She does like the sunlight. She does like the quiet at night when she wants to sleep. She does like to sleep. She does like hunger. She does like to go to the bathroom. And you reverse her complete negativism by adulterating it with a great many positive things. And there are so many positive things. She may dislike the colour of her eyes, but she liked her eyes."

Milton Erickson 1979
In The Room with Milton H Erickson MD
Jane Parsons-Fein 2018

Bugger Bugger Shit!

It was my first appointment with a dermatologist. My GP had advised me to have regular skin checks because my sister had died from malignant melanoma. I was 23; my sister had died two and a half years previously. I have blue eyes, red hair, very fair skin and a family history of melanoma, living in the country with the highest rates of melanoma in the entire world. I was a walking advert for skin cancer. I explained to her the family history and that I was now living permanently in Australia. "That's a shame." she said. Then she looked aghast, "I'm so sorry I didn't mean that to come out the way it sounded, I just meant that this is the very worst place for you to live, you should be back in the north of England." That did not help curb the significant anxiety I had about developing the disease after my experience with my sister.

Anxiety is a strange little emotion. It gets under our skin and into the back of our brains and whispers away, "You can't do this", "You can't say that", "People will think you're stupid", "What if I die doing that?". Anxiety eats away at our resilience and it is rising in epidemic proportions across the western world. We have to do something urgently to curb it if we are to have any long-term impact on the mental health and wellbeing of our communities; particularly our children.

What I frequently hear is, 'my anxiety' as if anxiety is an inextricable part of someone - it isn't; I have red hair; even if I dye it, I still have red hair underneath. It is a part of my genetic makeup. Anxiety is a feeling, an emotion; it is not an inextricable part of us. Yes we know the impact of epigenetics on sensitising babies in-utero to be susceptible to certain things but that can be changed, often with hard work and support, but it can be changed.

Anxiety Is Just An Emotion

In this chapter I, by no means, want to minimise anxiety; particularly for those who suffer from a diagnosed anxiety disorder which can be crippling and needs to be managed with the help of a health professional. What I do want to do though, is attempt to put some things into perspective and to give the reader a more helpful way of managing anxious feelings. We all have anxious feelings; we don't all "have anxiety".

Often there are two ways people deal with someone else's anxiety. The first is to dismiss it with usually, well-meaning, platitudes such as, "Just get over it" or "You'll be fine". The second is to avoid it or accommodate it, "Oh I know that you are worried about that, don't worry you don't have to do it". The problem is that in the world, we often have to do things that are uncomfortable or downright scary.

We cannot prepare the road for our children; we have to prepare our children for the road and that means supporting them to rise above the things that scare them. The scientists saw the pandemic coming; the average citizens of the world didn't. We were totally unprepared but some people managed better than others. I don't mean in terms of the physical aspects of Covid-19 but the psychological aspects of it. The people who managed the situation better were the ones who had been prepared for the road. They had been supported to build their resilience for years.

My fears and anxiety around developing melanoma were completely realistic. I am at a very high risk of developing it. Melanoma is unlikely to ever not be a risk to me. The way I have handled it however has changed over the years. There have been many occasions when I have had a suspicious mole that needed to be checked; what I used to do was put my head in the sand. If I ignored it, it would go away. All that did was dismiss my anxious feelings. It didn't actually help my feelings at all or build my resilience in this area. In fact what it did was to cause my feelings to amplify until they were a siren in my ears that I couldn't ignore. I felt nauseous

Bugger Bugger Shit!

constantly and I couldn't sleep until I finally saw the doctor who would invariably tell me it was nothing to worry about. I have had lots of skin lesions frozen off over the years; none of them were melanoma although some were pre-cancerous.

After about 10 years of being paranoid about melanoma, I decided something had to change. It was exhausting, if nothing else. I decided to get educated; I asked my dermatologist to explain specifically to me what were more worrying changes. She gave me a handout with coloured pictures of different moles with detailed descriptions of what they were and how dangerous they were. That meant that I could make an informed assessment on how much I needed to worry. I wasn't going to switch off the worry but I was going to dial down the volume on it.

The next thing I did was commit to going to see my GP immediately if I saw anything that was concerning. My GP would then reassure me initially and when I could get in to see my dermatologist, she would generally confirm the GPs opinion. Understanding my very real fears, she gave me permission to ring up and she would endeavour to make a space for me to see her as soon as possible.

On one occasion I did actually need that. I saw a new 'mole' and made an appointment to see my GP. My GP wasn't working on this particular day so I saw another, reasonably inexperienced, doctor in the practice. I showed her the lesion which was a dark black colour. She was extremely concerned and called my dermatologist whilst I was in the surgery with her. My dermatologist agreed to see me straight away, so with the GPs fears ringing in my ears I drove the 30 minutes to her. She ushered me into her rooms almost immediately and when she saw my skin, she had to contain her annoyance with the GP. It was nothing whatsoever to worry about and was a fairly common skin lesion that could easily be frozen off even though it wasn't at all dangerous.

Anxiety Is Just An Emotion

Afterwards I reflected on the whole saga; I realised that I was actually much less fearful than the GP and that if it was something sinister, I had discovered it early and it was unlikely to have such a devastating outcome as my sister. The anxiety I felt about melanoma is now completely managed. I am sensible but I am not paranoid. I have an annual skin check and if I see anything that looks unusual I still get it checked straight away. I understand that knowledge is power and avoiding or dismissing something that causes me to feel anxious is a completely unfruitful exercise.

When we understand that anxiety is just an emotion; like happiness, or sadness or disappointment and that it ebbs and flows, we can take hold of our feelings. We all need to change our language around anxiety. Instead of saying, "My anxiety" when we can say, "I am feeling anxious right now," it means that we will inevitably, at some point, not feel anxious.

The other fundamental thing to consider when supporting someone experiencing anxiety is that if we help them avoid what is causing them to feel anxious, we are denying them the opportunity of succeeding. One of the key elements of a resilient person is having overcome a previous difficulty. When we deny someone the opportunity of succeeding; by dismissing or accommodating their anxious feelings, we deny them the opportunity to build their resilience.

The only thing that avoiding something that causes us to feel anxious will do, is make our anxious feelings worse. Despite the fact that we are often acting out of love, we are actually causing harm. If we dismiss someone's anxious feelings, even if our motivation is love, we are causing harm because the person experiencing anxious emotions ultimately continues to feel alone and judged. The feelings don't just evaporate.

In Chapter 1, I talked about Emotion Coaching. Among other things, Emotion Coaching allows someone to 'feel felt'. When we emotion coach people who are experiencing anxious emotions, they feel that they are understood. We need to remember however, that the pivotal point to Emotion Coaching is the last point; Resolution or Problem Solving. Once someone 'feels felt' we then need to support them to work out a way to respond differently next time.

Eli Liebowitz, from Yale University, has developed The Space Program which is specifically designed to support children who are experiencing entrenched anxiety. What Liebowitz has found is that children and young people who experience long term anxiety have been systematically accommodated by their parents. The clinicians at the Space Program, even though it is designed for children and young people who experience chronic anxiety, don't see the children. They work with the parents to help them stop accommodating their child's anxiety.

They start from a place of offering an empathic statement and then lead into a courage statement; for example, "I can see how scared (this) makes you feel but I am totally confident that you can do this." End of conversation. This is essentially emotion coaching; parents support their children to 'feel felt'; they empathise with them but then they move into a place where they talk about what the child can do next time they feel like this - essentially a statement about courage. Of course there is more to the program than this but if we can all work towards empathically challenging our children, adolescents, friends and family then we will see resilience starting to rise. We want to accommodate the anxious feelings of those who are close to us because we genuinely care but we have to remember it actually causes harm.

When feelings of anxiety are entrenched, this is not something that will be fixed overnight. With patience, consistent support and challenge to people with feelings of anxiety, they can rise and build their resilience so that next time they can manage it a little better, and little better and a little better. When they experience success after long periods of feeling like they can't succeed or crippling anxiety, the feeling is tremendous.

I have a painting of a little girl seemingly leaping from a hill. The painting is called 'I'm Flying'. I love it but some of my friends have seen it and it scares them; they have said to me, "Oh no, what if she falls off the cliff?" My response is, "But what if she flies?" Fundamentally, we need to ask ourselves the question; do I want to support someone to increase or lower their resilience. Do I want to rejoice in their success? I think most of us would say that we really want our friends, our children, our family to experience success and to build their resilience; we just don't know how, so we make it up as we go along, unintentionally causing harm.

There are other ways we can diminish feelings of anxiety. The first one is to ensure we get good sleep. When we are suffering from lack of sleep the good DOSE chemicals that I mentioned in Chapter 1 are lowered; this means our medial pre-frontal context which manages feelings of fear and danger is not able to work effectively.

Secondly, we need to exercise, preferably outside. When we exercise, endorphins (one of the DOSE neuro-chemicals) are increased and these increase our feelings of wellbeing. Sunlight increases Vitamin D and helps to lessen feelings of depression. Believe it or not, singing is also a very helpful exercise in supporting brain health and wellbeing because it increases endorphins; singing with other people is even better because we are enjoying something in community which lessens our feelings of isolation. Finally our brain, just like our bodies, needs to keep hydrated so drinking enough water is essential.

It's important to note that anxiety is different to fear and they are both different to trauma. Anxiety is essentially an emotion that starts in the prefrontal cortex, when we think and ruminate about something; either in the past or a possibility in the future, that isn't actually dangerous. It then moves into the amygdala (the fear centre) and a feedback loop is created.

Fear, however, starts in the amygdala; the early warning alarm centre of our brains, that essentially keeps us alive in dangerous situations. I often give the following example to try and explain this; you are driving along and a fire truck comes round a corner, careening towards you with sirens blaring and lights flashing, it's on the wrong side of the road and if you don't take evasive action immediately it's going to crash into you. Your amygdala, in an instant, understands the danger and you turn the wheel to avoid the fire truck. Your heart is thumping, you might have sweaty palms and you might be breathing heavily. It was a terrifying experience. That is fear.

Anxiety on the other hand would be this; you are driving along and you see a fire truck with sirens and lights heading in the direction of your house. Your thinking goes something like this, "Oh no, that's heading towards home. Oh no, my house must be on fire. Oh no, did everyone get out? Did the animals get out? Did I pay the insurance premium?" And so on. The brain is ruminating and stressing about something that isn't real.

The way we deal with both of these scenarios is different but they do both need to be dealt with. There isn't room in this book to address in detail the ways they can be managed effectively but I have provided some recommended reading at the end of the book. Essentially, if we can manage our body's stress responses, and we can challenge our thinking then we can capture and control feelings of anxiety. If we can actively work towards lessening feelings of anxiety then we are fundamentally building a more resilient population.

Returning to the topic of the language we use around distressing events, one of the things I hear frequently is overuse of the word 'trauma'. Trauma is not the same as anxiety or fear or experiencing something distressing. I had a difficult childhood; I did not generally have a traumatic childhood. I

Anxiety Is Just An Emotion

have experienced some traumatic events but I do not 'have' trauma. Other people have had extremely traumatic childhoods and they may very well be dealing with trauma every single day.

Likewise when we use inflated terminology for what are essentially everyday annoyances, then we diminish the people who have experienced trauma and are living with the consequences. I could say something like, "The traffic was a complete nightmare today, I feel traumatised". No, I don't. I feel stressed, I feel annoyed but I have not experienced trauma.

Trauma is one significant event or series of events that cause us to feel terrified. What is traumatic for one person may not be for another; for example, I had a car accident many years ago; I was in the middle of a multiple vehicle crash. It was incredibly scary and yes I felt traumatised by it at the time. With some lovely support from my dad who helped me to feel safe and in control again, I recovered reasonably quickly. If a Formula 1 racing driver had a car crash; he or she would be unlikely to feel traumatised by it.

We are often afraid to address the feelings associated with trauma because we are worried about 're-traumatising' someone. If someone is currently experiencing feelings and experiences associated with trauma we're not going to re-traumatise them; they're already traumatised. We might however, make it worse, especially if we do nothing, ignore it or tell them to 'get over it'.

What we know about trauma, is that the support people receive during and after the traumatic event/s is one of the keys. When people experience trauma, their choice and control has been taken away and so the very first thing we need to focus on is helping them to feel safe and back in control and have professional support available for them. When we can do that, we are re-building resilience. When we support one person at a time to re-build their resilience, ultimately, we are going to build a more resilient society.

Chapter 20

That Offends Me

Humans are nervous, touchy creatures and can be easily offended. Many are deeply insecure. They become focused and energised by taking offence; it makes them feel meaningful and alive.

Michael Leunig

I am wholly confident that in the pages of this book there will be something I said that offends someone or said something else that someone vehemently disagrees with. It's completely fine if you disagree and I am more than happy at any time to sit down with you, a good cup of tea, and have an open, respectful and compassionate conversation about our differing viewpoints. I will not be offended and I will not try to change your mind. That's not my job. The job of all of us is to be open to new ideas and to respectfully listen, debate and maybe change our minds - or not, but at least we will have heard each other.

That Offends Me

When we can hold two separate viewpoints in our hands and respect the right of an individual to hold a different perspective than ourselves, we are truly resilient.

I don't think I'm exaggerating when I say I believe the Western world is experiencing an existential crisis, of its own making, when it comes to the mental health and wellbeing of its population. There are a myriad contributing factors to this; the way we think about and respond to mental health and wellbeing; the way we have embraced our own privilege to the detriment of others; they way we take offence at the drop of a hat; the way people with differing or opposing views as ourselves are demonised; our resistance to feeling uncomfortable; our determination that we are right therefore everyone else is wrong. We have lost our way entirely when it comes to compassion.

This might be difficult to read because they are ugly ideas to consider and to entertain the possibility that we might be part of the problem is challenging. No one is all evil and no one is all good; we all play a part. None of us can set ourselves apart as not being part of the problem. The encouraging truth though, is if we are all part of the problem we can all be part of the solution. This book is an invitation for you to take hold of the challenge and commit to making a difference.

Too often religion, politics and sex are forbidden topics. We have forgotten the art of debate, of how to have a healthy and respectful disagreement. We are so invested in proving everyone else is wrong that we say nothing. We are so invested in not offending someone that we say nothing. We are so invested in not losing face by admitting we don't know what we're talking about that we say nothing. If we all say nothing, how on earth are our children and grandchildren going to survive?

Bugger Bugger Shit!

In 2007, I lived in the electorate of Bennelong when John Howard lost his seat and therefore the leadership of the nation. Prior to the election, I was with the daughter of a friend in our suburb's town centre and some of Howard's team were there handing out balloons and election information for the Liberal Party. My friend's daughter, who was in primary school at the time, asked if she could have a balloon. I said no. She challenged me and said we should be supporting the Prime Minister. I still said no. She is used to me challenging her thought processes and teaching or showing her how to do things she hasn't learnt before - it's not always about politics; one of the most practical things I ever taught her was how to make a bed with hospital corners (as any self respecting daughter of a nurse will know how to do), which is handy because she's now a nurse.

The following weekend was the election and we all know the results. The Liberals were out and Labor was in. The following afternoon, I was at her house having a cup of tea with her mum. She wandered into the kitchen, looked at me and said, "Well I hope you're pleased with yourself". I laughed silently to myself at her forthrightness and replied, "I am actually". Later, I sat down with her and explained in simple terms how the government works in Australia, the privilege of living in a democracy, compulsory voting and the importance of researching in order to make an informed decision about who you vote for. I said I didn't care which way she eventually votes when she becomes an adult, only that she does her research and votes according to her conscience and not the way her parents vote, or I vote, or her friends vote.

A few months later came Kevin Rudd's apology to the Stolen Generation. Once again we were having a milkshake together after I picked her up from school. Of course the whole nation was talking about 'The Apology', including her school friends. Knowing I would take her seriously; she expressed concern that the apology would mean that reparations would have to be paid. No, she is not a child genius, she didn't use the term reparation, it was a much more roundabout and unclear question but that was the crux of it. I could tell that she had been listening in to the conversations that were swirling all around us at the time and I wanted to make sure she understood, as clearly as possible, the fundamental moral issue at stake.

I thought hard about how to answer her and in the end I said, "You know when you do something wrong, it's not ok and you choose to apologise to make it right. And even though you are really sorry about it you still might have a consequence". She nodded her head, "And it feels like it's unfair, and you don't like it but you know it's the right thing", more nodding, "Well this is the same thing. For a very long time the Australian Governments and the Australian people did things that were really really wrong to Aboriginal people and families. Some of them aren't even alive anymore but what they did was still wrong. They represented all Australians and so we all need to say sorry. The Prime Minister said sorry on behalf of all of us because it was the right thing to do, even though some people might not like it and might disagree with it. And yes, we might have to pay some money as a consequence, but it's the right thing to do and so if it comes to that, the Government will work it out and will pay the money that they're told they have to pay".

Over 10 years later, it was finally her first opportunity to vote in an election. She messaged me the night before and asked me how she should vote. I refused to be drawn in; she knew full well the way I would be voting. Instead I referred her to the ABC's election tool; a brilliant way to easily assist people work out how to vote. For those who don't know; it lists many of the major policy issues that are being taken to the election and asks voters to choose from the multiple choice answers which option is closest to their own values. She got her result and texted me with it. I wasn't surprised,

Bugger Bugger Shit!

knowing her as I do. She had numerous strong candidates to choose from and she made her own choice according to her own values. I was proud of her. She is one of the most resilient young people I know.

All of my nephews have had experiences in High School where teachers could have engaged in a process with them and their peers to build resilience; but disappointingly they failed. The first one was where one of the boys was disciplined for apparently bullying his friend. As is so often the case with teenagers, it seemed to be a complicated scenario; it wasn't. What complicated it was the response of the school leadership.

They jumped to conclusions, didn't fully investigate the situation and leapt in to protect a child who didn't actually need protecting and had done something questionable in the first place. There was no bullying; what our child had done was to 'call out' his very good friend on something he had posted on social media. The boys trusted each other, were good friends and the other boy was perfectly ok with what happened.

The school focused on the call out and took no effort in understanding the context; until I had a very frank conversation with them where I myself called them out for their behaviour and assumptions. I had to explain that bullying is a sustained and purposeful use of power over another person aimed at diminishing the victim and enlarging the perpetrator. Bullying is not a single difficult conversation or incident.

The second experience was very similar in nature. A classmate of one of the boys had made a very racist comment. The boys were in Year 10 at the time and possibly not the sharpest tools in the shed when it came to nuanced conversations. Our child 'called out' the other child about his comment by referencing the vast numbers of terrorists who have an anglo cultural heritage. Another child overheard the exchange between the two boys and made a complaint to the school leadership. Both boys were given consequences for being racist. This was a golden opportunity for the school to engage all three children in a teaching moment; they didn't.

The third incident was different in context but again very similar in nature. In an English class the teacher was leading, again Year 10 students, in a conversation about language and the situation where some groups of people can use certain terminology but others can't. Our child joined in the conversation by saying, "Yes, like the N word. Afro-Americans can use that term but others shouldn't".

Some of the other students goaded him multiple times by saying things like what's the N word? In the end, with absolutely no support from the teacher, he, very uncomfortable now, eventually said 'nigger'. The same children who had goaded him then accused him of being racist and later, made a complaint to the school leadership about it. The teacher said absolutely nothing, and allowed this to take place. What an opportunity for a debate and conversation about racism and ethical behaviour. It was completely lost.

The final example was with one of the boys when they were in Year 7. An English class again. The teacher was engaging the class in learning about pronouns. One of our children put his hand up and said something along the lines of, "Oh yes that's like for people who are trans…". He wasn't allowed to finish his sentence. The teacher shut him down and told him to stay behind after class. Sure enough after class he lectured our child about respect. Our 12 year old boy was confused by this and said to the teacher, "All I was going to say was that people who are trans often use them and their as the pronouns". Again, what an opportunity lost and what a disrespectful assumption of the teacher.

Now you might all be thinking these were the same teachers or school leaders. They weren't. All of the examples were different teachers, different school leaders and even different schools. It is pervasive. I am not criticising

Bugger Bugger Shit!

teachers in general here. What I am saying is that ALL adults are in a position of influence over children. We are the ones who should be teaching children to understand nuance, to develop critical thinking skills, to engage them in restorative justice but we have all become so worried about offending someone that our children are suffering.

My final story designed to provoke thinking and self reflection involves me. I facilitate training with many different groups of practitioners, teachers, medical staff, early childhood educators and community workers. On this particular day, I was running an all day training with a large group of practitioners. It's a training program I have run dozens of times.

During the session, one of the younger practitioners asked me for my thoughts about available support in schools for gay and trans young people; a current topic of debate in Australia and one with significantly polarising views. What a big question and really one that wasn't directly related to what we were talking about. I was very aware of how much content we needed to get through during the day and that the question was complex with a multi-layered answer that would take some time to process and in fact deserved the time to be processed, if I sidetracked to unpack this, then I would have had to compromise on something else during the session which would have been difficult and I needed to stay true to what the organisers had asked of me.

My response was to try and explain the situation, as briefly as possible, so as not to lose too much time. Five minutes later, she asked me again. I again said that it was a very complex topic that required time to unpack and we didn't have time today to do that but I would be happy to discuss it another time or facilitate another session around it. I tried to continue on but she stopped me again and expressed her frustration that I hadn't answered her question and was dismissing her.

I knew then I would need to deal with her concerns albeit as briefly as I could. I addressed them as succinctly as possible but my essential point was that these are complex situations for everyone involved; children, parents, the medical and educational systems and there are no easy or simplistic answers. As professionals in the field, we need to be able to hold the competing and different viewpoints of everyone; without judgement and support people to develop their understanding, compassion and ability to walk in someone else's shoes.

Three months later I received notice that she had made a formal complaint about me and accused me of being homophobic and transphobic. People who know me well would say categorically I am neither of those things. When I looked at her complaint in detail she had completely missed out any contextual issues, had cherry picked things I had said and completely mis-quoted me. I also provided the feedback forms which were overwhelmingly positive about the training. None of the forms expressed any concern about the things she had raised. I hasten to add that I have absolutely no issue with anyone choosing to make a complaint about me. How can we change if no one lets us know?

The thing that concerned me the most about this episode was that the practitioner involved chose not to engage in a conversation with me later, as she had been invited to do. Had she done so, we would have had an opportunity to have a healthy clinical discussion where we could both learn from each other. She chose not to. I did not say what she wanted me to say and therefore I was wrong because she was right.

It is no one's job, particularly those who are in a professional relationship with anyone or in a position of power over anyone, to persuade someone to our own way of thinking. With complex issues we need to allow people space to develop their ideas; to provide them with an opportunity to challenge themselves and have the grace to allow people to change their

Bugger Bugger Shit!

minds and their behaviour if they want to. Unsurprisingly, the complaint was not substantiated.

This pervasive attitude of 'I am right therefore everyone else is wrong'; eats away at the core of resilience. I need to be resilient enough to engage respectfully in a conversation with someone who has different values, beliefs and opinions to me. I need to be resilient enough to change my own thinking if appropriate. I need to be resilient enough to walk with grace if someone chooses a path that is different to my own.

Clare Fox has completed an array of research in this area and outlines in her book; "I Still Find That Offensive", among other things, the pervasive experience in universities where students make complaints about academic staff who discuss areas that the student finds uncomfortable. If we are to raise resilient, critical thinkers then this has to stop. School and higher education establishments are the very places where our views should be respectfully challenged, where we can move outside of our own echo chambers to consider experiences and opinions outside of our own.

Returning to the education stories; I don't have an issue per se with any of the individual staff members involved. I have an issue with a society where teachers are caught between a rock and a hard place. The curriculum is so full that teachers don't have time and space to debate and discuss ideas with children. They spend so much of their time pumping children with information so that children can perform in exams that they don't have time to teach children how to think; how to question; how to critically analyse; how to give and receive constructive criticism.

The other side that they are wedged between is parents who attack the teachers who do actually question children's thinking and values and beliefs. A system that is so focussed on protecting children's privacy that children and parents can't meet together to resolve an issue. A society where children are taught that they are entitled to so many things. Families where adults expect the road to be prepared for children rather than prepare children for the road.

Having said that; school and higher education leaders do need to be held to account for the cultures and behaviours that develop within their institutions. As does the medical profession, the community services profession, business, science, transport, disability, faith communities and churches; the list is endless.

In my quest for resilience, learning to not take offence at the drop of a hat has been crucial. It's a hard skill to develop but when we understand what's at stake if we don't, then I think we all have a responsibility to try our hardest to develop it. It's not that I don't get offended, I just pause when I do and ask myself "what is it in me that is responding to this situation?". When I have asked myself that, I clarify what is going on for me and I can then choose how to respond.

It's appropriate to get offended at the wanton disregard for humanity by those in power. It's appropriate to get offended at the state of domestic and family violence in this country. It's appropriate to get offended at the needless perpetuation of poverty usually because of the greed of others. Our offence in these situations however needs to motivate us to do something about it, not to just sit on the sidelines and watch. In order to do this, we need to build our resilience. It takes resilience to stick one's head above the parapet and call out unethical behaviour. If we are going to change the world and turn this lack of resilience around, we have to start with ourselves. I, for one, think it's worth it.

Chapter 21

The Quest

And I want you to choose some time in the past when you were a very, very little girl. And my voice will go with you. And my voice will change into that of your parents, your neighbours, your friends, your schoolmates, your playmates, your teachers. And I want you to find yourself sitting in the school room a little girl, feeling happy about something, something that happened a long time ago, that you forgot a long time ago

> **Milton H. Erickson**
> My Voice Will Go With You: The Teaching Tales of Milton H Erickson
> Sydney Rosen
> 1991
> Norton

I started the writing of this book with a quest; to find out what it was that made me resilient. If I knew what my resilience was founded on, then maybe, just maybe, there might be some lessons from my life for others to take on board. My friend asked me why I seemingly had it together and she and my other friend didn't. My simple answer to that question is that all

The Quest

three of us are brave, all three of us are resilient; it just looks different for each of us.

There is a fundamental difference in the structure of my friends' world and my world however; I live in Australia and my friends reside in the UK. In Australia, despite the many and often significant failings of our social welfare system and our medical systems; particularly when it comes to rural and remote communities and of course Aboriginal Australians, we do have a basic functioning and integrated health care system.

I live in a capital city and can easily access the care I need with minimal wait times. I know that if I needed it; I could turn up at our local hospital Emergency Department and within a couple of hours see a Psychiatric Registrar, be admitted into a Mental Health facility and be provided with the care that was necessary. I can see a private therapist, one within the healthcare system or one employed in any of the large NGOs with minimal wait times. I can seek a medical specialist either within the healthcare system with a bit of a wait or I can see a private specialist, pay for it and then claim part of the fee back on Medicare.

One bonus from the pandemic is the accessibility of virtual health and psychological care if we can't get to in-person appointments. I can choose which doctors I want to treat me and when I come across a terrible one, I can make a complaint and I can change doctors. I can take out health insurance so that I can access Allied Health supports and in patient services in private hospitals. As a person with a disability, I have access to the NDIS.

None of these things are possible in the UK and they're often unavailable or patchwork in many areas of Australia. Governments need to take note of this. If we are to build a resilient population and if we are to use budgets efficiently; early intervention and prevention are the keys. My beautiful friends are struggling because they haven't been able to access the professional support that they need. In the UK, if you need community

Bugger Bugger Shit!

psychiatric support, you go on a years-long waiting list for an opening in a therapeutic group, which is entirely inadequate. If it wasn't so serious, it would be a comedy sketch.

I often tell parents it takes a 'village to raise a child'. The villages have disintegrated by and large and so I challenge adults to build their own village and be the village for the children in their world. It's not just the children that need a village though; we all need a village and we can choose whether or not we accept the challenge.

I have a village. A wide and vast village made up of lots of different people. Whilst I haven't accessed therapeutic support, I have worked everyday with clinicians for decades. In addition to our formal clinical supervision, we continually offer informed informal support to each other; mostly about work but we cannot do the work that we do without bringing ourselves into the workplace. Like anyone else, I have formed caring and ongoing friendships with colleagues and we walk alongside each other. These individuals form part of my village, just as much as my family and friends outside of work.

Resilience can't be packaged up. Resilience is unique to every single person. We can't compare my resilience to yours and when we compare ourselves with each other, we ultimately fail. What we can do however, is learn from each other; not compete with each other. No matter how resilient someone looks, we all have vulnerabilities, things that make us wobble.

It is the radical compassion that we have for each other that makes a difference. It is our commitment to loving big; to challenging each other to be the best versions of ourselves that makes a difference. Resilience can ultimately be a choice if the structural supports that we need are available. I choose to create a village around me. I choose, despite my circumstances, to lift up my head and put one foot in front of the other; sometimes that is really, really hard.

What I have learned through the pages of this book, is that fundamentally, when it has felt impossible to lift my head, it has been the people around me who have helped me do just that. My friends, my colleagues, my family who have whispered in my ear, "Don't give up." I hope that through the pages of this book, someone will hear me whisper to them, "Don't give up."

My sense of humour might be genetic but my willingness to see the absurdity in life's tricky situations; my ability to laugh at myself are all things that I have developed over time. A lot of people assume that I am outgoing and gregarious; an extrovert. They are shocked when I tell them, on the contrary, I am actually quite shy and an introvert. I would much rather sit at home with a cup of tea and my special people than be out and about at large social gatherings. What I have done however, with the help of my extrovert friends, is find my voice.

There have been key moments in my life where I have been willing to step out of my comfort zone and take a risk. Each time I do it, it becomes easier. I am confident at work now because I have been doing what I do for over 30 years. I am confident to speak publicly because I was forced to do it as part of my job and I have now done it so many times that I actually love it. I am confident to sing to an audience because I have done it so many times. The first time I spoke publicly I wanted the ground to swallow me up; the first time I sang publicly I couldn't even stand up I was so nervous; when I first transitioned to using a wheelchair I was scared and uncomfortable, but I did it. Like Maya Angelou's poem, I made a choice to Rise; the key I have realised though, is that I didn't do it alone.

We cannot become resilient on our own. We choose to allow people to help us; we choose not to take offence; we choose not to stick with the status quo; we choose not to walk past the isolated and broken; we choose to call out injustice; we choose to laugh at ourselves; we choose to forgive and we choose to ask for forgiveness. When we take the uncomfortable opportunities to build our resilience, we make a difference in this world; it's not easy but it is better.

We all have voices in our heads; the voices of the critics but also the voices of the encouragers. It is so easy to hear the voices of the critics; they are usually loud and insistent. The voices of the encouragers are usually quiet, gentle, calm, compassionate and kind. What we need to do in this quest for resilience is to become practised at tuning our hearing to the quiet voices of the people who believe in us; so that those are the voices that go with us into our futures.

The Quest

Me circa 1972 Malta

Me today 52 years later successful in my quest for resilience

Recommended Reading

I am listing some books which readers may like to follow up in relation to some of the topics discussed in the book.

Fox, C., (2018). I Still Find that Offensive! London. Biteback Publishing Ltd.

Gottman, J. M., & Declaire, J. (1997). Raising an Emotionally Intelligent Child. New York, N.Y., Simon & Schuster.

Hoffman, K., Cooper, G., Powell, B., (2017). Raising a Secure Child. Guilford Publications, USA.

Liebowitz, E. R., (2021). Breaking Free of Child Anxiety and OCD. Oxford University Press, USA.

Pitman, C. M., & Karle, M., (2015). Rewire Your Anxious Brain. Oakland, Ca. New Harbinger Publications Inc.

Siegel, D. J. & Hattzell, M. (2005). Parenting from the Inside Out. New York, N.Y., Tarcher

Siegel, D. J., & Payne, T,. (2011). The Whole Brain Child. New York, N.Y. Delacorte Press.

Siegel, D. J., (2015). Brainstorm. New York, N.Y., Tarcher/Putnam

About the Author

Angharad Candlin, a distinguished Author, Thought Leader and recently retired Psychologist with over 30 years of experience, is featured on the latest episode of Authors in the Spotlight. Hosted by Justine Martin, CEO of Morpheus Publishing and Angharad's writing coach, the episode explores Angharad's new book, Bugger Bugger Shit. Justine interviews Angharad about the book's themes and her journey, providing listeners with an engaging look into the creative process and the dynamic between author and publisher.

www.ingramcontent.com/pod-product-compliance
Lightning Source LLC
Chambersburg PA
CBHW061733070526
44585CB00024B/2650